Are you a proper teacher, Sir?

Gary Boothroyd

Published by SportsBooks Ltd

Copyright: Gary Boothroyd ©
October 2004

SportsBooks Limited
PO Box 422
Cheltenham
GL50 2YN
United Kingdom
Tel: 08700 713 965
Fax: 08700 750 888
e-mail: randall@sportsbooks.ltd.uk
Website: www.sportsbooks.ltd.uk

Cover art work by Martin Ursell

Typeset in Minion

A CIP catalogue record for this book is available from the British Library.

ISBN 1899807 25 X

Printed by Creative Print and Design, Wales

He's the Man

Yes, He's the man.
He's the one to blame.
He's the reason
England hardly ever win a game.
It's his fault;
Erickson (Taylor, Venables, Hoddle, Keegan)
has a dodgy football team,
And why our batsmen cower like rabbits
in a headlight's beam.
He's at the root of why Tim never wins a crown,
the reason Kiwis, Boks and Aussies
trample us in the ground.
Now if you want to know this villain
and like the pundits spit upon his name,
There he is...
clowning in a tracksuit,
P.E. teaching is his game.

For Yvonne
...with thanks to Ann

To England's P.E. teachers, particularly
those in Aston, Birmingham, and
especially Howard,
– *you* know what I mean.

(Many names in this book have been
changed to protect the innocent.)

Contents

Chapter One

YOU HAVE TO START SOMEWHERE
(September, late 1990s)

I CANNOT believe it has arrived; that moment I have tried to avoid thinking about all the way through the six weeks holiday. You know, the one that everyone except teachers believes is far too long. I am standing with my bunch of keys, 27 in all (one for every year I've been here?), jangling loosely in my sweaty palm. I have that sinking feeling deep in the pit of my stomach. It's a sensation that seeped into my consciousness as I stretched out in 86 degrees of heat on a Côte D'Azure beach this time last week, even with bronzed, near-naked flesh to distract me at every turn of my head. Now it's churning in anticipation of the willpower and emotion I am going to have to expend in coping with wall-to-wall kids during the long year ahead.

I shake free the big brass key from the entangled bunch. Believe me, I am no jailer, for I'm about to set those children free... on me!

I turn the key and throw open the double doors at the end of the dark P.E. corridor with its brown brick walls and perspex covered noticeboards adorned with various sporting photographs, charts and statistics. I shield my eyes, as I peer out into the dazzling brightness of a gloriously sunny September morning and try to focus on the top of the short, steep flight of steps that lead up to the playground. There's no one there.

First lesson up, it's a Thursday; period two, as yesterday was a Staff Training Day. Up to this point the classes have been in their form bases receiving Form Tutor "welcome back", timetables and freshly printed School Rules, which will be placed carefully into the first transparent sleeve of their personal organisers. The children will carry these conscientiously for the first two or three days before the organisers disappear from their "Inventory of Essential Items to Carry in School". By then, *forbidden* accessories will have taken priority; the Walkman (which can be got away with providing it does not appear round a neck in class), the mobile phone (which can be easily hidden about one's person, providing it does not ring in the middle of a lesson) and Pokemon cards (the latest craze in collectables, which replaced the craze in pocket micropets that were in need of regular "feeding"). All the above items are expressly forbidden in school as they cause distraction, dispute and disruption. Equally, they are the prevailing currency, being lost, stolen and fought over on a daily basis.

In sharp contrast, personal organisers have no status at all. Even the flimsiest of research would reveal a concise scientific rule with regard to the loss of personal organisers in Holte School. This would state that: "The Velocity of Disappearance of a personal organiser increases with the age of the Owner".

I trot to the top of the steps that lead up from the tunnel-like corridor and see those distinctive, blue plastic-backed organisers heading towards me. They are in the hands of the Year Seven (first year) boys and girls appearing from the exit doors of the main school building. The loosely formed groups are clutching bags, coats and organisers, their excited voices rising as they descend upon me. I point the girls in the direction of their changing rooms as the boys mill about chaotically around the top of the steps. They're all mine now, for the next hour, anyway.

I stand there, perfectly still to emphasise my waiting. They have been lined up and escorted into the changing room by Howard and Andrew. There's still a buzz of conversation, with occasional questions fired in my direction.

"What we gonna do today, Sir?"

"I haven't got any kit!"

"My mum says I haven't got to do P.E."

I do not move. I just stand there with folded arms, surveying the scene and them. I have a determination never to answer questions this early in a lesson on the premise that everything will become apparent. I am determined not to waste a perfectly good voice that by the end of the week will begin to sound like a train announcer with laryngitis on the tannoy at New Street Station. I never forget that there will be several more classes where these came from, all lining up throughout the day, with the same questions that most of them know the answers to... attention seeking, I call it.

There are a few evil glares from Howard and one or two "shushes" from Andrew, then I clear my throat ready to shape their destiny in sport at Holte School. I take them in, the black faces, the brown skins, the occasional turban, the incongruous white complexion or fair hair among this gathering of multi-ethnic boys. They all look very familiar. I'm not experiencing déjá vu, for I have been here many times before. I am seeing replicas of every face I have ever seen at Holte School. I see the images of brothers, sisters, cousins and now, more worryingly, fathers and mothers, etched into the faces of the new intake whose eyes are fixed on me right now.

"Year Seven... Welcome to Holte School P.E. Department. I'm Mr. Boothroyd, head of Physical Education, this is Mr. Knight and over here Mr. Oliver. We will all be teaching you sport in your P.E. lessons during your first year at Holte. You'll be pleased to know that you've come to the best school in Birmingham for sport and if you like sport or are good at sport you're going to like it here and do well. If you *think* you don't like sport or *believe* you're no good at sport, then you're soon going to think and believe differently, because at Holte we believe everybody can do well and enjoy sport. We have fantastic facilities; a sports hall, a gym, a floodlit Astroturf, a dance studio, athletics track, multigym and fitness room and a hall full of table tennis tables, as well as swimming baths, close by at Newtown. We're the best school in Birmingham for cricket, badminton, hockey and table tennis.

"Our football teams are feared by everyone, and we have some great athletics and cross-country runners. We also have an annual athletics sports day and swimming gala to look forward to. When you get older you can choose to do GCSE P.E. where we have the best results in the school."

I have embellished a little for propaganda purposes, which does no harm at this stage.

"Any questions so far?"

"Do we do Kung Fu?"

(Good question, never had that one before).

"A good question from... what's your name, son?"

"Mohammed!", a chubby, bright-eyed, chirpy individual.

"Mohammed... well, Mohammed, we do lots of different sports at Holte, but unfortunately Kung Fu is not on the timetable... yet. However, the Leisure Centre has a lot of activities that you can join. I know Judo and Karate take place in the Dance Studio in the evenings. Mr. Oliver's an expert at Origami, so ask him about it afterwards. O.K.?"

"Oh and one thing, if you have a question always put your hand up first."

I think I'm doing all right, well I should be as I have had plenty of practice. I can still feel the spasms in the lower part of my stomach and the first irritation in my throat is forming as I'm projecting my voice for the first time in weeks. I need a vocal breather, so I hand over to Howard.

"Mr. Knight will now remind you about the kit you need for P.E. I know most of you will have sorted this out after the information you were given during your visit for the day in July. No, don't start getting changed yet, Mohammed, though well done for remembering your kit on the first day! Over to you, Mr. Knight... by the way Mr. Knight is a Birmingham City supporter so never upset him as Blues fans can be quite dangerous. (There's a total blank in their ranks). Mr. Oliver is a Manchester United fan (cheers; I have to wait for them to abate) and I support the greatest team in football which is... anyone know?"

A hand goes up directly in front of me.

"Real Madrid, Sir?"

"What's your name?"

"Mohammed... Sir." He is a tall, athletic, serious looking boy with spikey hair, who is already sprouting a moustache.

"Mohammed... Mohammed... Real Madrid? Who are they? Of course not. I'm talking about Huddersfield Town. (This creates a total air of puzzlement... oh well). As for all of you, forget Manchester United, Arsenal, Liverpool or all that rubbish, you will ALL support Aston Villa!" (Boos all round).

"What do you mean, booing, support your local team! We'll let off Mr. Oliver for supporting Man. United as he's from Shropshire, which is very sad, but as for you lot, from now on you'll all support Villa... over to you, Mr. Knight."

Howard steps forward and silences the conversations.

"Now you've all been told before what kit you'll need for P.E.."

He holds up the royal blue chequerboard silky shirt and I beat a retreat into the staff changing room at the back. I fill up a plastic cup with water and glance into the mirror over the sink. I notice my suntan is already fading fast and think "God... I used to have hair once".

"... so by the next lesson, next week, everyone here will have their full kit, O.K.?"

Howard and I have been a double act for more years than I care to recall – oh well, 22 if you really need to know and it is at this point that I return to the stage before he begins to describe the reprisals for failing to bring kit. I do not want him to get too "heavy" at this point in their first ever P.E. lesson. In the "Good Cop Bad Cop" scenario, I am definitely the "soft touch" of the partnership. Andrew is still a supporting act, having just completed an accident prone first year of teaching with the usual mishaps; lost keys, broken arm, car that won't start, stranded with a football team in a distant part of the city after Howard forgot to collect him with the minibus... nothing serious. Andrew stands to one side, still a little self-conscious in his zipped-up-to-the-neck Manchester United tracksuit top, the beads of perspiration evident on his forehead.

"... and if I find anyone in the corridor next lesson without their kit..."

"Thank you, Mr. Knight. I think we'll tell them about the punishments and tortures for that next time... the thing to remember, everyone, is if you haven't got kit or are missing any item of kit, tell your parents what you need. If there's a problem (and there's a lot of those, I know money for P.E. kit being low on many household priorities in Lozells) then tell us and we *will* help. Our main concern is to get all of you off to a good start so you enjoy coming to P.E. Any questions on kit?"

There is a hand up from chubby, chirpy Mohammed.

"Sir, I've only got a Manchester United shirt."

"Mohammed, I can tell Mr. Oliver is beginning to like you already... as for me, well I'm going to allow you to wear it until you get a blue one, which had better be soon, tell them at home." (I'm reluctant to say "parents"; I have made that error too often in the past).

"And that goes for all of you... if you haven't got the correct colours, don't worry, bring whatever you've got, but expect us to be nagging you to get yourselves into blue or else!"

I can feel attention is beginning to wander and fidgeting setting in. I glance at my watch and there are still 32 minutes to go. We move into part two of their initiation.

"I'm going to give you all a sheet of paper that I want you to look at."

I give handfuls to Howard and Andrew to distribute.

"If you look at these you will see that they are the same as the large posters on the walls: *Ten Targets For Success In Holte P.E.*"

Heads begin to turn and several boys stand up to see the brightly coloured posters on the walls above the hooks.

"O.K., sit down and let's go through these very important things for you to understand."

I thought about calling them the Ten Commandments, but I think that has already been used. I stand in the middle of the changing room and every one's eyes are fixed on me as I hold up a sample sheet.

Number 1. Bring Your Kit, Be Organised.

"Now you are at Secondary School, you're no longer little children. Part of growing up is taking responsibility for yourself. I'm making you responsible for your kit. If you forget it you are to blame.

"Look at your timetable the night before, get your kit together, put it in your bag and don't bring excuses for not having it. I think we've said enough about this one already!"

Number 2. Do Your Best.

"Whatever you do in life, if you do your best, you'll achieve something. In P.E. and sport this is especially true. If you try hard, you'll improve; you might even surprise yourself by how good you are. Whatever you do; swimming, basketball, cross-country, anything... I'm looking for you to give it your 'best shot'. If you've done your best then that's good enough for us... do you think that's fair?"

(General nods of approval, others fidgeting blankly).

Number 3 Set Yourself Targets To Improve Practice.

" 'The more I practise, the *better* I get'." (Not exactly as quoted by Gary Player, but near enough for my purposes).

"Expect us to do practices in everything. It's not just about playing a game. You don't think Shoaib Akhtar, the greatest fast bowler in the world, just gets out of bed, runs in fast and hits England's batsmen on the head by accident, do you?

"No, he practises. He goes to the nets, gets someone to dress up like Graeme Hick and he practises hitting him on the head, or on the hand or whatever... and Shoaib enjoys it.

"Enjoy practising and you'll see and feel yourself getting better. Try to give yourself a target for improvement... what do you think we mean by that... anyone?"

There's a hand up on my left, definitely not a Mohammed.

"Yes, son."

"It's one of those round things with different colours, like you use in darts or archery."

(Quick... think!)

"That's a great answer... er... er, what's your name, young man?"

"Leon, Sir." He is a lean, sleepy-eyed Afro-Caribbean boy.

"Leon... excellent answer, Leon. When I say target in this practising sense I mean like in... swimming for instance. For example, how many of you here can swim 25 metres? One length of the pool?"

Twenty or thirty hands go up all around.

"What do you think your next target should be once you can do that... Simon?" (He's sat in front of me, I know he's Simon, brother of John in Year 9. He's a sandy-haired, freckled and mischievous looking kid.)

"A mile, Sir?"

"Well, I think that might be a good target for the future, but a bit steep after only 25 metres, don't you think? Any other suggestions for a *reasonable* target to aim for?"

"50 metres, Sir?" (Leon again.)

"Yes, Leon. I think that would be a good target, don't you everybody?" (I look round the changing room and am met by vague looks in return; better move on).

"I'm sure you'll all get to understand the need to set yourself targets as we go along."

Number 4. Always Warm Up Before Exercise Or Playing.

"Why do you think we need to jog about and stretch before we take part in sport... anyone?"

Serious, spikey Mohammed, "'Cos if you don't you might get a heart attack."

"... well done, Mohammed, that's very true, isn't it Mr. Oliver, particularly if you're overweight?" (an in-joke as Andy's been ribbed unmercifully about his "bulk" ever since the head made a tactless reference about someone being obscured by Mr. Oliver's bulk in the morning staff briefing).

I think Andy was beginning to drift off there and he is startled by the attention he gets. He reddens slightly and mouths the word "bastard" almost imperceptibly in my direction.

"That's a good answer when you're thinking of someone who isn't very fit, but in our situation here, why do you think we should warm up?"

"So you don't pull a muscle and get your blood going round your body better?" (that's Leon again).

"Brilliant!... if you've come out of a warm changing room like this, onto the Astroturf, and you're a bit stiff... your body feels stiff, your legs feel stiff, then you go to kick a football or run after it and 'BANG', pulled muscle. When you see the players on Sky (they've all got Sky but 99.9% of them will never have seen a 'live' game)... say before Aston Villa v Liverpool, you'll see all the players jogging, stretching and then sprinting so they're ready to play. We'll be doing that too. O.K., we'll move on."

Number 5. Always Shower And Keep Good Hygiene After Exercise.

"Now you'll see through there..." I point into the shower area. Several boys get up and begin to walk across the changing room to have a look. "... sit down, go back, you can all look at them later (phew!). There are 16 showers in there and the water is nice and hot. I expect everyone to bring a towel because after every lesson you will all be going in the showers... together."

At this point I can feel the cogs whirring, the pennies dropping and the Court of Human Rights being faced with an excessive workload. There's also the possibility of picketing on the school gates by the mullahs from the local mosques.

"Yes, we will all be going in there together" (well not exactly; I will not, except to shepherd them or, in some cases, lever them in).

"... yes, without your clothes on."

There follows much discussion, giggling and laughing as they conjure up this sight in their minds.

"O.K., I know most of you will never have been in the showers before, but bear (bare!) this in mind. Do you think Ryan Giggs and Dwight Yorke (good multi-ethnic example) have their Manchester United kit on under their clothes?

"Do you think that after the game they put their Armani suits (they all recognise Armani in Lozells) back on over their football kit, then jump into their Ferraris and go home?

"Of course they don't! After they've beaten Birmingham City 7-0, in a friendly of course, Dwight and Ryan get in the shower together and wash off all the mud and sweat and have a laugh." (I am hoping they are not thinking what I am thinking, the way this sounds I do not want to seem to be promoting Clause 28 ideas here).

"... and that's what we'll be doing, to get clean, wash off the sweat and... all right, we don't have any mud because we don't have any fields, but you all get the picture, O.K."

"Any questions?"

A pale, white boy sitting to my left: "My mum says I mustn't have showers."

(It is the same boy who said, "My mum says I haven't to do P.E.")

"Sorry... what's your name?"

"Martin, Sir." He's a sickly, pasty-looking boy with straw-coloured hair who looks like he has spent his entire summer holiday in a darkened room bathed in the flickering light of a TV screen.

"Well, Martin... and this goes for everyone. You will only be excused from taking part in P.E., or showering, if you bring a doctor's note. I know people get a bit embarrassed going in the showers with everyone else at first, but you'll be surprised how quickly you get used to it... (Martin's looking totally unconvinced) and I am prepared to let you wear your shorts if you want."

Howard hates this concession to modesty and I can feel his hackles rising from here as well as the look with daggers aimed at the back of my neck.

"Any more questions?" (Please... no).

It's chubby, chirpy Mohammed. "What if you forget your towel?" (I'm ready for that one).

"Well, Mohammed, no one need worry about that... we have baskets of towels fresh from our school laundry, so everyone can always enjoy a shower, now let's move on to the next thing on your target sheets."
Number 6. Play By The Rules And Accept Decisions.

"Every sport we play has rules. The only way we can play properly and fairly is to keep to them. You have to know the rules and play to them otherwise it's pointless.

"If you are lucky enough to play for a school team, you'll accept all decisions, whether it's cricket, football, basketball or anything else. In these games, who will make the decisions? Put your hand up if you know."

A boy at the front: "The judge."

"Er... yes... in tennis, that's right, I guess. Any other ideas?"

"An umpire in cricket or a referee in football and basketball, Sir." Yes, it is Leon.

(From now on Leon is going to get to answer all the questions; it will save so much time.)

"Leon, excellent! In lessons, the referees will be Mr. Oliver, Mr. Knight and me and, in some cases, you. You may be given the whistle to referee a small game or umpire a cricket match. I expect everyone to accept all decisions even if you don't like them or agree with them and if you don't what happens?... Leon?"

"You get a yellow or red card."

I produce the above objects from my tracksuit pocket and hold them over my head as all eyes fix upon them. (Leon, you're a gem.)

Number 7. Show Good Sportsmanship; Be Modest In Success And Accept Losing In A Good Spirit.

"Anyone like to explain what this means?"

A new hand, that of a small, wiry Asian boy near the back corner. "Humayun, Sir. It means not threatening to beat up people if you lose." (He is clearly speaking from experience here; the receiving end of it, I would guess from his defensive look.)

"Yes, a good answer, Humayun. Remember this, boys, all of you. Here at Holte we believe we're the *best*. We expect to win and when we do, we don't make fun of the other team.

"We don't chant 'we won, we won. You're crap and you know you are.' (I wait for the laughs to subside)... No, we shake hands and thank them for the game and say 'well played'. All right, we know we're good, we know they're rubbish but we don't show it, O.K.?

"On the other side of the coin, when we lose, like Humayun says, we *don't* threaten to get them afterwards. We accept defeat and show determination to come back next time and beat them.

"The same goes for all lessons. Whether you're playing table tennis, hockey, cricket or any other sport, if you lose you shake hands (some hope), you don't go into a sulk (highly likely) or threaten to beat the winner up (very probable) or 'blaze' them (a local term for abuse) or their *mums*. I don't want to hear anyone say 'your mum*' (a certainty!).

"In short, we will show good sportsmanship here at Holte at *all* times." (I am in dreamland).

Number 8. Respect Others, Different Races, Religions And Cultures. We Will Not Tolerate Bullying.

"Look at us all here. Mr. Knight's white, Mr. Oliver's a bit red and me, I'm a lovely shade of brown because I've had three weeks on the beach in the South of France... and some of you are black. A lot of you are Muslim, some are Sikhs and one or two of you are probably Catholics. At Holte there are a lot of different religions, colours and cultures. In some way or another we are all *different*. The one thing we share is that we are all at Holte and we're all in it together... do you understand?"

There are some vague assenting nods from all around me.

"We will accept our differences... we will *not* abuse each other in any way and we will *not* accept bullying in any form." (There are whole variety packs of those and that is just among the staff and management).

There's a hand up from chubby, chirpy Mohammed.

"If you feel you're being bullied or picked on *tell us*. We can't do anything if we don't know about it, can we? Do you think that's fair... any questions?"

"He's just blazed my mum, Sir!" He points at the boy next to him, a malevolent looking Bengali boy who is probably beginning to tire of "chubby, chirpy's" close company wedged in next to him.

"I'll talk to you both at the end," I say as I stand over them, inviting the Bengali boy to sit in another confined space across the aisle. He moves willingly and squeezes himself in among the sardine-like bodies. (I feel a bit of bullying coming on, Mohammed).

Number 9. Enjoy Sport And Physical Activity.

"All I want to say on this (my voice is giving out) is sport is meant to be enjoyable. We want you to look forward to P.E. lessons. We want you to be successful. If you do your best you *will* be. Who knows, you might become famous. We've had many boys who go on to be professional sportsmen, boys who once were sat here like you on their first day at Holte. Mark Walters (his pictures are on the wall among the photographs of various school teams that

*The local culture of "blazing" is widespread. The most common form of abuse is the use of the phrase "your mum", which can cover a host of unspoken possibilities i.e. "your mum does it with you, the milkman, the neighbour's dog etc." The usual outcome to this is a punch-up. Those less willing to fight will continually report that people are saying things about their mums. As a teacher you will be required to investigate and be met with blank faces, denial or counter accusation. (A "Your Mum Tribunal" would be a useful addition to the Student Council).

adorn the walls under perspex) played for England, Aston Villa, Liverpool and Rangers and is probably a millionaire now." (He is now playing for Bristol Rovers, is going downhill fast, and at 36 severely dates me so I won't mention that).

"Whatever standard you reach, if you do your best and enjoy sport, you'll enjoy *life* much more... and that's a promise, and finally..." (I am on my last vocal "legs").

Number 10. Get Fit. Keep Healthy.

"For some of you, P.E. lessons will be the only exercise you get. Some of you don't even walk to school, you come in cars (not many, really)... nobody rides a bike to school (no chance... a certainty for mugging on the mean streets outside), you go home and slump in front of your videos, TVs and computer games. I know it's not true of *all* of you *but* we don't set homework in P.E. though I'm giving you some now!"

Eyes lift and there's a general air of puzzlement and interest at this announcement.

"The homework is... get yourself a ball, get yourself a bat, practise your cricket bowling and batting, practise your football shooting... run about, play games among yourselves in the streets and spare ground. *Get fit – not fat!*"

They get the joke and laugh, also with some relief that I am not expecting them to do real work at home. No, I will leave it to the academic staff to extract blood from stones. (I think I might be responsible for a potential rise in the numbers of children being run down by cars in the streets of Lozells, but I doubt it; streets and roads are to these kids what rivers are to fish).

I feel I cannot say much more but a glance at my watch shows 17 minutes remaining. (Always have a contingency plan to fill the time available.) We will have a quiz but this is one I prepared earlier... having been brought up on *Blue Peter*.

"Now I want everyone to take out your personal organisers."

There is a general atmosphere of puzzlement again.

"... the *blue* folders you were given with your timetable and school rules in, O.K.?"

A widespread shuffling and opening of bags now takes place as chirpy, chubby Mohammed walks out of the scuffle and stands in front of me.

"Sir, I've left my folder in my classroom."

My patience remains beyond reproach at this point in the school year, as we are still only 47 minutes into it. I am all sympathy and understanding.

"Now, Mohammed, what use is it in your form room? You need your personal organiser at all times, especially in the first week, so you know who you are, what lesson you have next and also to place in the plastic wallets anything that the teachers give you, like homework, for instance. Do you understand, Mohammed?"

"Yes, Sir... can I go and get it?"

"No, Mohammed, you can sit down and get it at the end of the lesson."

Smiling, I put my hands on his shoulders (in three years time it is likely to be his throat), turn him round and, in a friendly avuncular way, guide him back to his seat.

"Now, everyone!" I am speaking over the babble as Howard and Andrew settle everyone again. "I want you to place your 'Ten Targets' sheet in a plastic sleeve next to your school rules."

This they do, though it is all a bit fiddly so I have to wait for the fuss to die down again.

"Now I know I've said a lot to you today... and it's a lot to take in, but it has to be done today so that next lesson nothing needs to be said (if only!) and we can get down to what we're here for... to play sport.

"In the time we've got left we are going to have a little test to see who knows a bit about sport. Those who do the best will get a merit."

I produce a wad of typed sheets and again give Andrew and Howard a handful each to distribute to the outstretched arms. The quiz has been a useful stand-by with the new intake in their first essential, though, tedious, introductory lesson. I asked Howard to do the quiz once.

Sample questions:

1   Who won the Derby last year? (Nijinsky)

2   Where will the next British Open Golf be held? (Turnberry)

with more of that ilk. You might guess that Howard is a keen golfer/hacker and likes an occasional bet on the horses. However, horseracing and golf are not major pursuits in Lozells... though once I do recall seeing a golf club being swung in Aston... a youth was smashing a bus shelter with it.

Howard's quiz was not a success. I had no choice but to remove this responsibility from his extensive job description. I seem to remember giving him feedback on the quiz's alarmingly low scores.

"Howard, it wasn't meant to be fucking Mastermind!"

Well, my quiz is much more "user-friendly" and 'hands-on'. These terms come readily to mind as Staff Training Day was only yesterday.

My quiz: "Now boys, listen carefully this way! I have a box and in it are 15 sporting objects. I will produce them from the box one at a time and you have to say what they are and which sport they belong to. You do this by filling out the boxes next to numbers 1 to 15 on the typed sheet you've been given.

"Do you all understand? Don't worry about *spelling,* spelling doesn't matter as long as I can understand what you've written!"

(Sorry for my lack of rigour, Mr. Woodhead*)

At this point I should be differentiating, as some of the kids will barely be able to write a word. Giving them all the same undifferentiated task is not on, really, but after all, we're only the P.E. department, not the English department... and it is only a bit of fun, trying to fill the 10 minutes remaining... oh, you have a go, Estelle Morris†!

I reach into the big cardboard box that I've placed on the table. I take out a relay baton.

"It's a relay baton!"

"Leon... the idea is to write down the answer on your own sheet and keep your answers to yourself. Well done, anyway, but now we'll use that as an example, don't write it down!" (There's some crossing out going on).

"From now on, everybody, rest your answer sheet on your personal organiser and keep your answers to yourself."

"But Sir, I haven't got a folder to rest on."

(Guess who?... no, it's not a quiz question).

"Here, Mohammed, have a clipboard." (Contingency number two! Contingency number three is to have lots of spare pens, but for the first time in "the History of the World" everyone seems to have a pen).

"Sir, I haven't got a pen."

(Guess who?... you are wrong, it is my friend Martin whose mum clearly believes he should not carry a pen either. No, stop being unkind *now*!)

"Here you are, Martin... now let's get on, O.K."

There is no desperation in my voice. I am a true professional, I am a true professional, I am...

"Now no one is to speak, just look at the object, write down what you think it is and which sport you would use it in."

My hand reaches into the box and slowly I hold up object no. 1. It is a football shin guard. (You have to start with an easy one).

"I know this is an easy one, but write down what it is and don't let anyone see. Don't forget to write down the sport or game you would use it in." (I'm sorry for being repetitive, but I think we are getting there. Their heads are down, carefully writing, with much shielding of paper from prying eyes).

Object no. 2 – a rounders ball (easy to get wrong). And so it goes on as I work my way through the box. They are quiet and attentive with the occasional gleeful gasp of private satisfaction upon recognising an object that seems to baffle everyone else.

Chief Inspector for OFSTED
†*Education Minister*

Object no. 3 – an abdominal protector or box (some giggles).

Object no. 4 – a shuttlecock (vague recognition, generally).

Object no. 5 – swimming goggles (they've all got it).

Object no. 6 – a football stud spanner (they all attempt to get a better look. I have to tell them to sit down and I walk around to give them a close up view).

Object no. 7 – a hockey kicker (the majority are puzzled).

Object no. 8 – a trampoline spring (isolated "yeses!").

Object no. 9 – a gel ice pack (total bafflement I should not have used this, it is too difficult).

Object no. 10 – a table tennis post (some know it).

Object no. 11 – a foil (as in sword fencing, they all like that!).

Object no. 12 – a lacrosse stick (see number 9).

Object no. 13 – a gum shield (some start shadow-boxing. I have to say "don't give the game away!").

Object no. 14 – a hockey goalkeeper's mask (they are totally intrigued by this).

Object no. 15 (oh no! I need something because Leon was a smart alec at the start).

I dart into the staff area and quickly grab a hammer, carrying it by the handle; the metal ball, hanging from the wire, bangs along the floor. (Some seem to recognise it straight away).

"That's it everyone, well done! Don't forget there are merits for those boys who get the most right. Now make sure your name is on the top of the sheet. I also want you to write in the three boxes at the bottom of the paper your three favourite sports... got it?"

This they proceed to do, and in the minute remaining Howard and Andrew collect in the sheets of paper as I turn back several restless, impatient bodies who believe this is the signal for them to leave.

The bell rings.

I stand arms folded, waiting for silence and their attention. "Now everyone, well done. You've been very patient today as you've had to listen to a lot of information. Remember, next lesson... Friday, period 5 (roll on Friday, 3.30 pm) we are going to start. No talk, no information, no quizzes just *action*. Well done!"

We dismiss them, one area of the changing room at a time to avoid being trampled to death.

They have gone.

Andrew says, "They don't seem a bad lot to me."

Before I answer, chubby, chirpy Mohammed bounces back through the doorway.

"Sorry, Sir," he chimes in with a wide grin, "forgot to hand my quiz sheet in." He turns on his heel, having thrust his paper at me, then sprints out through the door, his foot-falls echoing down the corridor. The three of us shake our heads in unison and laugh.

I glance down at his crumpled sheet.

Name:	Mohammed Ali	7T
No 1	Fotball pad	Fotball
(several blanks)		
No 7	a shoo	running
(more blanks)		
No 11	a sord	sord fytin
(blanks)		
No 14	a massk	Hanibl Lekkta
Favourite Sports		
1	Kung Foo	
2	Snoker	
	Drats	

I place his sheet on the pile on the table-top. It is Year 10 next and a boy bursts in breathlessly.

"Sir... what we doin' today, Sir?"

P.S.   Leon won the quiz.

Chapter Two

HUGHIE: KEEP ON RUNNING
(Mid 1970s)

THERE WERE two things I did not see on the morning I went for an interview at Holte School, for my first ever teaching post; any pupils or Hughie Quigley. Perhaps the headmaster, Mr. Normington-Mitchell and his deputy, Mr. Stroud might have been worried that my apparent air of calm would have been unduly ruffled had I done so.

After all, a candidate for interview does not need to have any unnecessary clutter in his mind when about to undergo a demanding interrogation, namely, a glimpse of the children whom he is likely to be teaching or the Head of Department who is to be his mentor and set an example for him as he is about to embark upon his fledgling career.

I had spent an hour walking around the Lozells neighbourhood after the taxi had deposited me at the school's front gates beneath the sign *Holte Comprehensive School*, beneath which someone had written *Is Crap*. I had walked trance-like along the parallel streets of row upon row of red-bricked, terraced houses opposite the school. Many were boarded up, seemingly awaiting demolition. I had blinked at the multi-racial population inhabiting them and the lively bustle of the run-down shops of the Lozells Road. This scene was totally alien to me. It was another planet to which I had been transported. This was extreme cultureshock after four years in the leafy Georgian-terraced haven of Cheltenham and the six months in the quiet suburbs of Scarborough, Ontario, where I had sought a respite from school, college and anything resembling an educational institution.

I turned the corner, away from the market-stall style frontages of the shops. I was about to cross the street opposite the school's main entrance when I saw what I thought to be the entire school population filing out in twos from a distant gate further up the street. It resembled an ordered evacuation by the back door.

I could have been forgiven for thinking the school had been cleared specifically so I would face no distractions in the taxing interview that lay ahead. I sat outside the headmaster's study, cup of coffee in my trembling hand, five minutes later. Nervously, I asked the school secretary if the other candidates had arrived.

"Oh there are no other candidates, Mr. Boothroyd," came the encouraging reply.

It was December 21st, the last day of the Autumn term; the post had been advertised to commence from January 1st 1972. Being the sole interviewee, the headmaster and his deputy were able to put me through a particularly rigorous interrogation, as to my suitability for the post of Teacher of Physical Education in a school of some tradition. Well, it had "some"; one year and one term to be exact. The school had opened in September 1970, with three schools, Lozells Girls, Holte Grammar School for Boys and Gower Street Boys Secondary Modern merging to form Holte Comprehensive on the new purpose-built campus.

The interview lasted 15 minutes. It also consisted of several probing and pertinent questions. These were along the general lines of:

"Have you been to Birmingham before?"

"Will you require help in finding accommodation?"

"Have you received your travel claim form?"

I dealt adeptly with each question. The whole interview really posed one all-embracing query.

"When can you start?"

I seem to recall being asked if I had any questions of my own that I wished to ask, as they were now offering me the job. My mind was in turmoil from the "grilling" I had endured and the inescapable fact that I was beginning to realise ("I've got a job. I've got a job!").

The only question that came to mind was,

"Er, er, yes, where are all the children?"

"Oh, of course, they're all at the church, at the school carol service. Anyway you'll be wanting to catch your train now. Can we get the secretary to call you a taxi... don't forget to sign and give her your expenses form. We look forward to seeing you on January 6th, Mr. Boothroyd. Good luck!"

The headmaster rose from behind his desk, shook my hand, and his deputy ushered me out into the echoingly quiet corridor.

Hughie phoned me in Yorkshire the following day. I had returned to the tranquillity of my parents' bungalow on the rural outskirts of Huddersfield.

"Hello, can I speak to Gary Boothroyd, please?"

"That's me..."

"Hello there, Gary, this is Hughie Quigley... I'm the head of boys' P.E. at Holte School. I'm pleased to be speaking to you. Sorry I never got to meet you yesterday. I'm sure you're going to enjoy the job... it's a very lively school. I hope we can get together before you start after the Christmas holiday. When will youse be coming to Birmingham? Have you got yourself sorted for living yet, if not you're more than welcome to stay with me and Edith and the little ones..."

I cut him short, as his rapid Irish monologue seemed to need no pause for breath.

"Well that's very kind of you, Hughie... but I'm making some enquiries already."

Our conversation lasted the best part of half an hour with Hughie contributing approximately all of it, while I made the occasional sound at my end to indicate I was still breathing. Hughie told me all about the school, the kids, his kids, his wife and what they would be doing over the Christmas period.

"We're away to visit my family in Ireland from the 27th but we'll be back for the 2nd."

School started on the 6th so I was alarmed to realise I knew little (nothing) about timetable, groups, courses, syllabus, organisation or anything much relating to Physical Education at Holte School. I knew what facilities it had from the information pack the school had sent with my application forms; other than that, zero. I managed to persuade Hughie to meet with me two days before the new school term, though I felt a little anxious of the fact that Hughie had voiced the opinion that we could "sort me out" on the first day back and that,

"We could throw them a ball, while I fill you in and tell you what's what, so to speak!"

Hughie suggested a venue for my briefing after I rejected the above strategy. It was to be the *Jester* pub next to the Birmingham Casino, somewhere I ought to be able to find as a complete stranger to the city. Hughie gave me sketchy directions from New Street station which I hastily jotted down on my mum's floral notepad. We agreed upon a 12.00 noon lunchtime meeting for detailed discussion and information dissemination with regard to my anticipated role as a teacher of Physical Education at Holte School... or that is what I hoped.

He was standing inside the doorway of *The Jester*, sheltering from the rain. I recognised him immediately, even though I had never seen him before. Wispy, sandy hair, pale, freckled face, about my height, 5ft 8ins, wearing turquoise running bottoms and a white T-shirt with the motif, "*run for your life*", emblazoned across the chest.

Two hours later, three pints of lager consumed by me and one pint of mild by Hughie, I still knew little more than nothing about the mysterious workings and administration of the Holte Physical Education Department. What I did know was that Hughie was an affable, sympathetic Ulsterman from a small village in the north west of Ireland and that he had a wife and two "kiddies" and he lived out at Atherstone near Tamworth. I had also discovered that he ran.

Hughie was a runner. He ran long distances every day in all weathers. He ran from home to school and back (10 to 12 miles each way) some days. He ran in the lunchhour, he ran in non-contact periods and he had run to the pub. He had told me as he was jogging on the spot in *The Jester's* doorway.

"I've parked the car at school and had a trot into town... I needed to stretch my legs after all that Christmas and New Year grub. I'd better just stick to the one pint as I have to run back."

To put it simply, Hughie travelled light and I suppose if I had to run everywhere, I would have too.

The couple of hours in the fuggy atmosphere of the pub had just flown by and my lunchtime lagers and cheese rolls pushed to the back of my mind the questions I had urgently needed answering; "What is my timetable?", "Which groups will I teach?", "What will I teach?" all the usual minor queries on a teacher's mind at the start of a new term in an unknown school.

"Right, I'll be away then. I've enjoyed talking to you, Gary. Don't you worry at all, we'll sort the finer detail out the first morning. We'll throw them a ball and take it from there!"

Hughie's white T-shirt disappeared into the traffic as I stood in the grey drizzle. I took out my bus pass and headed back to my one-room bedsitter in Moseley, bloated, disorientated and with a definite sense of foreboding.

Hughie threw them the ball. In fact, he threw several balls. Every lesson for the first couple of days. He had jotted down a timetable that covered the first few weeks. It was scribbled on a piece of A4 paper, and he pinned it to the changing room noticeboard on that first morning. He had talked to each class in turn after I had been introduced; "Mr. Boothroyd, our new P.E. teacher." Dai, the other full-time P.E. teacher and I had stood at opposite corners of the changing area to quieten the excitable, noisy boys, dampen down the frequent laughter and generally discourage talking as Hughie embarked upon a rambling, humorous though generally incoherent monologue about expectations, arrangements and "organisation", for the half-term ahead. He said he would excuse them kit requirements for the first lesson but in the interests of "say...fur...tee", full kit and correct footwear would be required for the next lesson... "or else."

"Say...fur...tee, say...fur...tee", the pupils, particularly the older ones, would pick up on this lilting version of the word "safety" and immediately an undercurrent of "say...fur...tee", "say...fur...tee" would begin to emanate from pockets around the room. Hughie's references to "safety points" were legendary:

"Don't you run on the poolside... for your own say...fur...tee."

"Javelins must always be carried point downwards... a very important say...fur...tee point."

"For say...fur...tee, remain seated on the bus 'til it stops."

On every occasion it would trigger laughter and mimicry and Hughie chose to ignore it.

Having given his organisational pep-talk, Hughie would then produce two or three footballs and say,

"8R, a ball, sort yourself out, two sides on the playground Mr. Foster! 8S, a ball, two sides out on the Redgras, Mr. Boothroyd! 8T, a ball two sides with me over to the sports hall... let's go!"

Dai and I would attempt to quell the instant disorder and issue alternative instructions to our groups. We would sort out sides and the games of football would be played on the assigned locations in full school uniform, minus blazers, which were left hanging like rows of bats on the hooks that lined the changing room walls.

The first week was a bewildering morass of playground football through which I felt little more than "a wanker with a whistle", whose only role was to prevent or intervene in "punch-ups", take occasional abuse and answer questions in the vein of, "Are you a proper teacher, Sir?"

There I was, white trainers, blue college tracksuit, immaculate, white Fred Perry shirt, a good degree, F.A. coaching badge, overseeing "throw-'em-a-ball football."

At least I had a proper job... and I was going to become a proper teacher.

Disorganisation may have been one of Hughie Quigley's weaknesses, but one of his strengths was that he was prepared to fight for what he believed was right... literally. I had come down from my registration class one afternoon to hear the chants of "fight! fight! fight!" rising from the bottom P.E. corridor. I proceeded cautiously down the stairs in the direction of the mayhem in the slim hope that it might have resolved itself by the time I came upon the scene. In this instance, it had not, and I had to push my way through a circle of bodies to find Hughie and a fourth year (Year 10) boy engaged in a wrestling bout on the floor. Hughie was well in command of the situation, having his "opponent" in a convincing head lock. I managed to usher the spectators through the double doors and hold them back, allowing Hughie to regain his feet and declare himself the winner.

I subsequently ascertained that the boy had abused Hughie in the pre-lesson inquisition over absence of kit and had attempted to push Hughie out of the way. The fight had been the outcome of this misdemeanour. Eventually calm had been restored and the rest of the groups allowed to enter the corridor again. The pupil, a short-tempered Afro-Caribbean boy, had regained his feet and his breath and seemed to accept his defeat in the one fall or submission bout. A few months later I was to witness the same combatant head-butt a 6 foot tall science teacher, in a crowded corridor, but in Hughie he seemed to realise he had met his match.

Hughie was also not averse to fighting behind closed doors. At Holdford Drive playing fields, one autumn morning, he had locked himself in the groundsman's hut with his adversary, a "stroppy" boy of Scottish descent. The only feedback I and the rest of the groups got of the progress of this battle of Gaelic titans was a few bangs, grunts and clatters from behind the green doors. The fight ended when Joe, the ruddy-complexioned Irish groundsman, came over from his cricket square to find out what was going on. Joe, expressing concern for his equipment inside, particularly the tea-making items, persuaded Hughie to unbolt the door. He showed little sympathy for Hughie as Joe was from the Republic and had no time for those "over the border" in the North.

We somehow managed to arrange the pupils into double file to walk back up the long driveway from the playing field to the waiting West Midlands Transport, double-decker bus. The battered Scottish Challenger and the Irish Champion, bleeding slightly from the nose, bringing up the rear. The only information I could glean as to the cause of the bout was the possible questioning of the fatherhood of the referee in a hotly contested football match. Knowing Hughie's total lack of familiarity with the rules of football, the query may have not been without a great deal of provocation.

Hughie's most notable fight was, without doubt, an open-air exhibition in a half-full stadium. The Hadley Stadium, Smethwick, was hosting the annual athletics championships for West Midlands schools and Hughie, as a team manager, had driven his star high jumper to the venue early, in advance of the team bus. His intention had been to give his talented protegé a valuable warm up and practice before the event. Hughie had felt that the notice, "*no warming up or team managers inside the track during the championships*", did not apply at this juncture, as technically the championships had not started. Upon seeing Hughie infringing this dictum in the high jump area, the event organiser (let us call him "Nasty Bastard" because to everyone in P.E. circles locally, that is exactly what he was) had run over and given Hughie a good measure of verbal grief. Not content with that, he had made the mistake of giving Hughie a more serious prod in the chest.

The Holte team and assistant staff had entered the stadium only to be confronted by the spectacle of their team manager indulging in a wholehearted bout of fisticuffs against the blue mattresses of the high jump pit. Hughie and the high jumper were both banished but he had the full sympathy vote of all his P.E. brethren in attendance. "Nasty Bastard" had got the better of the meeting regulations but by far the worse of the fight.

In all other respects, when he was not fighting, and that was only infrequently, Hughie was the perfect gentleman, with the emphasis on gentle. Trish Exley, the head of the girls' department, ran easy rings around him in the organisational stakes and often referred to him as "Quiggles". The men were always at a constant disadvantage in terms of facilities, documentation and finance owing to Hughie's naivety matched against Trish's well organised, occasionally Machiavellian, manoeuvring. Hughie, when placed in an unfavourable position by Trish's arrangements, would just shrug and become wryly philosophical,

"Ah well, if that's the way she wants it, so be it", and turn the other cheek. Trish, to her credit, with her jet black hair and cold look borrowed from Cruella De Vil, would not gloat over her successes in always securing the upper hand. She just continued to play without handicap and trounce Hughie whenever there was advantage to be gained in doing so. In departmental "one up-womanship", Trish had no equal.

There was one area, however, that Trish could not better Hughie; two if we counted running. That was in the "discipline" of slippering. Hughie could have slippered for Ireland, if the event could have been granted Olympic status. Well, after all, Synchronised Swimming...

The key to successful and effective slippering was, not to expend too much energy, obtain full cooperation from the recipients and to make participants and spectators alike feel they were playing a part in a meaningful and character-building ritual. Hughie's technique was impeccable, and his selection without favour or prejudice. Kit miscreants would line up in the corridor:

"Where's your kit?"

"Forgot it, Sir."

Hughie: "Over there."

"Lost it, Sir."

Hughie: "Over there."

"Our house got burnt down, Sir." "Oh that's terrible luck you've been having son... over there."

"I have a note, Sir."

"Over there."

"... from the headmaster, Sir."

"Let's be having a look at it... you're lucky... next time, make no mistake, you're over there."

The "slipperees" would then be led into the changing room. In front of their braying, cheering peers, many of whom would be stood along the benches in order to obtain a better view, they would receive the "slipperrrr!" as Hughie would announce it. Each recipient would be requested to lean forward to an angle of 90 degrees. Blazers would be lifted to uncover the target area and the trousered buttocks would receive one smart "whap" from Hughie's running shoe. His choice of weapon was particularly important, being whippy, light and easy to grip.

Though I came to accept the routine of slippering as normal practice during my three years under Hughie's regime, I never felt comfortable with the spectacle. I did use it myself on a couple of occasions when I had been driven beyond patience by atrocious behaviour. I vaguely remember the target moving at point of impact, my chosen item of footwear being too inflexible to grasp and a semi-sprained wrist being the only tangible outcome of the fiasco. I never resorted to ritualised corporal punishment again. To the sudden spontaneous throat-grab, I have to plead, "Guilty, your honour."

Hughie had no such qualms and he had honed his technique through years of premeditation and practice. I once witnessed him slipper 21 boys in quick succession, before a lesson on a particularly wet and inhospitable February afternoon. Sixteen of them were members of my third year hockey group which Hughie had labelled the "Bengal Rifles" as the majority seemed to have ancestors from that region of the subcontinent. They all seemed none the worse for their "slippering" as I shipped them on to the waiting, double-decker bus to the playing fields. I do recall feeling a distinct odd man out in my tracksuit, shepherding virtually a whole group of hockey players, attired in school uniform, minus blazers and ties, as there was little spare kit to accommodate them. The Bengal Rifles showed admirable stoicism and no small hockey skills in less than ideal conditions, giving me an insight into why the British lost India.

Hughie's appetite for fighting and slippering was only surpassed by his unquenchable enthusiasm for running, and his ability to get pupils to run too. He would appear at the end of most school days, as a pied piper, trotting out of the main gates, a motley following of 20 to 30 boys of all colours and cultures trailing in his wake. Cross-country running was his speciality and during his tenure, Holte became one of the leading exponents in the West Midlands. The school teams monopolised Aston Championships, leagues and relays, won several county races and were always in the reckoning at any events held in rain and mud in the depths of winter. Hughie produced cross-country champions in an area of England where there was no 'country'. There was not even any grass, or what little there was could only be found a mile away. This was the grassy triangle of parkland dividing Wheeler Street, Great King Street and the "dabble with death" dual carriageway of the Middle Ring Road which was beginning to encircle the Birmingham city centre. This was Hughie's "country". It was along the pavements of Lozells, Newtown and distant, exotic Handsworth that Hughie's running club put in their miles. Before major events Hughie would run his teams to the huge Perry Hall playing fields to give his runners a feel for grass and softer going.

Cross-country in my own school days in the leafy vales around Almondbury, above the Holme valley, consisted of streams, woods and cart tracks with the odd worrying farm dog to encourage a lengthened stride. There, in the heart of Birmingham, cross-country lacked all the visual pastoral pleasures, but still included canine incentives to faster running. Stray dogs were plentiful and far more persistent in the chase than their country cousins. Dogs, traffic, fumes and abuse accompanied any training run and this was the environment in which Hughie revelled. He was as a fish in water, in his true element pounding the streets, pavements and verges, the feet of his entourage trotting on behind. The majority of his teams were black, and their silky, sweat-shined athleticism and stamina were a joy to behold, even though several had to be encouraged from their warm beds on cold Saturday mornings. Hughie was quite prepared to do the round of door knocking and verbal chastisement. Once in gloves and gold running vest these same reluctant bodies were relentless in grinding out the miles and wearying the opposition.

Hughie ran competitively, himself, but without fame or much accolade. He was a solid club runner for Small Heath Harriers at the time, and generally made up the numbers in competition. When pressed, he would admit to finishing 83rd or somewhere similar at a weekend meeting. One understood that the running was everything, his position relevant only in the sense of pushing in front of other teams' back-markers. There was no Victor Ludorum for Hughie, few medals but plenty of mileage. He would rack up the miles in his lunch hour, often heading for lessons sweat-stained and dishevelled. A new head of Lower School, spotting Hughie in the corridor one day, invited him into his office and attempted to counsel Hughie over his perspiration-prominent presentation. Hughie did not fight him, but did return to the P.E.

department bewildered by the reproach. Style and sartorial organisation were not high on his agenda. Organising the annual Aston cross-country championships was, however, at the top of it.

This task would be taken up by one school in the area, hosting all the various age-group races one Saturday morning, usually late in March. Hughie had been excited at the prospect of holding this event in the calendar at Holte for the first time. Several objections had been raised by other school team managers over Holte's lack of "country" and absence of grass that would effectively make the event a road race. Hughie had overcome the objections by promising that well over half the race would be run around the grass verges bordering the school's perimeter fence and would also embrace the verdant expanse of the 'triangle' previously described at the bottom of Wheeler Street. It had been agreed that Holte would host the event.

The morning of the championship revealed a grim prospect. A cold, heavy fog hung over the city, visibility was less than 20 yards and seemed to be deteriorating. Traffic was groping around the surrounding streets with headlight beams unable to penetrate the wall of fog. The cross-country enthusiasts of the other eight schools in attendance expressed unease over the conditions but were reluctant to press for abandonment. After a delay of half-an-hour during which the fog showed no sign of lifting, Hughie, detecting an improvement unnoticed by everyone else, insisted the markers in their bright yellow fluorescent bibs, should head off for their positions around the course in readiness to direct the runners. Hughie attempted to place all minds at ease by insisting that these boys marking out the course would be reliable and that he himself would run as a "hare", leading the echelon of runners round a very straightforward course.

My role was to be the Finish Steward. I had laid out a line of traffic cones in the shape of a funnel in the school driveway, 50 yards from the main gate. At the end of their race, the runners would enter the funnel and receive a numbered ticket from me, which would indicate their finishing position in the event.

I stood in the doorway of the sports hall as more than 200 boys of all ages from 11 to 18 assembled on the benches against the walls to listen to Hughie's final instructions prior to the races starting.

"Now welcome to you all, boys!" Hughie spoke through the megaphone. It was a striking spectacle to see all the multi-coloured vests. The gold vests of the Holte boys outnumbered two to one those of the other schools, the red of St. John Wall, the white of Cardinal Wiseman, the amber and black of Handsworth Grammar School, the yellow of Broadway, the green of Great Barr, the black and white of Holyhead and the royal blue of Aston Manor. It presented a patchwork quilt of colour topped with black, brown and white faces.

"I know the conditions are not good... but it's a fairly straightforward course if I can explain it to you now... so pay careful attention, boys."

Hughie pointed to a large poster-sized map drawn in black felt-tipped pen indicating the course with red arrows showing the direction to be taken by the runners. The map was pinned to a blackboard situated in the centre of the sports hall and all eyes, including mine, focused upon it. The diagrammatic map indicated the school, its boundary fence, the one road to be crossed and the distant triangle of grassland to which the markers had been recently dispatched. Pointing to the red arrows, Hughie outlined the intended path of the runners with his finger.

"Noy here's where we start... top of the tennis courts. You'll all be running down here and out of the gate behind the sports hall. You'll be turning right and following the fence, staying on the grass, (emphasis on *grass*!), you'll run all the way around the outside of this fence, past the tower block of flats here, until you'll come to the pavement. Noy here (tapping the map)... is the only road you'll be crossing. In the interests of say...fur...tee (some giggles from gold vests)... do NOT cross the road until the teacher gives you the O.K. That will be Mr. Edlington over there... he will see you over. D'ya understand, noy, this is the only road you'll have to be crossing. Once over the road it's straight doyn Wheeler Street, on the pavement until you come to a marker here (tapping the chart). You'll all be running off to the left up the grassy bank until you reach another marker here (tap, tap), where you'll be turning right, keeping on the grass... On your left here is the main dualcarriageway... again for your own say...fur...tee do *not* run on the road, keep on the grass.

"Noy at the end of this stretch you'll come to another marker where you'll turn right again heading back towards Wheeler Street. As you can all see (his hand drew the shape)... you'll have run round a triangle on the grass area. You'll noy be heading back up the road, on the pavement to where Mr. Edlington (Mr. Edlington waved) will again see you over the road. You keep going straight up to the school gates. Turn right here and down the driveway, here, is the finishing funnel where Mr. Boothroyd, over there by the door, will give you your finishing ticket. Be sure to hang on to your ticket as that's the position you've had in the race and the number of points you've scored... The first six runners in from each school will count for the final points total. Don't forget to give your tickets to your team manager after the race... I think that's it. Any questions?"

Hughie lowered the loudhailer as the boys began to raise themselves en masse from the long line of benches.

"I think you're going to run as a hare, aren't you, Mr. Quigley?" I had to shout across to him. He quickly raised the megaphone to announce over the increasing noise of nervous, excited runners.

"Ah yes... boys... hold it noy! Although you've all seen how simple the course is... because of the fog I'm going to lead you roynd the course. The front runners can keep me in sight... those who'll be further towards the back of the field, just keep your eyes on the vest in front and take directions from the markers... they'll all be wearing the yellow bibs. That's it. Junior race first, first and second years... follow Mr. Boothroyd to the top of the tennis courts!"

I opened the heavy, steel-plated door and led the stumbling, shivering mass of bodies to the furthest end of the tennis courts. The shock of the cold blanketing fog had brought audible gasps from the runners as they left the warmth of the hall.

"Go!"

My arm dropped sharply and the 110 runners in the junior race propelled themselves like sprinters after the shape of Hughie who jogged ahead into the gloom. There were one or two fallers in the tangle of arms, legs and bodies in such a congested start, but they scrambled up from the uneven tarmac and staggered after the rest of the field, disappearing into the fog.

I walked over to the fence. Two minutes later, on the other side, Hughie came trotting by. He was half-turning to see the green vest of a Great Barr runner some 20 yards behind, the limit of any visibility at this point. This boy, David Clarke, was an outstanding runner. I knew him from previous races, he was always at the front and previously unbeaten that season. Hughie had to accelerate as David was closing the gap between them. A few seconds elapsed before a white vest, then several gold, another white vest then a continuous flow of colours well bunched together, emerged and quickly disappeared on the small area of grassy border I could see through the netting of the fence. A few stragglers, coughing and gasping, followed on behind, but within a minute all the race contingent had come and gone in the fog, heading for the road crossing.

I groped my way across the tennis courts and playground, feeling reas-suringly for the finishing tickets in my anorak pocket. The yellow tickets with black numbers were secured in order, 1 to 130, by a large bulldog clip. I walked past the funnel of cones to the front gates where the front runners would re-turn in approximately 20 minutes' time. The intermittent cars were still cau-tiously feeling their way, as if blind, through the shroud that had enveloped everything. The line of terraced houses across the street was still not visible.

"They're coming!"

Some 15 minutes later, one of the team managers came jogging towards the gate as the mist seemed to thin slightly. I ran back to the funnel, tickets in hand, anxious not to spill them from the clip. Hughie came into view down the driveway. He ran towards me at a comfortable jog, breathing easily. The first young runner appeared... the inevitable green vest. There was enthusiastic applause from the gathering group of team managers and senior runners, who would be setting off next. Young Clarke sprinted into the entrance to the funnel then slowed to a walk. I offered him the number 1 ticket, which he took in his black gloved hand, then his knees buckled as he crouched gasping for air. The clapping continued.

A few seconds later, a white vest of Cardinal Wiseman entered the funnel of cones and then another; two in the first three was a good return for Wiseman. The first gold vest appeared (Tony Bailey, our best runner) then another, Roy Marshall, his black face wet with perspiration, his tightly curled black hair beaded with the damp from the mist. Two more gold vests followed, which added up to four in the first seven runners to return, a fantastic effort. Half a minute elapsed then another gold vest took a finishing ticket, followed by two more in quick succession. No matter how long the time period lasted, in which no runner could be seen, it was always a gold vest which was next to be applauded, emerging from the fog at the entrance to the funnel. Holte had entered 27 runners in the race, all of whom achieved a place in the first 30... it was incredible. A few worrying minutes elapsed before a blue vested runner staggered into view.

"Everybody's got lost!"

The boy grasped his ticket and sank to the ground.

The senior race was abandoned as team managers, myself and Hughie plunged into the "pea souper" and jogged down Wheeler Street. We headed for the direction of the Newtown "Bermuda Triangle" where a whole cross-country race had disappeared without trace. To our relief, all were found safely.

I became head of Holte Boys' Physical Education when Hughie Quigley left to take a promotion at a school in Coventry. He was running home one day, when a van mounted the pavement, hit and killed him.

Chapter Three

HOCKEY, SHOWERS AND NO EXCUSES!
(November, late 1990s)

YOU HAVE caught me at a bad time.

It is the morning after a week's half-term holiday and it's a decidedly "dodgy" November morning. Heavy rain is on the horizon and I have a five period day of lessons ahead of me; hockey, swimming, swimming, badminton and football. Year Nine, Year Eight, Year Eight, Year Ten and Year Eleven, followed by a Year Seven football match after school, which I foolishly arranged before we broke up for the holiday. It did not seem a bad idea with a week's holiday to come, but from my position now on a bleak Monday morning, I feel I could well do without it.

I enjoy taking the team; they are keen, likeable and quite promising and they have even won once, but at the moment my mind is not right. Over the weekend my daughter announced that she is returning to live at home after living with her boyfriend for 18 months. Added to that prospect is the admission of my 17-year-old son to having smoked the forbidden weed with his pals at a party. I am faced with some heavy twilight conversations in the parental home this week. Worst of all, Huddersfield Town lost at home on the televised Sky match yesterday, a heavy thrashing from local rivals, Barnsley (*Barnsley*!). I spent a restless night of intermittent sleep with the three crises outlined above taking it in tormenting turn to infiltrate my consciousness. Please have sympathy.

I turn the key in the double doors and push open the right hand one against a strong southwesterly wind, very ominous. First down the steps is Juned, a cheerful, friendly Bangladeshi boy with a ready smile only matched by his sadistic streak.

"Sir, did you see Huddersfield Town on TV yesterday? What a thrashing!"

Why I ever broadcast my allegiance I will never know. I should have kept it as a private grief.

"You're in the relegation zone now you know!"

Juned, to his credit, knows almost everything that is going on in the Premiership and Nationwide football leagues, and amazes me with his up-to-the-minute comment and analysis. His major failing is his passion for all things Manchester United.

"United won, did you see it, Sir? 4-1 against West Ham... what about Beckham's goal... brilliant!"

His Birmingham accent just adds to the incongruousness of his Manchester loyalty and I have to come back at him.

"Anyone can support Manchester United."

I know this sounds very churlish and that he has every right to devote his football supporting life to whoever he wants. I suppose it is my misfortune to have been selected by Huddersfield for a life of torment. On the rare occasions United lose, Juned appears openly unhappy, a state of mind he does not share with me at that moment. He is completely oblivious to my jibe.

"... and Roy Keane signed a new contract you know; we're going to hammer Anderlecht on Wednesday!"

Fortunately I do not have to listen to any more of this as the rest of Year Nine begin to arrive. I really believe that Juned ran ahead of them just to gain maximum effect and satisfaction from his weekend's winning hand.

The tide of bodies begins to push down the steps past me and I direct Group C to the sports hall changing rooms, where Alan, our other young P.E./geography teacher, is to teach a badminton lesson. We have two groups in the main changing room; Group A football and Group B, my group, who are to do hockey.

"Sir, what we doing, Sir?"

There are various enquiries. I make a general announcement over the bodies descending the steps.

"Group A, football, Group B, hockey!"

I say this twice through force of habit.

"Sir, can we play in the sports hall?"

"Sir, Sir, it's going to rain!"

"Sir, can't we do football too?"

I ignore all these comments.

They have all piled in and I pull the door open to confront the anticipated scene in the corridor. Yes, they are all there, the "Usual Suspects". They are referred to in P.E. policy documentation as "potential non-participants", but Howard and I know them colloquially as "dossers'" A quiet calculation reveals that there are eight of them. Not good, then again, not bad for the first day back. I am just about to begin the necessary interrogation when the doors are thrown back violently and in strides Mobasser.

"Here's a new boy, Sir!"

Mobasser points to a small mixed-race boy who has just followed him in through the doors. The boy has the tense, cowering look of someone for whom school has held out nothing much more than a catalogue of suspicion, chastisement and failure. Trust me, I know the look.

"He doesn't look very new to me, Basser... I'd say he's about 13½ ."

The boy almost smiles, Mobasser guffaws.

"Oh, Sir, you know what I mean... Miss Carver's sent him down with me. He's just come this morning. I've got to take him round with me."

Mobasser visibly puffs out his chest with the importance of this task. If ever there was a case of the blind leading the partially sighted, this is it, but I smile and say, "Right... and what's your name, son?"

"Jeremiah..." in a barely audible grunt.

"Mmm... Jeremiah, I'll sort you out in a moment. Leave him here Basser, you go in and get changed."

"Sir, I haven't got my kit!" (Make that nine)

"Never mind, go inside and get some kit from Mr. Knight." That reminds me, I have not seen any sign of Howard yet.

"But Sir, I've got a bad leg!"

"Where's your note, Basser?"

Mobasser is a chubby boy of Pakistani origin. He has spikey, dishevelled hair and several double chins. He is generally known as a bit "barmy". He's outspoken, and swears frequently though he does not realise it as he speaks. He is hyperactive when he should not be (between lessons), totally inert when he should be active (during lessons) and likes a joke, particularly if it is at someone else's expense, preferably involving pain.

He always has a strong reason for not doing something and can be totally stubborn in attempting to resist any attempts by staff to assert their authority.

"Don't call me Basser, Sir!"

"O.K., Mob... where's the note?"

"Sir!..." We have developed a rapport whereby we get on reasonably well.

Mobasser fumbles in his leather bomber jacket – it is not school uniform but it is black so everyone has turned a Nelson eye. After much searching he produces a piece of paper. It is the brown, sticky flap of an envelope. Not the envelope itself, but the "V" part that seals it. I take it from him and make great play of attempting to read the small writing.

It reads:

"Dear Mr. Botroyd
Mobasser cant do P.E. today as he has a leg."

It is not signed. I read it again and verify that is exactly what it says.

"Mob... I know you have a leg... you have two of them. You also have two arms, a head inside of which is a brilliant brain which is very important for hockey... go and get some kit inside."

"But Sir! I've got a bad leg."

I show him the note, pointing to the error.

"Oh... yeah, it should say bad leg."

"Who wrote this, Basser?"

"I did, Sir."

"You did... why didn't someone at home write it?" (I am still prone to asking silly questions.)

"My mum can't write and my dad's gone back to Pakistan for a funeral."

"Couldn't anyone else have written it for you?"

"No... they were all at the airport to see him go."

At this juncture I need to draw upon all my years of experience, empathy and counselling skill to conclude this potential impasse with a troubled youth.

"Go in the changing room and get some kit."

"Sir, no Sir... I won't be able to run."

"Tell you what, Basser, get the kit, give it a go... have a walk about and *if* it's too bad I'll let you come off, O.K.?"

Amazingly, he accepts my proposed compromise and bounces off into the changing room, bad leg instantly forgotten. The noise from inside is getting louder. Where is Howard? Two boys come out of the changing area in a partial state of undress proffering me their valuables. I send them back in, insisting Mr. Knight should be here soon to take their watches. I move along the line of "potential non-participants".

No. 1 – Shaun, a pale, gentle Afro-Caribbean boy.

"Sir, I had an asthma attack over the weekend."

I know he has no note but equally I understand his condition.

"All right, Shaun, sit at the table over there and I'll give you some work in a minute."

(Why is it whenever I hear "asthma attack" I'm reminded of that terrible joke: "I had an asthma attack once. I was walking through Aston Park and got mugged by three asthmatics." I think I am sick.)

No. 2 – Amar, a lazy boy, overweight, quite intelligent, but has done everything possible to avoid physical activity from the start of Year 7. He has improved, though, with much cajoling, particularly in hockey.

"I forgot my kit, Sir. I thought it was Week One."

At this point I must explain that Holte operates a 10 day timetable. This consists of Week One and Week Two which are constituted entirely differently. It is possible to be confused if you are not well organised or live from minute to minute, with no long term view, as many pupils often do. We once operated a four period day, five day week but this proved to be far too straightforward. We went from this arrangement to a five period day and then on to the natural progression of a two week, 10 day timetable of five periods each day with the incessant changeovers and pupil movement which that arrangement required.

The reasons for this were... I have forgotten. However, it was for everyone's benefit. I recall Mr. Weeks, the deputy head timetabling aficionado, promoting its advantages to a staffroom virtually unanimous in opposition.

There were many points raised to question its desirability, the most prominent one being that pupils would tend to forget whether it was Week One or Week Two, both genuinely or when the purpose suited them. Mr. Weeks did not subscribe to this negative or cynical viewpoint. His faith led him to believe fervently that the pupils' organisational skills coupled to the use of the omnipresent personal organisers would make these fears unfounded. The proposal of a 10 day timetable was voted upon informally, rejected almost unanimously and of course came into being a few weeks later.

Mr. Weeks has been absent on extended sick leave, rumour has it, owing to a bad back and palpitations. This has been a source of some staffroom resentment, not through his having left us with a legacy of a 10 day timetable, but through having utilised two perfectly good excuses at once.

Amar had also been left with the problem of not knowing whether it was Week One or Week Two.

"Amar... how can a boy as bright as you not know whether it's Week One or Week Two?"

"I've lost my personal organiser, Sir!"

I know that I have no kit large enough for Amar so I am going to spare me grief and him the embarrassment of trying to squeeze into a skin tight shirt and shorts that would make him resemble the Michelin Man.

"Right, Amar, just this once, I'm going to let you stay here. Sit over at the table with Shaun... don't forget your kit on Friday."

Amar sidles over to the table barely able to hide his glee at this success and flops down with a sigh onto one of the moulded plastic chairs.

No. 3 – Dwight, a Group "A" pupil who is a strong, athletic Afro-Caribbean boy, and a regular in the school football team. It is very unusual to see him here in the malingerers' lineup.

"I stayed at my dad's over the weekend so I couldn't get my kit, Sir." (The family are separated and I know he lives with his mother.)

"O.K., Dwight, go and get some kit from inside."

I have no problem there as he wants to play. He quickly disappears through the changing room door.

No. 4 – Intikhab. I had seen him immediately after I had come in and I was not looking forward to reaching this point in the queue. Intikhab is a small hunch-shouldered boy with a perpetual frown. I have tried, but it is difficult to find anything to like about him and any attempts at being positive quickly dissipate when I have to deal with him. He is reluctant to do anything, can deliberately provoke others, is quite devious and is openly suspicious of any attempts to encourage or show goodwill towards him. He tries to avoid any real involvement in P.E. and can be openly disobedient when he is in a particularly obstructive mood. He is semi-permanently on pupil report, yellow or red. Here we go!

"Intikhab, have you had a good holiday, then?"

"What..."

"Never mind, Intikhab, why aren't you doing it?"

"I've not got any kit."

"Where is it?"

"I've lost it."

He hardly ever brings kit, so this statement is debatable in its authenticity because he would have to find it and bring it to lessons before he could lose it. This makes me remember... I must not lose it with him.

"All right, go and get some kit from Mr. Knight."

"I don't want to do it."

"Why not, Intikhab?"

"I've got a cold."

"Where's your note?"

"I haven't got one... I'll bring it tomorrow."

Intikhab's chin is on his chest and his hands are firmly jammed into his trouser pockets.

"There's nothing wrong with you, go and get some kit."

"I don't want to... mumble, mumble."

I fail to catch the end of his sentence.

"Come on, Intikhab, there's nothing wrong with you and we're doing hockey... you know you're good at hockey... come on!" (I am almost pleading and I am definitely not winning this.)

"I don't wanna do hockey..."

"Intikhab, go in there and get some kit!"

Silence.

"Are you on report, Intikhab?"

He produces a red report. There are two kinds of report; yellow means a pupil is on behaviour or attendance report to the head of year, red is danger, one step from exclusion, being on report to the senior teacher (pastoral) for serious misbehaviour. (Got him!)

"Intikhab, you're on red report to Mr. Holland. If you don't take kit I'm going to send you up to him and he won't be happy... will he?"

Intikhab grimaces. I can feel him weighing up the pros and cons. He turns and trudges into the changing room, but not without giving me a malevolent glance. (Phwew!). Next...

No. 5 – Waheed, a boy of very low academic ability who is slow on the uptake but quite lively and athletic in P.E. He has five brothers, all of whom are in the process of going through their careers at Holte. They all struggle to bring kit and it is apparent that they share it between them as each different year group's lessons come around. Waheed has no bag of any kind and does not carry an organiser.

"Forgot my kit, Sir!"

I "do a Dwight" and there is no problem. (Where is Howard?)

No. 6 – Wayne, a white boy with a newly cut, razor sharp hairstyle. He was a regular in the school football teams during his first two years but seems to be developing into a hypochondriac. Wayne started with colds, graduated to 'flu, complained of headache which became migraines, suffered from pulled muscles and was prone to groin strains and a persistent bad back. He always seems to enjoy telling me about his latest ailment.

"Sir, I had a heart murmur at the weekend. I haven't to do any games for a couple of weeks 'til the results come through from the hospital."

I am all concern.

"Oh no, Wayne... that's a shame. We were hoping you'd be able to make your comeback in the team for the cup game on Wednesday."

"I couldn't anyway, Sir, I sprained my ankle playing in the park on Saturday, before I had the heart murmur on the night."

(My jaw has dropped... can I believe all this?) Time is pressing and I definitely do not want to hear about the events of Sunday, so I direct Wayne to the non-combatants table.

No. 7 – Shariful and Wajid. I lump them together as they may as well be designated "conjoined twins" They are inseparable in the social sense. Their joint careers are one of classroom laziness, absence of equipment, frequent truancy, virtual non-participation and an inability to complete homework. The case for the defence might be that these two Bangladeshi boys have few literacy or numeracy skills, came directly from abroad, the former in Year Seven, the latter last year and speak English only as a weak, second language. However, I am the prosecution in this case.

"I thought Week One, Sir!" Shariful volunteers.

"Week One, Sir", Wajid echoes the sentiment.

"Go in... get some kit... now!"

Case dismissed.

They turn and attempt to go through the door together, almost jamming themselves shoulder to shoulder in the frame.

This leaves only the "new" boy.

"Now Joshua..."

"It's Jeremiah"

"Sir, if you don't mind, Jeremiah... I'm sorry about that. Now have you been told what you need for P.E. here at Holte?"

"No... Sir."

"Well, you need full blue kit and trainers. Mr. Knight, the other P.E. teacher will tell you the details of how to get it and the cost, when he comes along in a minute. Do you have kit from your last school?"

"No, I lost it... Sir"

I am determined not to add to his educational career of harassment yet.

"Well, Jeremiah... I'm going to give you a week or so to sort yourself out. Today you can come along outside with my group, Group B, who are doing hockey. Mobasser's in that group so you can see what goes on, O.K.?"

He leans against the radiator and nods.

"Stay here 'til the hockey group comes out."

I have dealt with the queue and am about to plunge into the noisy changing room which is now emitting raucous laughter when Wayne chimes up from the table by the door.

"Sir, what we gonna do? I can't write very well!"

Wayne holds up his right arm to reveal his wrist, swathed in a grubby white bandage.

I turn my eyes to heaven and my body in through the springheld door. Everyone seems to be changing but there are hoots of laughter coming from one corner. I push in to a small group of bodies to find the source of the hilarity. It turns out to be Ashley, a mild, good-natured Afro boy with "locks" to match.

His large, Mickey Mouse boxer shorts are the cause of mirth. I do not believe they are standard Rastafarian issue. I raise my voice to tell them to quieten down and get on with changing. There are still laughs and exchange of banter but I give up on it and cross to the staff changing room door where the kit defaulters are still waiting for the absent Mr. Knight. (Where is he? I am definitely getting irritable now.)

I push past the waiting group at the door and take in valuables first. Howard should have done this.

"Any valuables?"

I take seven or eight watches, small amounts of money and one Walkman, placing them in brown envelopes. Each envelope is numbered and I tell the depositor his number which he will repeat to me to obtain the return of his valuables at the conclusion of the lesson. (A perfect, foolproof system, except when fools forget their numbers, then it's "What was in it?" "A watch." "What kind of watch?" "Don't know, but it had a silver strap." etc. etc. etc.)

Next, the kit queue. (Where the fuck is Howard?) I have a cupboard full of freshly laundered shirts, shorts and socks. It is all old school team football kits and is yellow, which discourages pupils from forgetting to return it. The other insurance against long-term borrowing is the taking of an item of clothing in exchange. This is usually a school tie which acts as a "'deposit" on the loaned equipment.

Dwight gives me his tie and I hang it on a hook by the light switch. There are easily a dozen ties there, all unclaimed, another demonstrable flaw in my attempts to arrive at the "perfect" system. I give him in return; a shirt, shorts and football socks. He does not require trainers as he is wearing his own to school instead of shoes, good for P.E., excellent for style rating but a broken school rule as shoes are meant to be worn at all times.

I kit out Shariful, Wajid and Waheed using the same procedure. Waheed has no tie so I take his holey jumper as security. (That is holey in the sense of having several holes around the armpit region as opposed to holy in any Muslim way.) I have to lend them all training shoes. Along the wall, inside the doorway, are three narrow shelves all housing pairs of trainers in neat lines. They are almost all my old size eight Reeboks in white or black with one or two other sizes I have secured from lost property, which were long unclaimed. "Potential non-participants" are remarkably amenable to the requirement of using this rather uninviting secondhand footwear. I do get the occasional "refusenik". I remember a sullen individual snapping at me on one occasion,

"I'm not wearing no verruca pumps!"

I thought it was a fair comment as they clearly had accommodated a thousand previous borrowers, so I allowed him to take part in his Doc Martens. Needless to say he did not perform very well in the hurdling lesson which followed. I didn't have plasters big enough for the grazes on his knees.

When it comes to loaning out footwear I always ask, "what size?" (I am referring to their feet.) Most "potential non-participants" will not have a clue, for the majority will not know which day or week it is. (Sorry for being so negative, Mr. Weeks.) Some will say size five or size nine-and-a-half, but generally I am met with a confused look by this question. When given a definite size, let us say size six-and-a-half, I look carefully at the rows of footwear and give out a pair of size eight.

(Speaking of eight, where is the eighth Horseman of the Apocalypse, Intikhab?)

There is no sign of Intikhab. I stride purposefully into the changing area where most of the groups are attired in blue and ready to go. I cast my eye around but fail to sight him. I venture into the toilets, the smell of urine reminds me I must get some bleach sorted out... and there he is. Intikhab is leaning forward over the sinks, looking closely into the mirror, carefully combing his hair.

(That fucking does it!)

I try not to shout as it is just too early in the day for emotional turbulence, but I do raise my voice meaningfully.

"Intikhab, go out and get up the stairs. There's a chair outside the P.E. office by the gym. Go up there and sit on it until the end of the lesson. I'm wasting no more time on you."

I definitely do not want him sitting by the non-combatants at the table outside. He trudges out, dragging his heels deliberately, while mumbling under his breath something I am determined not to hear.

And now everyone is changed. I have them all sat down. I hastily give worksheets to the "theorists" at the table outside and a football magazine to Wayne. I produce my register with its neat rows of ticks and assorted codes. We are 12-and-a-half minutes into the lesson. Yes... *so far*!

Howard bursts in rather breathlessly.

"Sorry, Gary... thought it was Week One!"

Registration having been taken, Howard calls out his group. He carries a large red Umbro bag, full of footballs, over his shoulder. I invite my group to come and get their hockey sticks. They line up, with a little pushing and shoving, along the wall by the staff door where I gave out the kit. The staff room has to double as a storeroom as well as staff changing and shower. The boarded windows, glass long gone from numerous break-ins, have vertical metal bars for security. It is our Fort Knox of games equipment.

I hand out the hockey sticks one at a time from inside the steel locker, inside the double locking door, opposite the training-shoe shelves. Each boy, in turn, thrusts out an eager hand and there is always the same response. The recipient will give the stick close scrutiny. If it is a new stick, highly possible at this early stage of the year, there will be a look of triumph. If the implement handed over shows some kind of wear and tear, the grip being ragged or loose, the boy will attempt to pass the stick back to me with a:

❑ "Can I have a better one than this, Sir?"

❑ "This stick's too small, Sir!"

❑ "This stick's too heavy, Sir!"

❑ "Can I have one for Abdul too, Sir?"

(Please tick appropriate box)

The last option is a cunning ploy to obtain two sticks from which to choose. The discarded stick will be found later, jammed down the back of a radiator.

Of course, I always accede to these requests.

"Take the one you're given... *next!*"

Occasionally, I take a stick back, make as if to put it back into the locker, only to give the petitioner exactly the same one in return. It rarely fails... amazing.

I give the basket of hockey balls to a "trusty". This is likely to be someone who can be relied upon to carry them to the Astroturf without spilling the whole contents over the playground or surrendering to threats from others to let them have a ball on the way out. I give them to Ashley, the "dreadlocked" boy with the Mickey Mouse underwear. I lift a set of bibs from the various row of colours on hooks along the storeroom wall, pick up a pile of marker discs on an aluminium pole and, with whistle round my neck, head out behind the stick-wielding cohort, locking all three doors after me as I go.

By the time I have jogged out to the playground, two distinct groups have formed during the minute which has elapsed. One consists of boys lining up by the Astroturf gate as they are always expected to do, the other, mainly remnants, including the "conjoined" Shariful and Wajid, are bashing empty drinks cans and other playground detritus around the tarmac. Amongst those following correct procedure by the gate, one or two are pretending to machine gun each other in a loud headache-inducing manner,

"Da, da, da, da, da!"

I silence the machine gun battery with one shouted order,

"Shut that flaming row up, Mobasser!" then deal with the can hitters.

"If those sticks are broken, you'll all be paying for the damage. I've told you before, do *not* hit cans or stones with the sticks... you'll break them."

"How much they cost, Sir?" (Ignored)

Order is restored, they are all lined up, though there is some gentle tapping of sticks on the high, wire fence. I can feel the first spots of rain in the air.

I tell them all to run to the centrecircle of the football pitch.

Howard is down at the far end of the Astroturf with his football group. I can see him demonstrating keeping the ball up on foot, thigh and head as his charges stand in a semicircle, each boy with a foot on a white ball. Howard's ball goes slightly askew and in trying to reach it with outstretched toe, he flips it up too high and it goes over the 10 foot high fence. I hear the laughter from his group.

I assemble my hockey players around the centre circle. I insist on them holding their sticks with both hands as they jog round the circle for a warm up. They keep to the line of the circle as they jog one way, then the other, forward, sideways and backwards following my shouted instructions. The warm up serves two purposes:

1   It gets the blood flow circulating to the muscles, and gently increases the heart rate and respiration.

2   It encourages them to shut up as they soon have no breath left to speak.

(You will not find this second factor in any Exercise Physiology textbook.)

The conversations die down as they settle into a rhythm of jogging and coughing which is only disrupted by the intrusion into our midst of two footballs from Howard's balljuggling group. I call my joggers to a halt and we all execute a few different stretches while holding our sticks.

"Legs apart... stretch forward... gently... rest your stick on your feet... stretch up... hollow your back, hold it for five seconds... twist gently from the waist... this way... now the other way... *good*!"

I do not allow them to put their sticks down as invariably someone will appropriate another (better) stick and an altercation will result.

I assemble them on the halfway line, backs to the football group (good organisational point) and demonstrate what I want them to do.

"Keep both hands on the stick, Indian dribble... reverse the stick this way... that way, like so... keep the ball inside the centre circle. Keep control of your own ball, don't run into anyone else."

I give them a ball each and they are away. There are one or two collisions and several balls elude the controlling sticks, rolling away towards the fence, each with a boy in pursuit. I give a blast from my whistle.

"Stop... gather in... let's look at it again."

I invite Raj, a really skilful and intelligent player, to demonstrate, which he does, far better than I did.

"Now look at Raj... well done. Look at his hands, how he keeps his head still and over the ball. See how close his ball is to the stick... brilliant, Raj.

Right, we're going to try again and anyone whose ball goes out of the circle... five *press-ups!*"

The demonstration, coupled with the threat, has focused minds and for an impressive two minutes they are concentrating totally and not a single ball goes astray. I change it so that every time I give a blow on the whistle, they have to stop the ball dead. Again, they do this well. This group of boys have a lot of hockey skill, particularly when they concentrate and talking is off the agenda... and so the lesson develops.

I organise a series of passing and moving practices in threes and fours with the better ones taking on more difficult patterns. We move on to three or four versus one in a grid, demarcated by the coloured discs. It is all going satisfyingly well until Mobasser refuses to be the "one" in the middle, when his turn arrives. At that point, I have the bibs ready and the marker discs laid out for two five-a-side games in one half of the Astroturf, so I stifle the possible Mobasser crisis at birth.

"Right, everyone... well done. Gather in... put all the balls in the basket... we'll have a game."

There are a couple of cheers as the balls are hurriedly rammed into the basket.

The rain is beginning to fall more heavily, but that is not all that I have noticed. The girls are coming out. (Oh, no!) I had completely forgotten about the girls. Understandably, as they had been on the swimming, gymnastics and dance programme before half-term, leaving us with a monopoly of the Astroturf.

Now they are entitled to their half of it. I run over to Brenda, the young, athletic, Demi Moore lookalike, woman P.E. teacher with whom I get on very well. (Where have they been 'til now? We're halfway through the lesson... flippin' heck!)

"Sorry, Brenda, I'd completely forgotten about the girls coming out. Look, I've just laid out my markers... any chance of you sticking to the playground as there's not long to go?"

"No!" (We don't get on *that* well.)

Brenda is suitably sympathetic, however, and agrees to accept one third of the surface, which means I have to get my "conjoined twins" to collect all the markers again. As they are completing this, the girls begin to file on to the Astroturf and line up, shivering and looking decidedly unenthusiastic, inside the fence.

(I could not help but notice that there was an absence of machine-gunning or tin can hockey as they came out.)

They are almost military in their order as they form up in their pristine blue aertex blouses, navy blue skirts or tracksuit bottoms. The uniformity extends to their hair, which is wholesomely sleek, black and flowing with the exception of two athletic Afro-Caribbean girls who both sport threads of coloured beads in braided strands which brush their foreheads.

My hockey group are now lined up loosely along the fence adjacent to the girls whom they are eyeing up with interest. I am just about to hand out the bibs as I have decided to settle for one game (sorry, Mr. Woodhead) when Brenda does it to me. (Brenda, no! Please, Brenda, no!)

The girls put down their hockey sticks and begin to jog across the turf towards the opposite fence. Any instructions I try to give now fall on completely deaf ears as all eyes are fixed on wobbly bits, that in some instances move extremely agitatedly under aertex blouses. It would appear that sports bras are not "de rigeur".

There are several self-conscious laughs and one or two lascivious comments that I do not quite catch the detail of but understand the sentiment. (I hope that is Ashley's stick protruding under his shirt.) I decide against a short lecture on equality of opportunity and a critique of male chauvinism in favour of trying to reassert control and reduce adolescent libido by selecting two teams and goalkeepers. This does not prove easy as there is much jockeying for position to be selected for the perceived strongest side or better still, to be lined up alongside friends. I do this arbitrarily to avoid the embarrassment of "picking" and the psychology of rejection this embraces. I try not to ride roughshod over allegiances but try to achieve two teams of parity likely to produce an even competitive game. However, I do stick Mobasser in goal.

He keeps reminding me, at ten second intervals, to be exact, that he cannot run. I have to put him on the blue team as he refuses to wear a bib.

The two teams line up impressively, having been organised by the self-appointed captains Ashley (blue) and Raj (red bibs). The reds hit off as the rain begins to fall steadily. I can no longer see the summit of the Post Office tower near the city centre, a sure sign the rain has set in for the day. None of the players are complaining, however, as the game immediately achieves competitive momentum. The yellow hockey ball zips crisply around the green baizelike surface as the players demonstrate good control and passing. (They must have been taught very well.) Play moves towards the reds' goal as I glance behind me to the top end. I see Mobasser hanging by his (no, not his neck, sadly) hockey stick, from the crossbar of the steel hockey goals, both feet off the ground.

"Basser... get down!"

A cheer goes up, 1-0 to the blues, I missed it. The reds seem to accept the validity of the score as the ball is returned to the centre spot. I look over towards the girls to see the whole throng crowding through the gate and beating a hasty retreat back to the changing rooms. I look at my watch and I estimate that they have been out for between five and six minutes. (Thanks, Brenda. Mind you, I am beginning to think that retiring to the warmth of the changing rooms is not such a bad idea as the wind seems to have got up and the rain is now lashing down.)

I am torn between two juxtaposed Physical Education standpoints with regard to lessons in adverse climatic conditions:

(a)   Playing in dire weather is desirable in the important process of character building. To show any weakness will undermine future attempts to encourage participation in bad weather.

(b)   If I take them in, it is really me who wants to come in, not them.

It is really me who wants to go in as no-one is showing the least discomfort or desire to abandon the match.

"Can I go in, Sir? I'm getting wet"

It is Jeremiah. He had been watching the proceedings through the fence.

"Oh, sorry, Jeremiah. I'd forgotten all about you... er yes... go back into the P.E. corridor where the boys are writing and wait 'til we all come in."

He runs off at a pace I suspect he has never replicated in any P.E. lesson.

The game continues to ebb and flow as these kids are really beginning to show a grasp of hockey skills, space and movement. Any passer-by, if they could see through the stair-rodding rain, might be quite impressed by the quality of play. The ball continues to rattle backwards and forwards on the greasy, now puddled surface. It is still 1-0 to the blues and I am thinking of blowing the final whistle. We have 12 minutes left and Howard and I are going to have to put everyone through the showers.

"Last minute... come on reds, one last effort for an equalizer!"

The ball is flicked forward by the reds and finds Ali who has been goal-hanging. (A term for staying up near the opposing goal, not the activity previously ascribed to Mobasser.) He has adhered to this advanced position not through any tactical nous but simply to keep out of the way of the ball and the action. Unable to avoid reacting to the proximity of the ball, Ali controls it adroitly. He pushes it firmly with his stick in the direction of the goal, 10 yards distant... which is entirely devoid of a goalkeeper!

The ball trundles into the empty goal and rattles against the wooden backboard. The reds run around, sticks aloft, and begin to submerge the slightly embarrassed Ali with hugs and backslaps. The blues, like me, look around for the errant goalkeeper... and there he is, limping across the playground, a bedraggled sight, trailing his stick behind him along the tarmac, heading for the changing rooms.

"Mobasser...!"

We clatter back into the corridor, rain dripping from our hair, eyebrows and noses. Some of the boys begin to hug the warm radiators as I fumble with my keys. The blues are quite philosophical about the manner in which they conceded the late, late equaliser.

Led by Ashley, they have one philosophy... they feel the need to separate Mobasser's head from his body. I placate them and prevent them from pursuing this excessive course of action by shepherding them in through the changing room door while shielding Mobasser from their venom. I take him to one side.

"What did you do that for, Basser?"

"I was freezin'... soakin' and me fuckin' leg was hurtin'... Sir."

(This sounds almost reasonable to me.)

"Well, you could've waited for the last whistle... there was only a minute to go, Basser... and don't swear."

"I didn't swear!"

"Yes you did... you said 'fucking'!"

"No I didn't!"

"Oh yes you... oh just go in!"

I wade through the soggy bodies trying to hand over their sticks and I reverse the process of exchange, replacing them back in the metal locker. Some boys have not bothered to wait and have just dropped them on the floor near the door. I get Jeremiah to retrieve them which he does, reluctantly.

I return to the centre of the changing room and as the steam begins to rise from their bodies I give the instruction:

"Right, everyone... in the *showers*!"

This inspires a rising tide of groans which swells to a flood when the football group troop in. Howard adds his exhortations to mine.

"Get in the showers, my group... now!"

I turn the large stainless steel tap on the mixer valve and walk through the showers pressing buttons which make the jets of cold water hose across on the tiles behind me. I put my hand under a stream of water and begin to detect the first traces of warmth.

"Come on lads... in you get... while they're hot!"

A few bodies begin to enter the showers gingerly, with towels tucked round their waists. The majority are sheepishly taking off wet games kit and some are even beginning to pull on trousers and their white school shirts.

"Get those clothes off now and *get in*!" (that's Howard.)

"You've got five minutes left and no one's leaving here until they've had a shower!" (that's me.)

More reluctant showerers enter the white tiled area. By now, the steam is rising and there are the sounds of laughter and horseplay emerging from the hot streams of water behind the walled partition.

Howard is much better than I am at encouraging showering, so I leave him to winkle out the last pockets of resistance while I make a quick visit to the laundry. I haul out a large metal basket of freshly laundered towels and as I struggle back clutching the wire meshed container I see Mobasser sat at the table with the non-participants, keeping his head down, pretending to work. He is fully attired in school uniform.

"Mobasser, you've not had a shower."

"I have, Sir... look, my hair's wet."

"That's just the rain... get back in the changing rooms and get those clothes off... you're having a shower."

"But Sir... I've bloody 'ad one!"

"Don't swear, Mobasser!"

"I didn't swear!"

"******* ****"

I have an armful of urgently needed towels. We have three-and-a-half minutes left before the bell rings. I am soaking wet; appropriately, I am going swimming next.

Well, what would you do?

"Right... Basser... next lesson I'm going to personally stand over you while you have a shower."

(This does not sound right at all).

Exasperated, I turn and scuttle back into the shower area, where I drop the basket of white towels onto the wet floor. Howard is holding the naked bodies back as over half of them do not have their own towels. The black and brown shiny figures emerge from the steam as we throw a towel, each time an arm is extended in our direction.

There is a tangle of drying and rubbing before the wet towels are dropped in a pile at our feet. Some boys try to squeeze between the two of us in an attempt to return to the changing area with a towel still encompassing their waists, but this is met with: "get dried in there... no wet towels in the changing room."

Howard is a stickler for this rule. If it is an act of supreme willpower to succeed in getting everyone into the shower, extracting the remnant "shower-holics" requires virtual SAS tactics.

"Come on out you lot... we've only two minutes left... come on, hurry up!"

Three or four black bodies still under the hot jets of water are barely visible through the now superheated steam. They are in no rush to reach the next lesson as we have just provided the perfect "late" excuse.

"Sorry we're late, Miss... Mr. Boothroyd made us have showers."

I will be getting a good quota of telephone grief from the humourless Science department later in the day. They are still not rushing to come out so I turn the temperature dial to the blue sector.

The cold water brings screams and a quick exit of black bodies now demonstrating "St. Vitus Dance'". I throw them a towel apiece and retain one myself as I begin to dry my flattened lank hair. I try to make a quick change of clothing while giving out valuables. Howard helps me take back returned kit and he hands back the ties.

"Sir, can you sign my report?"

It is Mobasser and it is a yellow report. I snatch it from him, irritably. In the designated boxes I tick YD4 ($Y = 2$ minutes late, $D =$ behaviour totally unsatisfactory, $4 =$ work poor.) I then write a comment in the space provided for each lesson throughout the day.

[Apart from failing to bring kit, forging a note, swearing occasionally, refusing to wear a team bib or taking part in a practice as requested, leaving the lesson without permission and refusing to have a shower Mobasser has been a model pupil!]

(I have overrun into the science segment.)

I thrust it into his chest, not quite constituting assault. (Suspend me on full pay, pending a full enquiry *please*.)

"Sir, what's this all say?"

The bell rings.

"Off you go to your next lesson, Basser... don't forget your kit and *towel* on Friday."

He turns and troops off, Jeremiah following him,

"Fuckin'... mumble... fuckin' school!"

I cram a handful of spare swimming trunks and towels into a holdall then remember I've left my waterproof suit in the P.E. office upstairs. We have a one-and-a-quarter mile walk, to the baths, in the rain, ahead of us. I dash through the changing room still half full of bodies in a state of semi-undress.

Howard is stood over them menacingly: "Everybody out... I'm giving you one minute!"

I gather up the worksheets and Wayne's magazine from the table outside. The non-participants have rushed off to Science.

I have to ease my way through the multitude of girls leaving their changing room at the opposite end of the subterranean corridor. There is a heady aroma of cheap perfume and talc, not entirely unpleasant after the sweaty smell of the boys area.

"Excuse me girls... sorry... pardon me."

I edge through them and take the steps up to the office two at a time. Then I see him. Intikhab, hands in pockets, swaying back on the rear two legs of a blue plastic chair, propped against the gym door. He's chewing.

"Intikhab... just go!" (I will get him later.)

Chapter Four

A ROUND WITH HOWARD
(Summer, late 1990s)

"On the golf course a man's soul is laid bare and every facet of his character, however well disguised, will eventually be outed."

Lauren St. John

THE HOLTE Open Golf Championship is now entering its 25th year. The honour of being Competition Secretary falls upon me because I am the possessor of the Links Card. This is the passport that permits pre-booking of tee-off times at the Championship venue, Hill Top Municipal Golf Course, West Bromwich.

Not unlike all major golf tournaments around the world, the Holte Open has a rich and colourful history. It was inaugurated 25 years ago when Howard, a young probationary Physical Education teacher, invited his Head of Department, the present incumbent organiser, to play a round of golf at Moor Hall Golf Course on the outskirts of Sutton Coldfield. Howard was not discouraged by my confessing to having the minor handicap of never having played golf before, being a little unsure of rules and etiquette and more pertinently not possessing any golf clubs with which to play. Howard, in his usual positive way, discounted all these reasons for reluctance on my part by offering to lend me his brother's clubs, saying he would tutor me on rules and etiquette as we went along and that my cricket boots would be perfectly satisfactory footwear.

It was only after 18 holes that I truly understood Howard's underlying motivation – he loved winning.

Moor Hall was an immaculate, beautifully manicured course. Had it been someone's lawn, I would have been reluctant to place a cricket boot upon it. Howard admitted that this mode of footwear contravened the rules, when

I questioned him in the locker room beforehand, but he was adamant no one would notice, the course being deserted at our early morning tee-off. Howard's application of golfing etiquette has been known to be flexible on certain occasions.

My errant footwear gave Howard the first psychological advantage in a game that he insisted should have a competitive edge. I felt as conspicuous as a clown wearing size 20, turned up slippers and was relieved to be concealed from view by a row of neatly trimmed leilandii on the first tee.

I was permitted a few practice swings and felt a certain rhythm flowing through my legs and arms helped by Howard's coaching point of keeping my head still while watching the ball. This two minute coaching "clinic" had definite effect, for I went on to destroy the course; not in the way a Tiger Woods, Ernie Els or Colin Montgomerie would lay waste to a course, by posting unimaginably sub-par figures. No, my destruction of the course was executed through a series of excavations along the length and breadth of the pristine greensward. Fortunately our early start meant that few golfing members were able to witness my hooks from the tee, hacks down the fairway, and total misadventures in rough and bunker alike. My putting was solid. I hit the ball firmly and it just about remained on the green.

To give me a chance, Howard generously donated one shot every hole, which allowed him to beat me by a rugby score rather than one of cricket proportions. I did middle a tee shot beautifully on one occasion. I watched with awe as the ball soared into the blue yonder, with that wonderful feeling when everything has clicked, only to see it plunge straight into the only lake on the course. The lake wasn't even meant to be a hazard on the hole we were playing.

Howard was overjoyed at having played one of the best rounds of his life. As we came off the course he insisted that I should not be too downhearted. He told me I had done well and that with regular playing – he never mentioned practice – I would definitely improve. Afterwards, in the non-members' bar, we agreed we would play again the following week. That is how the Holte Open was founded, from a very inauspicious beginning.

Since that original match, the championship has been held at numerous venues in Birmingham, including Gay Hill, Edgbaston, Handsworth, Kings Norton and even the world-renowned Belfry (I took 121 – Howard won by 10 shots). The margin of my defeats gradually receded as I improved. The only time the championship left the region of the West Midlands was on the occasion of a school visit to Alton Towers. An impromptu competition took place over a very testing 16 hole Crazy Golf links (two holes closed owing to vandalism). Howard retained his crown on the very last hole, the notorious

Windmill, where the ball has to enter apertures in the rotating windmill sails in order to gain access to the elevated green. Howard's 8 to my 10 left him 1 up and it was here that we changed the whole format of the tournament from Medal to Match play. The competition has benefited greatly as a result, for a player's interest in the competition is no longer brought to a sudden end by including an horrendous 10 on the scorecard.

The championship has become a regular fixture in the P.E. department calendar, though there have been fallow years. Both of us had the good fortune to get married and this, together with the compromises needed for wedded bliss, the advent of young families and other sporting commitments, particularly at weekends, meant golf playing opportunities became severely curtailed.

The subsequent divorce settlements placed financial restrictions on our ability to play the more civilized well-heeled Birmingham courses, as green fees escalated with golf's growing popularity.

It was financial expediency that took the championship to the less vaunted venues of the Municipal Tour; Hatchford Brook, Pype Hayes Park, The Lickey Hills and Cocksmoor Woods. The perfect venue was discovered at Hill Top Golf Course, West Bromwich. This course had numerous advantageous qualities:

The course was only 15 minutes drive at 60mph from the school gates (down the Walsall Road, turn left at *The Scott Arms*, slowing only for speed cameras) thereby enabling a tee-off before those arriving from work descended in obstructive numbers. (The course was generally considered too far for students and the unemployed to reach, not being on a public bus route and was quieter, with an air of greater exclusivity than other more central municipal courses).

By purchasing the previously mentioned Golf Link Card a pre-booked tee time could be arranged and at a discount. (This allowed far more generous prize money beyond the £1 of earlier traditions).

These crucial factors led to Hill Top becoming the "Home of Golf".

It should made clear that the Holte Open has been "open" only in the way the World Series in baseball in the U.S.A. is a reflection of "world" competition. To obtain the privilege of playing in the Holte Open one must have some firm connection with the Holte Physical Education department.

The tournament has attempted to move with the times by encouraging female participation. No one can accuse the committee of being unaware of the importance of Equality of Opportunity.

It was only last year that an invitation was offered to Brenda, one of the female half of the department. Howard had objected to my unilateral invitation and interjected that he had nothing against Brenda or women per se (he did say Brenda, the last bit's my interpretation of his sentiments) but that (quote):

"It would devalue the competition" (unquote).

Howard talked it through with Brenda and offered her the opportunity to walk the course and perhaps caddy, in the manner of Fanny Suneson to his Nick Faldo, in order to gain insight and experience. She declined this generous offer with an ungracious "Piss off, Howard!" and refused to speak to him for a week, thereby proving Howard's other point that women were temperamentally unsuited to golf. (I am only reporting this).

Remarkably, the last five opens have been contested by four competitors, me and Howard (the champion), Andrew, our young, "jinxed" P.E./history graduate and Powelly, a Welsh Geography teacher. Having outlined previously that qualification for the competition depended solely on P.E. membership criteria, the committee have made an exception in Tony Powell's case. He is 6ft 1ins, plays rugby, football and badminton with a kamikaze death wish, drinks heavily, is a devotee of Channel 5 erotica and for no particular reason follows the misfortunes of Ipswich Town. It is obvious that he was a P.E. teacher in a previous life and therefore satisfies the committee as to his eligibility.

Also it has always been felt that the tournament would benefit from the foreign influences of flair and flamboyance.

We were also encouraged by the fact that Tony had hardly ever held a club in his life and were confident that there was little chance of the title going abroad. It has been the recent acceptance of Tony and Andrew into the fray that has led to the introduction of "The Wooden Spoon". Powelly is already five times the holder and is finding golf character building.

Unfortunately today's championship is back to being a matchplay "two hander". Andrew has had a flood in his house. His kitchen, downstairs carpets and soft furnishings are all ruined.

This would not have been recognised by the committee as an acceptable reason for non-appearance, but Andrew cut his fingers trying to break in through the kitchen window. (On discovering the cascade of water and finding his phone wouldn't work, he'd dashed out to a telephone box to call an emergency plumber. He'd come back to find himself locked out and lacerated himself attempting a break-in.)

Howard, in sympathy, had offered Andrew four more shots in consideration of the cut fingers. Andrew had tried but he just could not grip the club.

Powelly will also have to retain the "Spoon" as he has to attend a geography department meeting and has run out of convincing excuses for his non-attendance.

So it's head to head, toe to toe, no quarter given or asked for – a slug it out confrontation between Howard (The Champion) and me (The Challenger) for the honour of being acclaimed "Holte Open Golf Champion".

Monday Evening, Late June

Tee-off Time:	4.17p.m.
Weather:	Dry, partly cloudy, moderate westerly wind, temp 66°F
Venue:	Hill Top Golf Course, West Bromwich – Par 71
Competitors:	H. A. Knight (The Holder)
	G. D. Boothroyd
Absent:	A. Oliver (scratched – injury)
	A. Powell (scratched – wooden spoonist)

We stride down the rough cinder track trailing our golf trolleys behind us. I follow in Howard's wake. He always rushes to the first tee. Primarily, because Howard always rushes everywhere but also, in this case, owing to our mutual fear that someone will beat us to the tee, and as a result be faced with a slow round, having to play behind hackers.

Hackers are a blight on our championship. We can relax, however, as there is no one to be seen and in addition there are no other players following us down from the clubhouse. The pressure is intense enough without having to be observed by other pairings as we play our first tentative tee shots.

Howard selects a club from his bag. We have agreed the rules in the car park.

1. We are to play straightforward Match play

2. No shots will be given to either player

3. £2 prize money will be awarded to the winner (plus the honour of "Champion")

4. Placing in bunkers to be allowed. (The bunkers are awful following the heavy rain during recent weeks, with sand resembling concrete).

I take out my two wood as Howard strides on to the tee. He presses his tee peg into the tufty ground between the two yellow markers designating the men's tee-off area.

"How about an extra £1 for the front nine and 50p for a birdie?"

"Howard... we've agreed the format... let's leave it at that eh?"

I am having none of these potential complications as I am focusing on the daunting task ahead; that of wresting the title from Howard's grasp over Hill Top's "Holes from Hell". I swing my club in a leisurely arc, neatly decapitating a dandelion in the sparse grass alongside the trolley track. My career record against Howard reads:

Played: 39   Won: 7   Halved: 2   Lost: 30

(I am a compulsive record keeper in my diary).

It is not going to be easy, but I feel quietly confident. The reason for my optimism is that I have been (whisper it)... practising. To any true devotee of golf, the need to practise would be considered an essential prerequisite to success on the course and vitally important in preparation for a "major". It is quite routine to hear of Nick Faldo or Sergio Garcia spending hours practising chips, putts or drives after five hours on a championship course, having just posted disappointing 69s. In our case, practice, particularly in the hours preceding the game is looked upon as tantamount to cheating. (It must be acknowledged, however, that with reference to Andrew and Tony, practice is positively encouraged by the two "seniors". The last time the four of us played together, the two tyros had spent an evening at the local driving range and dispatched a hundred balls apiece. Andrew came into the tournament with a stiff back as a result of this endeavour and Powelly had two very nasty blisters on his left hand. Andrew shot his worst ever score and Powelly wanted to retire on the 16th (wooden spoon). Practice does not always make perfect.

A confession to Howard of having practised by myself would only lead to intense animated debate over shots having to be conceded. This would also lead to a perceived sense of injustice, ill-feeling and mental hurt not conducive to a peaceful state of mind on the first tee. It is with these crucial psychological factors in mind and a desire not to disturb Howard's equilibrium that I omit to mention my recent practice sessions. These consisted of:

A one-hour fling with my two wood, seven iron and pitching wedge at Holdford Drive playing field yesterday. (I'd reluctantly had to finish when some gypsy children from the caravan encampment in the middle of the running track had come over and pestered me to let them have a try too.)

Half an hour in my "free" period this afternoon, hitting balls into the throwing net in the sports hall. (I had sneaked my clubs over during the lunch hour while Howard was in the dinner hall.)

I swing my club backwards and forwards, loosening up my shoulders, trying to create a rhythm through hips, legs and arms.

"God, Howard... I feel really rusty!"

1st Hole – Par 4

Howard takes three or four practice swings on the tee. His grip on the club is terrible. His hands are at least four inches apart. He is a left-hander and being 6'1", adopts a slightly bent-kneed stance, as if his clubs are too short. (They probably are, as he admits to having played with them since his youth.) He always looks as if he is about to play his favourite cricket stroke, the sweep shot. Even with his ungainly stance, unorthodox grip and short clubs, Howard possesses a powerful swing that can propel the ball some distance further than that of which I am capable, when he times it well. His first shot is totally lacking in timing and his strong bottom hand causes the ball to lob high into the air only to flop down in heavy rough, just to the right of the fairway, only 50 yards away. (Not good.)

Howard extracts his tee peg and stumbles stiffly from the grassy plateau.

"Didn't time that at all... I feel tight."

I line up with the two wood behind the ball after taking my two regulation practice swings. My Vardon grip feels comfortable; hands interlinked, thumbs in line, fingers interlocked. My club goes back, head still; striking the ball with a follow-through that feels the metal shaft touching my left shoulder. I look up and there it is! The Max-Fli no. 2 is sailing into the blue yonder. I have played a superb drive. (Practice *does* make perfect.)

"Great drive..." Howard notes admiringly.

"Yeah... I can't believe it!"

I stride off, tugging my trolley, leaving Howard to search for his ball in the clinging deep fringe of the fairway. He finds it without too much difficulty and hacks his next shot a further 50 yards onto the middle of the fairway, still a good distance behind my perfectly positioned first shot. I feel I can just about reach the green with my four iron, which I draw from the bag, wiping the club head with a beer towel.

Howard takes his third shot and strikes a beauty, clean and straight but which runs through to the back of the green. I have two shots on him. I "top" the four iron. (I did not practise with my four iron!) At least it went straight, though only 40 or 50 yards. Now it is down a divot mark (Damn!). My five iron extracts the ball from the hollow in the fairway (too many of these hackers do not bother replacing divots) and it follows Howard's through to the back fringe of the green. Our balls lie four feet apart.

"It's you."

"Come off it, Howard, yours is further away, look where the flag is." (It is definitely him to play.)

Howard walks round to the left of the green and eyes the distance between ball and flag.

"It's you to play... look at it from this angle."

He wants to see the line and pace of the green by watching my putt first, but I do not want to get involved in this amount of negotiation at the first hole so I snatch out my 9 iron and gently chip the ball towards the flag. It is downhill all the way but the shot has no "legs" and my ball rolls to a halt a good eight feet short (Crap!).

Howard takes his putter and stabs the ball out of the inch high fringe. I watch as his ball rolls inexorably towards the hole. (It's a good putt – shit!) It stops two feet short.

"Pick it up, Howard."

(I am giving him this missable putt as I may require payback later, when the heat is really on.)

I now have this to halve the hole.

(Yes, I am one down! I hit it too firmly and it lipped and I cannot believe it... after that tee shot too! Damn it!)

"Bad luck, Gary... after that great drive as well. I learnt something from your chip from the edge of the green, you know..."

(*I know* you did, Howard!)

(*Howard 1 Up*)

2nd Hole – Par 4

Howard's honour again. He has no timing, and though his tee shot goes much further than at the first, it has a lot of hook in its trajectory and plunges to the right into more thick rough. Again, I hit a very sweet two wood straight down the middle.

"Your drives are looking really good... I just don't feel right on the tee yet." (Well too bad!)

We have to look for Howard's ball and after a couple of minutes I spot it.

"Over here, Howard. It's in a bit deep, this will take some shifting." (Sow the seeds of doubt in his mind.)

Howard stands over the ball. He gives a mighty slash and a clump of grass and ball travel all of 10 yards into more of the similar terrain. (Perfect.)

"Bad luck, Howard."

His next shot partly retrieves the situation, leaving him an approach to the green of approximately 30 yards.

(Come on! This time... forget the four iron.)

I select the five iron again and the ball soars away, bounces once and rolls off the right front edge of the green, into longer fringe grass than I would wish. Howard plays an uninspiring pitch to the back of the green at least 10 yards from the flag stick.

(He's had four to my two... now for the important shot, Nike... just do it!)

My practice with the pitching wedge, of lifting gentle improvised shots from the tufts, results in a perfectly weighted subtle chip; with a quarter follow through, which leaves the ball three feet from the hole.

"Great shot, Gary... but it's not dead yet. Mark it. If I can hole this..." (No chance, Howard.)

Howard had no chance, his putt charged way past, on the left. (One to me!)

(*Even*)

I keep to my "on the tee" routine. It is my turn to go off first. I line up the ball from behind, resting it on the specially shaped tee peg that guarantees consistency of tee height. I make sure the maker's name is at the back of the ball so I can focus on it.

I flatten the ground with a firm foot behind the ball. (This gives me confidence that I won't hit any undulation behind the ball on my downswing just before impact.) I make my two practice swings and on the third... I take a great divot six inches behind the ball. The said object limps abjectly with three or four bounces, coming to rest at exactly the point where the fairway begins, a full 35 yards away. At least it went straight. (Where did that HACK come from?)

"You hit the ground behind the ball."

Howard is very observant.

"I fucking know!"

Howard's three iron fails to fire again and he slides off the fairway to the right, into rough and in front of a huge electricity pylon. He is still 75 yards ahead of me.

The flag, even though it is downhill all the way to the green, looks like it has been placed in another country, so far away does it appear. I try to take my own advice, that of playing every shot on its own merits, forgetting about the debacle of the previous effort. I hit a majestic three iron that disappears over the crest and descends out of view onto the lower fairway. (That's more like it!)

Howard is faced with a puzzler. The electricity pylon offers no relief (local rules). He has the choice of attempting to hit through the forbidding framework of the metal giant, taking the chance that the ball will evade all crossgirders, or he can decide to take the safe option and chip onto the fairway, thereby sacrificing distance. He has seen my impressive second shot hurtle past him down the hill. (Very interesting decision, Howard.)

Howard takes the first option and gives the ball an almighty crack. He has clearly hit it well because the "Boiiiing" from the pylon's metalwork is quite resounding as his ball rebounds back from it for a distance of at least 20 yards (Yes! Yes!). Howard is beside himself with self-reproach.

"I knew I should have chipped out... I knew it! I was really unlucky though... another yard to the left and I'd have had a clear shot down the fairway."

Howard scythes the grass with his club as he trudges over to his ball. (We've had two each, now.) His next shot fades round the pylon and his ball comes to rest 20 yards behind mine, out on the open fairway. It is at least 150 yards to the front of the green. Howard's fourth shot looks perfect but takes a bad kick on the last bounce, his ball diving into a bunker to the right front of the green.

"Did you see that?... (Yes, I did!)... it was straight on line... I hit it really well and then that bounce... I don't believe it."

(Victor Meldrew eat your heart out!)

My third shot does not reach the green, but my next, a seven iron run on, leaves me a comfortable two putts for a creditable six. Howard's bunker shot, after he has placed it on a neat mound, explodes out but stays off the putting surface by coming to rest in a small thicket of grass on the down slope from the bunker. His putter snags in this, leaving his ball well short of equalling my bogey and I am *one up*!

(Boothroyd 1 Up)

4th Hole – Par 3

"How you won that hole after that drive... I'll never know. They ought to give a free drop for that pylon... I've always said that. It's an unfair penalty... it cost me two shots that did."

On and on he chunters as we trundle our trolleys to the next tee.

"You're not driving well though, Howard, are you? Let's be honest... if you'd hit the fairway, the pylon wouldn't have mattered, would it?"

"It's still an unfair obstacle on a golf course... I don't care."

I hit a five iron from the tee... it is straight. My follow-through pose is held perfectly as I watch admiringly as my ball lands in the heart of the green and with one cushioned bounce, stops dead, pin high (what a great shot! I am in awe of myself, as Greg Norman once remarked on his play).

"Great shot, Gary."

Howard's ball follows mine exactly but he has over-clubbed. His ball lands in the middle of the green only to run on and come to rest on the steep bank at the back. It refuses to roll back down on to the putting surface.

"Damn! I thought about taking an eight iron too, with that breeze behind... I knew it!"

Howard's putter from the bank is pure guesswork, through a clump of thickish fringe grass, on to a downhill, sloping green. His ball seems to gather pace as it runs well wide of the hole and 12 feet past (not good... for Howard). I have a sliding putt from a similar distance and get near enough for a "gimme'" which Howard does.

"Pick it up... this for a half."

He misses.

"I don't know... I just don't feel right."

Howard rams his putter into his bag and his trolley begins to run away down the hill. Howard has to run after it in hot pursuit. (This is all looking *very* promising.)

(*Boothroyd 2 Up*)

5th Hole – Par 4

The Canadian geese show no interest in returning to the ponds that border the left hand side of the fifth. Hitting a birdie on this hole is a rare event and these "birdies" seem to display disdain for the chances of being hit by a tee shot from the golfer about to play – me. There are approximately 20 geese to the left of the mid-fairway bunker. This trap is in a perfect position to sucker the average golfer with a well-struck tee shot. I operate on the secure principle that my drive will be neither well struck nor dead straight. I take deliberate aim for the oval shaped sanded area. My rhythm and timing seem perfect, reflected by an arrow-like trajectory of the ball into the bunker with a degree of accuracy I have never experienced before.

"You're striking it too well, Gary." This is said with a little too much cheerfulness for my liking.

Howard is always intimidated by the threat of water on the left at this hole, so overcompensates by aiming far to the right. True to my expectation, that is exactly where he lands his ball, just in the rough, slightly backward of my distance in the sand trap.

My trolley creaks as I reach the bunker. The geese have not moved. They all seem to be sporting a look of amused satisfaction as they turn as one to watch my next shot. I practise a few desultory swings with my sand iron as Howard plays his second shot far off to my right. He has made another clean strike and his ball wings its way along the top side of the sloping fairway, falling away conveniently to bounce to the front edge of the green. I can feel the aura of satisfaction emanating from him even at this distance.

I inspect my ball. It is sitting up very nicely. I begin to think a seven iron could be used. The extra distance would give me a chance of taking something, even a half, from this unpromising position. (A seven it is!) I swing and hit. (I do not know what happened there. Did my head go up?) My ball has hit the front lip of the bunker and is now positioned in a dire situation under the overhang. Howard has come over to assess my plight. He remains silent (just as well!). Twenty pairs of goose eyes beam with joy (... or am I being paranoid?)

I take my sand iron, watched by the largest crowd with which I have ever been faced. Although it is a difficult lie, I lift a wedge of sand complete with ball which lands comfortingly on the safe haven of the fairway. There is no applause from my brown-feathered friends, only an air of disappointment that I did not spend more time with them in the sandpit. They waddle off to wait for someone else to appear on the tee.

Howard is waiting up ahead as my next shot with the four iron never gets off the ground and trickles lamely along the sloping fairway. I have now had five to his two. (Hole over.) We go through the motions of putting out. I am thinking that if I had missed that bunker, the whole scenario of the hole and my resultant feelings might have been entirely different. I return the flag into the hole having taken an eight. I suddenly remember. (You *prat*! You could have placed the ball in the bunker!)

(*Boothroyd Still 1 Up*)

6th Hole – Par 4

"I can feel it coming back!"

Howard tees up his ball and strikes a very impressive three iron, straight down the middle of the left to right, sloping fairway.

"You've just lost the hole, Howard."

"How d'you mean?"

I had not noticed, until he had played his tee shot, but he has just driven off from the red tee markers, the ladies' tee; not the yellow markers 20 yards further back.

"Oh come on, Gary, you could've told me before I teed off... you walked over here too... come on!"

After negotiations and recriminations that fall just short of requiring the intervention of a U.N. peacekeeping force, I concede the argument and agree to play from the red tees too, without penalty for Howard. (I am not being totally magnanimous for at the back of my mind is the possibility that this concession may prove an important trump card in my hand over the crucial closing holes).

My own drive is not a bad one but I feel I have lost the initiative somewhat, the snap and certainty of my previous tee shots having dissipated. How quickly rhythm disappears. ("Hacker's Hypertonia"). Howard's three iron again dispatches another, depressingly accurate second shot that sees his ball stop on the upslope a few yards in front of the highly elevated green. I attempt the same with my three iron, but another mistimed effort scuttles along the ground, leaving me over 70 yards behind Howard. The steep hill in front of me now renders invisible the green and flag on the summit.

"You're lifting your head now."

"I know."

(I am also losing my backswing, locking my wrists, and failing to follow through; apart from that I am flying!)

Another trundling shot later and I see my ball disappear over the top of the hill in the direction of the flag which I know is there somewhere. I have now had three shots to Howard's two. His putt from 15 yards off the green has the correct line but stops 12 feet short.

I walk onto the green behind him with only one question on my mind. Where is my ball? No... it cannot be. I stride, with heart beating, towards the flag. I peer into the hole. (No, it isn't). The ball is not in the hole. I trudge heavy-legged to the back of the green, up a slight incline and peer down the steep bank that falls away for 10 yards to thick grass. (Yes, there is the bastard!)

Howard holes with two putts and I play an irrelevantly good chip with my pitching wedge expertise. I should have stood firm over the tee shot issue and I would now be two up. Instead, it is...

(Even)

7th Hole – Par 3

We play two indifferent tee shots over the V-shaped valley to the elevated green. We follow these with two grubby approaches from the semi-rough on the upslope. We then proceed to three putt from distant positions on the best green on the course. (Thank goodness the TV cameras do not follow us this far into the country!)

(Still Even)

8th Hole – Par 4

Howard hits another straight, confident three iron and if we possessed a swingometer, I feel there would be a 25% swing apparent, towards him winning the match at this stage. However, I try to recall my earlier rhythm on the tee... and fail miserably. I deliver a complete slice into the trees on the right. I have to accept three off the tee. My second attempt is a real peach, being straight, high and long, bounding along the fairway and passing Howard's ball by 20 yards. There is an immutable "Hacker's Law" that states "Having played a woefully errant tee shot with accompanying penalty the second attempt will induce the exclamation, 'why couldn't I have done that the "effing" first time!'"

"Great recovery shot, Gary, you can still win this hole."

This is very worrying. Howard is beginning to encourage me. He must have read the swingometer readings too. But even swingometers can "crash" and Howard's next shot proves it. He has a straightforward nine iron to the large green but produces a horrible slice. (Beautiful from my perspective). His ball disappears into long grass to the left of the green *and* there is now a nasty bunker between him and the flag. (Even Tiger Woods might struggle with Howard's next shot.)

My own seven iron is straight and true. (It is all coming back!) My ball rolls to a halt 10 feet from the hole. (*Yes, Howard, I can still win this hole*). I may have had four to his two but he is a yard into six-inch high grass. There is a flurry of flailing limbs and flying sod. When everything settles to earth it can be seen that his ball has managed to escape the tangle and lies in the open. He is left with a delicate chip over the bunker with plenty of green to play with. I offer up a silent prayer for his success.

I could play his shot with my eyes closed after all my illicit practice of this very situation. Alas, Howard lacks the finely honed touch required for this delicate shot. The ball is scuffed disappointingly into the sand. (Thank you God!) He is flummoxed and I have got him. He blasts it out and takes two putts for a seven, leaving me with two putts to win the hole. I do not need the second as my 10 footer slides precisely into the cup. I can't help feeling this is a criminal waste of a good putt and that I could have done with saving it for the last hole with all to play for... oh well.

(Boothroyd 1 Up)

9th Hole – Par 5

Howard is rattled by his unexpected misadventure as we pull our trolleys up the very steep cinder track to the ninth tee. I should have a breather as my legs feel jelly-like from the climb, but I press my tee peg in briskly and hit a confident drive, straight down the middle. I have just performed a routine that the professionals appear to perform on almost every tee. I swagger back to my trolley and ram my club back meaningfully into the top of the bag. I extract a small bottle of lemonade from the zip pocket and in unscrewing the cap, there is a loud explosion of fizz from the bottle... just as Howard is coming down in his backswing.

Howard's sliced ball travels a good distance, but at a definite 45 degree angle to that which he intended.

"Christ... I can't have that!"

"Sorry, Howard... I hadn't realised you were just about to hit it."

"Oh come on! You've got to let me take that again... I mean... I was distracted."

This time I stand firm. The noise was not intended. He was well into his swing and I am not convinced his slice was in any way the result of the erupting lemonade. (Well, not much). I add, as support to my case, that if Colin Montgomerie had hit a bad shot from the tee, he could hardly expect to have another go just because there had been a noise in the galleries. No, Colin would just have to accept it and would stamp off towards his ball and sulk. This is exactly what Howard proceeds to do. He slams his three iron into his bag and stomps off in a leftwards direction. I am determined to maintain my righteousness and be unfazed by his tantrum. I stride purposefully up the centre of the fairway, sipping my lemonade.

Howard hacks out of the rough, and then blasts a three iron up the middle. I follow with yet another topped effort, virtually cancelling out my initial advantage. My third shot is little better and we are now both 60 yards short of the green, having taken three shots apiece. Howard plays first and sends a soaring pitch into the heart of the green, his ball stopping pin high. I decide to play a seven iron runner which takes a bad second bounce to come up short on the front edge of the green. I then leave a long putt eight feet short. Howard holes a magnificent putt that breaks slightly left to right, which wins him the hole.

"Great putt, Howard."

"Thanks."

(I should have let him have a second tee shot... now look what I have done... I have psyched him up).

(Even at Halfway)

10th Hole – Par 4

We stride along the gravel path that leads through the trees to the 10th.

"It's great to be moving so quickly... much better when there's no one in front to slow us down, eh?"

Howard's cold enmity is quickly defrosted, particularly after having played a killer 20 foot putt.

"Yeah... and it helps when we're both playing well. It's a good game, this."

We emerge from the trees and are confronted by a sight of unimaginably appalling proportions. There are two players in the middle of the tenth fairway.

"Where the fuck have they come from?" I query.

"I bet they've not paid... this is always going on after six o'clock, they can't be seen from the clubhouse."

"Fucking hell!"

We are united in hatred against a common foe.

"If they look for a ball we're playing right through 'em!"

"Too fucking right!"

We decide to delay our tee shots to allow them to gain some distance away from us. I tuck into a ham roll I had saved from lunch while Howard devours a banana.

"Pity Andy and Powelly couldn't make it," Howard opines through a mouthful.

"Yeah... the battle for the spoon would have been very entertaining. Ha! Ha!"

The two intruders can be seen on the distant green in the process of replacing the flag stick. Howard is now on the tee and his three iron produces a flat, hollow sound as he dispatches the ball.

"Too fat!"

His ball goes skywards but plops down in semi-rough only 50 to 60 yards away. I resurrect my challenge with another straight, towering drive.

"That's what happens when you're disrupted like that... all your rhythm goes."

(Well mine didn't, Howard... pick the bones out of that!) Howard has to look for his ball and cannot find it. After a couple of minutes have elapsed I drag myself back to help him and locate it almost immediately. Howard hits an unconvincing shot no great distance.

I have a yardage of perfect range for my five iron, but make a total hash of it with a half slice and hack into rough 50 yards short and right of the green. (Intruders, then having to look for a lost ball... my rhythm has been destroyed, *damn it*!)

I nudge my third shot onto the green after watching Howard's mediocre effort. We both have trouble with long putts and pass up the chance to take the hole. We are of one mind as to the cause of our two miserable "double bogeys". (*flipping intruders!*)

(*Even*)

11th Hole – A Very Short Par 3

Whenever we play this hole I always think of the joke; "Yes, Howard and I don't always talk about sport you know. Once we had a serious discussion about love and sex. We ended up questioning each other about the most unusual place we'd ever made love.

Howard always prefers to go first so he admitted it was with a very well-endowed young woman on the 11th hole at Hill Top Golf Course. I said, 'Yeah... go on... what was it like?' Howard went on to describe it as a short par three with two nasty little bunkers in front of the green. He'd played it the previous week and taken three to get out of the one on the right. We never got back to talking about love and sex!"

In this round, Howard avoided the bunkers. We both hit the green and two putted for all square.

(*Still Even*)

12th Hole – Par 5

The intruders are well ahead and look like presenting no obstacle to the progress of the championship.

I find this hole very intimidating as I am not a long hitter and it always takes me four shots to get anywhere near the green, as it is uphill all the way. Howard has taken out his wood. No, I am not mistaken, it is his wood. At this point, the reader may be forgiven for imagining that Howard holds only two clubs in his bag (yes... the three iron and putter), but he does have a full set. If there was a Two Club Challenge event, Howard would be unbeatable as he would use his three iron to play all shots over 100 yards and reserve the putter for everything else. I have witnessed him putt from the fairway, 50 yards from the flag. I have seen him putt from bunkers and once from six inch deep rough. Andrew and Powelly are united in their derision of his safety first, conservative approach.

"It's all about winning, lads... not playing to the gallery," is his usual riposte to their baiting.

But it is a wood he is swinging now and I cannot resist.

"What's this, 'H', are you giving me a chance?"

"No... I think I'm going to give it a blast."

And he does. He hits it 'miles' but the ball fades slightly right to land behind the other electricity pylon on the course.

"That's no problem. I'm quite happy with that."

One drive and three three iron shots later I am on the front of the green and Howard is in the bunker on the left of it. He had learnt from his earlier mishap with the metal monstrosity and played a no-risk seven iron onto the fairway. He had followed that with a mid-iron that unluckily hit the wrong angle of a greenside bank, his ball falling into the bunker.

"I'm just so unlucky... another foot the other way and that would have rolled all the way to the flag." (But it did not, Howard... so bad luck).

I have had four to his three. He manages to scuff the ball out of the bunker then leaves his putt four feet short. I succeed in getting my ball down in two putts after persuading Howard to "gimme" a one-and-a-half footer.

"That was missable!"

"Come off it, 'H'!" (It was).

Howard is left with a tormenting short putt to halve the hole. It appears to be rolling in dead centre without a problem, but having been struck a little strongly, his ball hits the back of the cup, does a 180 degree turn and stays out. Half of his ball seems to be hanging over the edge but it refuses to drop into the hole. Howard stands over it in disbelief.

"Well... we can't keep waiting for a gust of wind, Howard... bad luck."

"Bloody hell! I've played this hole so well and you've hacked it all the way... and I've lost the hole... and that putt of yours wasn't a 'gimme' either."

It is all water under the bridge now and I try to reduce his understandable rancour by reminding him,

"That's me one up!"

(Boothroyd 1 Up)

13th Hole – Par 3

My honour, I know this hole very well. It is a five iron, perfect for my purposes at this stage and so it proves. Line, length and eventual bounce are all on cue as my ball drops to the turf, possibly 12 feet from the pin. Howard is still muttering about ill-luck and life's unfairness. (Always put it behind you, 'H'.) He hooks his eight iron slightly, misses the green and drops into very punitive rough. (I am definitely looking at going two up here!)

Howard's body language gives me cause for further optimism; his head shaking at injustice while he swings his pitching wedge, slicing the heads off wild flowers as he trails over to his ball.

His pitch from the rough is not too bad, landing on the fringe of the green, but still 10 yards from the hole. I had a casual look at my 12 footer but am enjoying Howard's discomfiture too much to pay more than an admiring glance at my ball.

Howard swings his putter and the ball looks to be following a good line on the hole and then... it drops in.

"Yes! Yes!... Yes!"

Howard dances a jig around the green, his arm raised saluting the non-existent galleries saluting his success. *(I do not fucking believe it!).*

"Now the pressure's on you... yes!"

I crouch behind my ball, mark it, polish it on my trousers, and replace the marker with the ball. Somehow, the 12 feet I had estimated seems to have doubled.

All my thoughts of winning the hole have evaporated. I just think, "put it close". I do, but not close enough, three feet past to be precise, with never a hope of sinking it.

Howard's satisfaction hangs like a cloud over my head as my predicament becomes apparent.

"This to halve." (Thanks for reminding me, Howard).

And so major championships are won or lost.

(Even)

(I missed)

14th Hole – Par 4

(I've fucking blown it... no you haven't... come on, just play the next shot... I've fucking blown it!) Howard strides to the next tee, every part of his body language shouts "champion!" and I am in mental turmoil.

"What a great putt, the mark of a true champion."

"Yeah... that was a real killer, 'H'... but it's not over yet." (It is).

This is Howard's favourite hole, one of the four on the course suited to his left-handedness. It has a dog-leg left, so he is able to hit over the trees that form a "knee" into the middle of the fairway. I always revert to playing safe, well to the right. He hits a "creamer" and although I try to follow him over the trees I seem to have subconsciously shied away from danger by ending up well to the west of the angle.

I am a long way from the green. Howard plays a good approach after I have hacked a nine iron from semi-rough. It is no contest on this hole and his par against my double bogey speaks volumes in expressing the degree of force in Howard's favour as to the likely outcome of the competition.

(Knight 1 Up)

15th Hole – Par 4

"That's two pars in a row now... I'm on a run... a real charge."

"Yeah... you're looking good, Howard."

Somehow I have got to hang in there and level this up. Howard hits a solid, straight tee shot which puts more pressure on me. Mine curves off slightly right into the area of staked trees separating this fairway and the next hole's adjacent one.

When I reach my ball I find it is lying in an unplayable position in a clump of grass, six inches from the base of a small sapling. I am about to pick up my ball to obtain a free drop (staked tree), when Howard strides over, elbows pumping.

"That's not a staked tree."

"How d'you mean... look at them, they're all staked trees."

I am 99% correct in my assertion. They are all staked except this one. *(Someone's taken the fucking, bastarding stake!)*

"Look, Howard... it should be staked. It's got two belts on it, but someone's removed the fucking stake."

"That's your bad luck... no stake, no free drop. You have to play it as it lies... or take a one shot penalty drop, not further than two clubs length away."

I know that a "free" drop is now crucial to my having any hopes of remaining in contention for the Championship. I feel I should call for the Match Referee, but the officials of the Royal and Ancient are unavailable so I use the next best alternative.

"Hang on, Howard... I gave you a break on the sixth when you teed off from the wrong markers."

"   "
".....

"If you don't give me a free drop, the fucking tree gets it. Ha! Ha!" I lift my club menacingly as if to lay into the sapling.

"All right... pick it up."

Howard returns to his own ball as I carefully drop my own onto a conveniently bare area enabling me to produce my four iron and hit my best shot of the round to the front edge of the green. The sapling standoff has upset Howard's momentum and he is only able to produce a lame mid-iron shot that finishes well to the left of the green.

We match each other by taking three more shots apiece to halve the hole. *(Knight Remains 1 Up With Three To Play)*

16th Hole – Par 4

I never play this hole well. It is a long par four up the slope to an elevated green.

"You never play this hole well."

Howard likes to confirm my innermost golfing insecurities.

"Thanks for reminding me, 'H'."

He produces yet another straight well-drilled three iron. (I will bet we've seen the last of his wood for this competition). My own tee shot lands well short of Howard's and my second heads unconvincingly to the foot of the steep rise leading to the green. Howard's second shot is cleanly hit but runs through to the back of the green. A good chip and run with my nine iron gives me a chance of a surprising par. Howard faces a long downhill putt.

"Tend the flag will you, please, Gary."

I extract my putter, mark my ball and stand holding the flag in front of me, its bottom tip on the edge of the hole.

"No, Gary... can you hold it from the side."

I sigh resignedly and stand arm outstretched, holding the flag at a slight angle.

"Can you hold it up straight, that's putting me off... and your shadow's across the hole."

(Any more of this and it will be straight up his fuckin'...).

Howard strikes his putt well and to my chagrin I have no option but to pick up his ball and lob it over to him.

"Great putt, 'H'."

"Yes... my putter's hot... your putt to stay in the match."

My possible par putt is now a "must". I hit it straight but short, an unforgivable sin at this point. I smack it with the back of my putter in the direction of my trolley.

"Dormie", Howard chimes up.

(Knight 2 Up And 2 To Play)

17th Hole – Par 4

I am not surrendering. It is not good but I can still square the match.

"You can still square the match, Gary." (It is uncanny).

I can most definitely still halve the match as Howard slices his tee shot into the trees on the left. (A definite lost ball.)

"I reckon I can find that." (Get lost, Howard).

My tee shot is a good, solid one, which comes to rest a few yards from the black and white marker post on the hill in the middle of the fairway that serves the purpose of indicating the line to the green from the tee.

"You'd better play a provisional, Howard."

"I'll find that don't worry... but I'll play another anyway."

His second attempt is a careless hook into quite punitive rough interspersed with mature bushes.

We fail to find either of his balls.

"I know it's here somewhere." (From the woods).

"I'm sure it dropped in this area." (From the bushes).

I indulge in an indifferent prod around in both areas but my only concern now is to halve the match.

"You'll have to play another, Howard."

"I'm not going back to the tee... it's got to be here somewhere." Howard's voice is coming from somewhere in the bushes.

"I'm playing mine."

I smack a comfortable five iron on to the centre of the green. (There is nothing to this game). Howard is still poking around in the undergrowth with his three iron, a very versatile club, and as I am about to rejoin him among the tangle of branches, I see his ball sitting snugly in a deep tuft of grass, but clearly playable. I am torn between two courses of action:

1. To tread firmly on his ball, thereby making it virtually impossible to extract, even with this putter.

2. To ignore its presence and help him look for it in the bushes.

I choose the third option.

"It's here, Howard!" (He is three off the tee).

"I knew it was near here... thanks."

Howard's determined searching proves irrelevant as he plays a horrible hack, which leaves his ball deeper in the rough. He sees my ball in the heart of the distant green and concedes the hole. (I took the trouble to hole out for an immaculate par four).

(Boothroyd 1 Down And 1 To Play. Come On!)

18th Hole – Par 4

(We consider this totally unacceptable – it is a par five. It is uphill, wind against, legs tired, we are emotionally drained. Forget the yardage, it is a par 5.)

I perform my tried and trusted routine. Ball on tee peg, foot flattens ground behind ball, look intently into distance à la Ballesteros and give it one almighty heave.

Somehow, everything comes together as I hit a thundering drive straight into the open acres of the 18th fairway, dappled with the long shadows of a midsummer evening. This is the greatest game. The joy I feel is nothing compared to that which fills my heart as Howard demonstrates a snap hook from the Hacker's Textbook of Technique. His ball flies over the staked trees and onto the adjacent first hole fairway, where we started three-and-a-half hours earlier. (This game is still on!)

Hill Top's benignity comes to Howard's rescue as he is able to stage a 3 iron recovery of 150 yards back onto the 18th fairway where his ball finishes rolling a few yards in advance of my earlier majestic effort. I still have a one shot advantage on him.

(This is the crucial shot of the championship).

I will not be one of Sam Torrance's wild card selections for the next Ryder Cup. My head went up and I topped it. I trudge after my ball, which finished only 30 yards further up the fairway. Suddenly I feel as if I am wearing divers' lead-weighted boots. Howard's predictable three iron "Exocet" to the green knocks all the strength from my body. My arms begin to ache with fatigue and it takes me two more inelegant hacks to reach the putting surface. I manage to putt to two feet and Howard flicks up my ball with his putter, giving me a six.

"Well played, Gary... three putts for the championship!"

Even Powelly, with his ability to misjudge line, length, weight direction, slope and speed, would have struggled not to get the ball into the hole in three attempts from Howard's position 20 feet away. Howard almost holes it in one. I hold the flag, pick up his ball and shake his hand.

"Well played, 'H'... you're the champ."

"You've just got to be able to take the pressure."

(I'll just have to keep practising).

Howard bought the first round in the pub.

Chapter Five

GONE SWIMMING
(December 1999)

I SLAM the laundry door shut behind me. We are going swimming and the large red kit bag over my shoulder holds a couple of dozen towels and spare swimming trunks. I am taking these as the usual form of insurance against those scholars who have had too much on their minds to remember their swimming kit. It is the last swimming lesson before we break up for the Christmas holiday so I have an announcement to make.

"Line up over here everybody... get into twos against the fence."

I have to wait for the boys who have been chasing each other across the playground to finally register my presence. They amble over to the back of the line forming by the high metal gate. Two of them try to push into the middle of the queue of excited Year Seven bodies.

"You two... go to the back, don't push in there. Everybody find yourself a partner to walk down with. Quiet and listen!"

I drop the bright red football bag containing the spare kit and towels onto the tarmac in front of me.

"Today is your last swimming lesson before..."

"Can we have a free play, Sir?"

"... your last swimming lesson before the Christmas holiday, so I am going to explain what we are going to do today."

"Are we going to be tested, Sir?"

"We will not be going swimming again until the summer, because it is the girls' turn to go again next term. So after the holidays when you all come back to school... *remember*... do *not* bring your swimming kit... you are *all* to bring your full games kit."

"Sir! I've forgotten my swimming kit, Sir."

"I have spare kit for anyone who has forgotten theirs."

Howard and Andrew walk across the playground escorting two other boys as I continue my monologue.

"Some of you will be going to the baths for trials for the swimming gala next term..."

"I don't want to be in the swimming gala, Sir!"

"... but that will only involve the best swimmers."

I wait for that information to sink in and conversations to abate.

"To help us with that today, everyone is going to swim a distance test."

"Sir... I can't swim, Sir!"

"... even if you might only be able to swim five metres, I want everyone to have a go. There will be certificates for those who achieve five metres, 15 metres or 25 metres. The strongest swimmers in the top group can try for longer distances if they want. Once we have done the tests... and *if* you have *all* done your best... *then*... we will have a play session. Any questions?"

"Sir, when are we going to do cricket?"

"Shanawaz... it's winter. We will be playing cricket later in the year, I told you yesterday. Don't worry, you'll get your chance."

"Sir, do you think I'll be in the team I'm a good bowler you know."

"Right... is there anyone here who hasn't got a bag?"

Raphael, a rather drowsy, smiling Afro-Caribbean boy, puts his hand up, directly in front of me.

"Here, Raphael... You 'ave now!"

I hand him the big red bag and the boys around him laugh as he tugs it over his shoulder. He grins good-humouredly at this imposition.

They are now all lined up in pairs with the help of Andrew and Howard's shepherding. I open the padlock on the double gates as Howard begins to tell me: "We caught Zabbas and Farooq trying to wag it... they were hiding in the bushes by the main hall. The little sods... we could hear them talking as we came out of the doors. Can you believe it... they said they were looking for their ball?"

We both laugh as we know their acquaintance with football is on a par with their interest in homework. They avoid both like they would a virulent disease. We know them both as a devious pair, even at 11. I look over and see them standing sheepishly together at the back of the line-up.

I swing the gates open and lead the way alongside the "twinnies", Ismael and Ishaq, who always seem to be at the front on our trek to the baths.

"Twinnies... slow down, don't run!"

I have stopped trying to call them by their correct names for they dress identically, are inseparable and look a perfect mirror-image of each other. If

I say, "Ishaq, hold your stick like this", the retort is sure to be "Sir, it's Ismael, Sir."

I have even tried a system of using the first name I think of, "Ismael", and deliberately saying "Ishaq" instead, but it will invariably be the wrong choice. I asked one of their pals how he recognised them apart and I got excellent advice:

"Sir, Ismael is the sad-looking one."

I give up, they both look pretty happy to me.

"Twinnies... *stop!* Wait for the rest to catch up."

We come to a halt to allow the other 56 to close the gap that has appeared as we prepare to descend the pathway to the road 100 metres away.

Andrew maintains a position alongside the middle of the battalion while Howard brings up the rearguard, pointedly chivvying along the two thwarted ball-seekers, Farooq and Zabbas. We proceed in much better order to the pavement that runs between the two rows of modern terraced houses, where gardens with low paling fences flank us on either side. It was here last week that we had to make a detour. We had been confronted by a barrier of blue and white tape which completely encircled the gardens and barred access to the pathway leading to the road. In each garden had been a policeman attired in baseball-style cap and blue overalls with *POLICE* stitched on the breast.

Each officer had hold of a rake or similar instrument and was searching for bullets, cartridge cases or weapons from a shooting that had occurred the previous night. The perpetrators had apparently run through the school grounds, scaled the gates and had been witnessed running in the direction of Newtown Baths along the route which we were now attempting to follow. The police contingent, as one, had stopped their meticulous search to observe our approach to the "pass" between the gardens. I had offered a breezy "hello" and congratulated them on the police's willingness to get involved in the Community Gardening Project. The nearest 'gardener' had replied with a mock serious tone

"Yes, this area has been nominated for the 'Britain in Bloom' contest next year... these lads are the Elite Gardening Squad."

Everyone had enjoyed a chuckle as we had made a sharp right turn, to take the next alleyway between the houses, the echelon of swimmers gaping agog at the large police presence.

There was no obstacle to our progress on this bright December morning, except the constant inattention and sluggishness of the back-markers. I look back to see a little group behind Andrew, who are walking in a knot, five abreast.

A clear gap has developed between them and the orderly file in front.

"Stop! You boys... yes your gang... get back into twos and keep up. On the pavement... stay on the right or no one will be able to pass us. Move on!"

We are off again, past the *Cross-Guns* public house on the opposite side of the road. It used to be the focal point for staff in evenings, after school, and a "watering hole" for office workers in their lunch (two) hours. It is now barricaded with metal shutters, having been long closed after frequent episodes of late night violence, twice involving deaths, as the drug culture moved in. Situated next to it, incongruously, is the "Butterfly House", which draws everyone's attention.

It stands out from its neighbouring pebble-dashed council houses with their drab frontages and drawn curtains behind small grimy windows which look out onto uniformly ill-kept gardens, full of flotsam discarded by passing pedestrians. The "Butterfly House" gardens are carefully tended with winter pansies and primula along its neat borders. The fences are covered with neatly trimmed ivy and clematis , now hibernating. The windows reveal curtains that are an elaborate ruched bouffant of pink and cream satin. Most striking is the additional feature, that of the whole house frontage being covered in butterflies. They are of various hues and sizes and are dotted at different heights on the front of the house. Some appear to be made of pottery, others of plastic and gauze. They present a striking array of colour in an unendingly dreary concrete landscape. The house draws head-turning looks as we pass.

"The big one's a red admiral, Sir."

"How do you know that, Kamran?"

"I saw one in a book from the library, Sir."

"Well done, Kamran... what about that small one by the bedroom window, what's that?"

"Don't know, Sir."

"Cabbage white!"

I lick my thumb and rub it on my jacket for emphasis.

I continue to lead the Indian file past the plot of waste ground on our right. It is covered with house-bricks, black dustbin liners bursting with rubbish, drink cans and other discarded junk. I notice that since last week it has gained a mattress, supermarket trolley and a TV set.

"Hey, Shanawaz... go and turn on the telly and see what the Test score is!"

"Sir, it won't work, Sir... it's bust."

"Oh, pity."

"Sir... do you think I'll be able to have a chance to bowl for the school team, Sir? I took a 'hat trick' for my last school, Sir... you know I..."

(Me and my big mouth) "I'm sure you're a good bowler, Shanawaz, just wait 'til the trials."

We are approaching the main road and I deliberately lengthen my stride to evade further cricketing queries. We halt at the road junction to allow the formation to close ranks. I hear Howard chastising Michael who is bag-toting Raphael's partner in the line.

"Why are you eating those crisps now, Michael?"

Michael is a small, chubby Afro-Caribbean boy with wide, rolling eyes and a perpetually quivering mouth that suggests he is never far from tears. Howard is not a total ogre; for in this instance the situation has some history. Howard has a Special Educational Needs (SEN) responsibility and Michael is a definite "special". He has a reading age of five and a personality to match it.

Howard met with Michael's mother the previous week and it was discovered that he had been spending his daily £3 dinner allowance on sweets, crisps and fizzy drinks.

This diet was clearly filling him with sufficient chemicals and "E" factors to do little for his powers of concentration in school. There was also the allied possibility that his tendency to hyperactivity might be linked to this misuse of funds. Michael always seemed to have a sweet or gobstopper in his mouth. We were forever asking him to open his mouth to prove he was not sucking on some sugary monstrosity. His multi-coloured tongue was never a pleasant sight to behold, when held out for inspection.

Michael's mother had consented to Howard's monitoring of her son's eating habits and in so doing keep a regular check on Michael's dinnertime budgeting. Howard was appointed Michael's Mealtime Mentor.

"Put your crisps away, Michael... save them for after swimming. You're going to end up being sick in the pool. This is a lesson now, it's not break-time you know."

Howard goes on at him relentlessly and Michael, now glassy-eyed, jams the half-emptied crisp packet into his Ninja Turtle rucksack. I lead the wavering black and grey line of boys down the path alongside the road which forms part of the Inner-circle bus route. We are neatly hemmed in by a three-foot high red brick wall that helps to form a narrow corridor between it and the higher walls of the houses' back gardens.

It is ideal for reforming the line into twos as there is only room for two people to pass through side by side. I use this 20-metre stretch as a 'sheep pen'. I stand on the wall at the end as the swimmers fill up the channel. Andrew and Howard stand at the rear of the group and everyone is nicely penned by the two walls. (I cannot help feeling two experienced sheepdogs would serve me just as efficiently... the kids are particularly fearful of dogs, in contrast to their unconcern at threats from P.E. staff).

We walk on a further 50 yards and reach the pedestrian traffic lights. I press the button on the panel which lights up *WAIT*. Behind me, four or five other hands have a press on it too.

"You don't need to press it any more... it won't make the lights change any quicker!"

"Can't we go over... there's nothing coming, Sir."

"No Ismail, Ishaq... wait for the green man."

I have seen cars speed through the red light many times here and have learned to completely disregard the green flashing man, the accompanying "bleeps" and the flashing of approaching headlights indicating it is safe to cross. We do not put a foot in the road until vehicles coming from both directions have come to a complete halt.

The lights turn to orange and there is a "toot, toot" of a horn from the car slowing in front of me.

"Bootroyd! Bootroyd!"

The driver of the car, which is a taxi, identified by the ubiquitous sticker in the front windscreen, leans out of the passenger side window. I immediately recognise the smiling features and dazzling white teeth of an ex-pupil. I lean over to the window as a black hand with chunky gold rings on each finger reaches for mine. We shake hands and he continues to hold my hand firmly as my memory bank begins to clear.

"I know... it's... Delroy... no, Leroy. How you doing Leroy... good to see you!"

"Ya still doing this Mr. Bootroyd... you're the man!"

"Yeah, 'fraid so... any chance of getting this lot in the back and running us up to school after swimming?"

Leroy laughs, still shaking my hand. Another horn sounds, but this one signifies impatience so I tap on the roof of the car and withdraw my hand.

"Better get going Leroy... nice to see you."

I cross to the other side and leave Howard to hold back the traffic from the middle of the road as the lights have now changed back to green. Many pairs of eyes are still trained on Leroy as the pairs cross the road in front of the taxi. I experience a short dart of satisfaction on being remembered fondly by someone who had been a real rogue during his school days.

I could not help but recall a car stopping in similar circumstances, some time ago, and the occupants, all ex-pupils, threatening Howard with the possibility of an unspeakable future demise. A month earlier he had bravely made a statement to the police as a witness to a street robbery, having recognised one of the perpetrators. Being well known in the community can serve as a two-edged sword. Howard hopes the "contract" is no longer out on him.

"Don't run... stay in twos!"

The last few bodies stumble to safety as the traffic begins to flow again. We are now close to our destination and as we move along the pavement outside Newtown Swimming Baths feet begin to move faster in anticipation. The swimming pool forms a small part of a precinct that has now been totally rebuilt. Only the baths and the Community Centre remain of the original 1960s architectural horror, which consisted of a concrete warren of pedestrianised underpasses and alleyways linking high-rise flats and windblown bunkers, that passed for a shopping mall.

The rabbits proved to be the shoppers and small businesses that tried to share some commerce there. They proved easy constant prey to the villains and muggers that skulked around. These predators would take what they wanted with sudden violence and escape down the suitably designed "rat runs" and subterranean passageways.

The banks had been the first to leave, followed by the supermarket and smaller shops. At the last, only a few gallant indoor market stall-holders remained. It had become a "no-go" area in which the Job Centre, adjacent to the baths, began to look like the set from *Fort Apache, The Bronx*, it had so many grills and bars on windows and doors. The staff that worked there could often be seen through the swimming pool windows making a discreet exit by a steel door at the rear of the building. All that was lacking was a heavily armed escort.

The wholesale demolition had taken six months and even the four floor, multi-storey car park had been bludgeoned to rubble. In fact, this concrete abomination had been the first thing to be levelled. I am certain no driver ever ventured to park a vehicle above ground floor during the car park's existence. To park above that level was surely to invite disaster... or worse. Occasionally, one would be able to hear the screech of tyres, handbrake turns, burning rubber and the hard revving of a stolen car being put through its paces on the upper floors. Other than that, Levels 1, 2, 3 and 4 were "no-man's land".

There was one occasion when our attention was drawn to the alfresco fourth floor, by the Findlayson twins. Howard and I were stopped at the traffic lights waiting for the change when we and our double file of swimmers heard it.

"Hey, hey, Knight... you bastard!"

All eyes, including Howard's, had searched the surrounding area for the source of the "greeting".

"Knight... Knight... up here!"

We could just make out the shape of a head above the parapet on the top floor of the concrete car park.

"Knight... you bastard! I'm up here... and I'm shagging a girl!"

This was followed by the cunning statement: "And it's not me... it's my brother!"

The following day, Howard cracked the case by consulting the register and confronting the two twins together. They were united in brotherhood, blaming each other. The Findlaysons were a curious pair and in no small way stimulated Howard's future interest in Special Educational Needs.

Having turned the corner, our walking file has broken into a trot to cover the last 50 metres to the baths entrance. I hold them back, and over the noise of the heavy traffic passing on the Walsall Road give final instructions.

"Walk in quietly! If you have 50p get a token for the lockers. Any sick notes... wait in the foyer!"

I go to the reception desk, sign the sheet indicating our numbers then hand over my pound coin in exchange for two locker tokens. Howard and Andrew follow the bustling boys through the double swing-doors into the changing area while I address the task of dealing with seven potential non-participants. I reach into the red bag and give a pair of trunks each to Zabbas and Farooq who look at them suspiciously as they disappear through the swing doors.

A frail looking Bangladeshi boy, Ali.

"Sir, I've forgotten my kit, Sir."

"Straight in and get some trunks out of the kit bag."

Raphael.

"No kit, Sir."

"Raphael, take the bag through and select some trunks for yourself... in you go."

Shanawaz:

"Sir, my arm's hurting me. I can't do swimming."

"Oh no, Shanawaz... but tell you what, swimming is the best thing there is for stiff muscles... particularly for fast bowlers. Go on in and give it a try, borrow some trunks."

Shanawaz goes in through the doors, gingerly turning over his bowling arm. Next is Shawn, a doe-eyed Afro-Caribbean boy.

"I had an asthma attack last night... can I be excused, Sir?"

"O.K., Shawn, go upstairs and sit in the balcony."

Rahin, a large, corpulent-looking boy.

"I can't swim, I'm fasting."

"Pardon."

"I'm fasting, Sir."

"Fasting? What do you mean, you're fasting? We have 56 boys here and nobody else is fasting."

"Our family have a special fast, Sir."

"Well, Rahin... you can still swim just like we do during Ramadan."

"But Sir, I can't swallow any water."

"Rahin, I'm not asking you to swallow the water, in fact I don't recommend it... it tastes horrible because of the chlorine. You and I both know the rules; you can shower, walk in the rain and go swimming. You aren't breaking any fast if you don't take water in your mouth deliberately."

"... but, Sir!"

"Rahin... in you go, now."

He goes, kicking the doors half-heartedly, which I ignore. I am not risking a Fatwa here as I have a printed sheet in my mark book folder giving the "dos" and "don'ts" in relation to Muslims and fasting with regard to Physical Education. It is produced by the Muslim Society, so I am on fairly firm footing when it comes to fasting.

Succeeding in getting children to participate in the face of the frequent intrinsic discomforts of sport and physical activity of various kinds takes a combination of willpower, motivation and outright bluffing. In the multi-cultural institution of Holte large amounts of each are required according to circumstance. I feel I live on the edge of having my bluff called all the time. I settle for having the door take the brunt of Rahin's frustration as I follow him into the noisy changing rooms.

Howard comes bursting out to meet me, almost knocking me backwards with the swing door.

"Where's Michael?!"

We both turn to look around the foyer and see him at once, pushing coins into the drinks machine. A can of Coca-Cola rattles in the trough at the bottom.

"Michael... what do you think you're doing?"

Howard shouts across the foyer as Michael extracts his can quickly and with his shuffling walk comes towards us.

"Why are you getting drinks before the lesson? You know you wait 'til the end... I just don't believe you sometimes!"

Michael's mealtime mentor continues to remonstrate with him as I leave them to it.

"Go in and get changed now!"

"Sir, I haven't got any kit."

I pause to see what effect this will have on Howard, whose veins are at near bursting point in his temple.

"No! But you have your crisps... you've got your drink... just wait 'til I see your mum again."

Michael's eyes seem to double in size and become watery as his tears begin to well up.

"Michael... don't start," I intercede.

"Put your can in your bag and get some trunks from Raphael's bag... go on in."

He pushes through the double doors, rubbing his eyes to wipe away the tears as an exasperated Howard and I follow him in, our ears being met by a barrage of noise.

"Right! Quieten it down! Any valuables to Mr. Oliver, those who need trunks get them from the bag. All reports to me. Once you're ready go through the shower and line up on the bath side at the bottom end!"

Andrew is quickly submerged by half-naked bodies requiring security for their watches, money and Pokemon cards, the new European currency. I am handed four yellow reports which I tuck away in the locker with my track-suit bottoms and waterproof jacket. The boys who forgot swimming kit have delved into the red bag and are holding up and trying on trunks from the selection available.

There are some small pairs from Lost Property but the majority are my old Speedos, thin and faded from the sun and salt of the Mediterranean. Shanawaz has put on a pair of these and pulls the tie-cord round his 22" bony waist. The 32" waistline of the trunks leaves some space down the front, which he is now peering down.

"Shanawaz, those are miles too big... here, put these on."

I select him a pair, bright green, just right for his skinny undeveloped lower body.

"Look, they're Pakistan Test team trunks."

His eyes light up as he holds up the lime green trunks for inspection. He pulls them on and strides proudly towards the showers.

It takes a further three or four minutes and many "Hurry ups!" from Howard before we succeed in assembling the entire company of swimmers on the bath side. The shivering, brown bodies sit squashed together against the cold tiled wall at the shallow end. I wave to Gary and Dave, the two resident swimming coaches. They are both leaning against the dividing rail that separates the main pool from the learner pool, clutching mugs of coffee. Both of them amble over as I give instructions to the seated swimmers.

"Right... as I said at school... today we're going to have a little distance test. We're going to see how far everyone can swim. You are all to do your best... then we'll get some play time. Anything you want to say, Mr. Gary or Mr. Dave?"

Gary is about my height, 5' 8", lean featured with a ponytail and the classic triangular build of a waterpolo player, a sport at which he boasts international honours. He is a lively character, well liked by the kids as he is always happy to have a laugh and a joke with them.

"Yes, Mr. Boothroyd. Remember, boys... when we get the play mats out for the fun session, no-one is to stand on them – it's dangerous. Also, no mats are to be taken past the rope at the halfway mark. When the whistle goes at the end, put the mats on the nearest side and climb out. Don't pull the plug out on the bottom or you'll empty the pool... Right, those boys who normally have armbands go and get them from the basket now, you're all staying in the learner pool with Mr. Dave."

Gary takes a drink from his cup of coffee. I have the final word.

"Except for the armbands... everyone else go and line up at the top end of the pool... DON'T RUN!"

"Michael, are you chewing?"

Howard makes Michael spit out a bright orange glob into the bin on the side.

At the deep end, Gary sends the swimmers off one at a time at 10 metre intervals. I position myself on the bath side, halfway down, with my recording sheet on a clipboard. Howard and Andrew keep an eye out for "quitters". The swimmers enter the water with a dive, jump or belly-flop according to choice, and in varying degrees of competence swim round the 60 metre circuit of the top half of the pool.

"Sir! Sir!... how far have I gone?"

"Ali, keep going, don't talk... save your breath."

Gradually the whole group are in the water and swimming. At various points individuals stop and grab the rail, their test being ended, a distance logged after being shouted out by myself, Howard or Andrew.

"Matthew... you've stopped, get out... 40 metres!"

"Van... 50 metres, well done!"

"Sir, he stopped, Sir, I saw him."

"Ali, concentrate on yourself... stop shouting out."

And so it proceeds until only two boys continue to circle the pool as the rest sit on the bath side, test completed.

"Ivahn, Ali... you can keep going, well done! 180 metres... keep away from the side, Ali!"

I read out the distances achieved, 15 metres, 25 metres, 60 metres, according to the point at which each boy made a clear stop. Some gave up a little too readily for my liking, having had one eye on Gary as he levered the large yellow and red play mats into the shallow half of the pool.

"Right, well done everyone. Now remember... no fighting or wrestling in the water. No standing on the mats. You can dive in the deep end once Ivahn and Ali have stopped."

The shallow end becomes a raging sea of spray, waves and splashing as it fills with bodies trying to be first to reach the mats. Gary also throws in some thin purple foam "logs" which are meant to be laid on or wrapped around the chest as a flotation aid. Immediately several boys start whipping each other with them.

"Raphael, Matthew... stop hitting each other with those logs... play properly!"

The staff and lifeguards stand around the poolside watching the foaming mayhem, shouting occasional instructions or threats:

"Don't stand on the mats!"

"Come back into the shallow end... don't cross the rope!"

"Don't run on the side... stay in the water!"

"Stop hitting each other with the floats!"

"Raphael... get *off* him!"

It never ceases to amaze me how quickly freeplay becomes experimentation in inflicting pain. Two boys are sent out for having each other in persistent headlocks.

"Sir... we were only playing."

Howard is unmoved.

"I don't care, you were told no wrestling or fighting in the water... get changed."

Out they go, muttering.

"Sir, how much have I done? I'm getting tired."

"250 metres if you can reach the steps, Ali."

He manages it and hauls himself up the rungs onto the side, then lies flat on his back, gasping.

"Sir... what... did I do?"

"250 metres, well done Ali."

I lean over his prostrate body.

"... but if you'd have saved your breath a bit and not spent half the time shouting out, you'd have done even further."

Ali is a cheerful, endlessly talkative Bangladeshi boy who is completely irrepressible. He staggers up from the floor.

"Oh Sir... can I do it again?"

"Ali, not now... of course you can't. You've got five minutes playtime left... *don't run!*"

He jumps onto a vacant mat and disappears under the water in the resulting tidal wave.

Ivahn, a persevering Afro-Caribbean boy, continues his lone circuit of the deep end.

"Well done, Ivahn... 550 metres... keep going!"

I feel a tapping on my shoulder.

"Sir, Mr. Gary's sent me up for a test."

It is Joshua, a small, polite African boy who has been in the armband group. He has come from Nigeria, joining us only three weeks ago. He borrowed trunks in his first swimming lesson, telling me he was a good swimmer. I had taken him into the top group at the deep end as I still fall for it occasionally, even with all my experience.

He had gone in head first and had not come up again. He sank like a stone. Gary, standing by me, had quickly grabbed the rescue rod and fished him out like an expert angler landing a prize catch on the pier. Joshua had coughed and spluttered but seemed none the worse for his five second "drowning".

"Joshua, I thought you said you were a good swimmer, you twerp!"

"Sir... in river... easy!"

He had never swum in a pool before. Perhaps he needed the incentives of anaconda or similar stimuli to aid a successful swimming performance.

Here he was again. This had to be a Gary wind-up.

"Now, Joshua... I don't think this is a good idea, remember what happened last time."

"Sir, I can now do it."

I grab the rescue pole.

"All right, Joshua, sit on the steps and slip in... we'll see how you do. Grab the pole if you start to go under."

He is in like a flash and among much thrashing of arms and legs, his inky black body submerged in foaming water, he moves perceptibly forwards along the rail. I trail the curved pole in the water just in front of him as his bobbing and rolling head continues to make progress towards the steps at halfway. Amazingly he swims the 15 metres to the rope dividing the pool and grabs the side rail.

"Well done, Joshua... 15 metres... brilliant!"

He climbs the steps and slumps on the bath side. I look across to Gary who raises his cup as if to say "cheers." I laugh and give him the "thumbs up".

Below me in the water Ivahn is still relentlessly pulling himself around the pool with a leisurely back crawl. He is about to collide with a mat that has strayed over the rope into the deep end.

"You boys... watch out... get that mat back down there!"

On the mat are the three Vietnamese boys, Van, Phuc and Duc. I find myself unavoidably thinking of "boat people".

"Keep going, Ivahn... you've got two more minutes. You've done 800 metres."

He nods in acknowledgement, head back, arms plodding.

There are three sharp blasts on the whistle from Howard and the turmoil in the water gradually subsides. There are a few more flails with the "logs" across unsuspecting backs and some boys have taken to trying to squash each other with the mats. Extracting the last few bodies from the water sees instructions turn into threats.

"Ali! If you aren't out in 10 seconds, I'll lift you out by your ears."

The cold air blown in by opening the emergency doors encourages the stragglers to make a rapid tiptoe into the warm showers. From there they have to be prised like limpets from under the hot shower jets. Inside the changing room itself it is now towel-flicking time.

"Stop flicking towels, Ali... Raphael! If I did that to you... you'd be the first to complain."

Andrew gives back valuables as I sign reports and complete my register. Howard shouts: "You've five minutes to get ready. Anyone not changed in that time will not be allowed to buy refreshments, or we'll be late back to school. Hurry up!"

There's a flurry of dressing activity at the unpleasant prospect of starvation.

I am writing down the distances in my mark book when Gary appears and beckons me.

"Here... come here and have a look at this."

"What...?"

He motions for me to follow him and I walk on behind as we reach the poolside. He points to the learner pool.

"Someone's left a present."

Then I see it. A brown object, two to three inches in length. (It's a "floater").

"I don't fucking believe it... crikey!"

We are laughing as Dave comes out of the store cupboard with a long pole and net attachment. He quickly manages to "scoop the poop" from the surface.

"Have I to take this into the changing room to see if anyone wants to claim it?"

We are all laughing uncontrollably as Dave flicks the excrement up and down in the net. I am the first to stop as I begin to register two contrasting sights; the first is Ivahn still circling the top end of the pool, the second can be seen through the open door at the far corner leading into the foyer. I see

Michael wearing only his shirt, feeding coins into the chocolate bar machine.

Howard is bellowing at Michael as they re-enter the changing area, the latter clasping his chocolate bar. His brown, stubby legs protrude beneath his white shirt tail and he is crying. Ivahn enters from the opposite end, a towel round his shoulders.

"Well done, Ivahn... we'll call that 1,000 metres, sorry I forgot all about you."

"When will I get my certificate, Sir?"

"Everyone will get them after the Christmas holidays in register... but I'll make sure you get yours in Year Assembly as you did so well."

The last few stragglers are finishing getting changed, pulling on coats or attempting clumsily to knot ties. The majority are now in the foyer stuffing coins into the vending machines.

"Sir... I can't find my soxes."

"They must be here somewhere, Ali... look under the benches."

Ivahn taps me on the arm, shivering.

"Sir, I can't open the locker."

I take his key and have a try myself, but the door refuses to open. I give the door a thump with my fist but it appears that something is jamming it.

"Sir... I still can't find them... someone's stolen my soxes."

Time is going, we have five minutes to return to school, a feat now a virtual impossibility. I am confronted with one naked shivering boy and another minus soxes, sorry, socks.

"Right, Ivahn, put this extra towel round you to keep warm."

I pull one from the bag and he flops down on the bench covering his stomach and thighs with it.

"I'll go and get the baths attendant to try and open your locker. When he's done it, get changed but stay here. I don't want you going back to school on your own... just wait until we come down with the next group in 15 minutes' time, O.K.?"

Ivahn nods, his teeth chattering audibly.

"Ali... you put your shoes on and I'll try to find your socks next lesson. We'll check if anyone has them in their bag by mistake."

He is not happy, but accepts the compromise. Howard and Andrew are shouting commands to the waiting gathering in the foyer. Poor Andrew has a history lesson next so jogs out of the front entrance to try to get back in time for the start. He has got no chance.

"No more drinks or sweets... don't put any more money in the machines."

Howard blocks the machines with his body to prevent access to the more persistent latecomers.

"Save your money for the tuck shop at break-time. Right everybody... outside and line up by the window, on the pavement!"

I have to push my way through the crowd of bodies eating crisps, unwrapping chocolate bars or tentatively holding hot drinks in plastic cups. They follow me out while Howard clears the foyer.

"The Great Return Trek" begins. We are in twos, the twinnies again at the front. I stride out to the first corner trying to set the pace and tone of urgency for getting back. By the time I reach there, the file has disintegrated behind me with a dawdling mass spread across the pavement. Howard comes steaming up from the back where he is escorting a tearful drinkless Michael. He berates them to get back into pairs. We are all halted at the corner and I assail them.

"Right... listen! We have three minutes left before the next lesson starts. We're going to be late. Anybody else who holds us up by strolling, walking out of line or messing about is going to lose their break... Let's go!"

We look a bit more ordered and urgent as we cross the road at the traffic lights, but Howard is still having words with the three Vietnamese boys at the back who are walking too slowly, trying not to spill their cups of hot chocolate. I decide upon a detour between the high-rise flats after we are all across.

"Why we going this way, Sir?"

"Because it's quicker... Ismael."

"It's Ishaq, Sir."

"... Ishaq!"

"Sir, Safdar says he's going to womit."

The twinnies continue to lead on at a brisk pace as I turn back to find Safdar crouched over a parked car. I put my hand on his shoulder, consolingly.

"Safdar, you O.K. son?"

"Sir, I feel sick..." he mumbles back from his hunched position. I have to tell a group of interested onlookers to keep moving.

"Breathe deep, Safdar... perhaps you swallowed too much water."

Too late – for up it comes, a mixture of water and chocolate bar.

"Hey... get that kid away from my car!"

I do not believe it. It is the "Jobsworth". He is a short, stocky man in blue overalls and flat cap, one of the caretakers from the flats. He is in his late 20s going on 55.

"He's been sick... it's nowhere near your car."

"... and it had better not be either."

"You're a gem, you are", I mutter under my breath as I crouch over Safdar who retches again.

"Nothing... come on Safdar."

I guide him back onto the pavement and we try to catch up with the line of boys now 50 yards in the distance. Jobsworth stands hands on hips, watching us go. Perhaps he does not remember, but I do. We had crossed paths a couple of years ago in similar circumstances.

The swimmers had just got over the road and I had seen two boys, thinking I had not noticed, heading for an alleyway with clear intent to "wag". (truant the next lesson). I had stopped the file, jogged after them, hauled them back and was in the process of giving them the sharp end of some advice. Jobsworth had apparently observed some of this spectacle, waddled up and began to berate me.

"I saw you... fuckin' manhandling those kids. You teachers... you're always fuckin' beating up kids. My fucking P.E. teacher at school was just the same. Well, I'm fuckin' 'aving you fer this. You two... you alright... we'll have your fuckin' teacher back at school!"

I remember that we had walked back to school with Jobsworth chuntering at me all the way. The swimmers, including the two attempted "waggers", were all totally bemused.

I have to admit they were the quietest group that I had ever walked back from the swimming baths. All I can recall replying in the face of his continuous tirade was: "You know it all you, don't you... you want to give this a try for a couple of weeks. You have a go and I'll watch you... you can show me how to do it."

We had arrived back at school and I dispatched the boys to their next lesson. I had taken the Jobsworth to the Deputy Head's office in order that he could present his case. The Deputy, sat at his desk planning the timetable, looked a little nonplussed when I introduced my new associate.

"Sorry to disturb you... there's an arsehole here would like a word with you."

I had returned to my next lesson and awaited the repercussions with growing uneasiness. I had no cause for anxiety as Dai, the Deputy, had given the complainant short shrift though reassuring Jobsworth that his "citizens arrest" would be noted and that I would be warned as to my future conduct. We had both had a despairing chuckle when I gave him the details of the whole saga. I did take it as a salutary lesson in not chastising miscreants in public places.

Safdar and I stumble away leaving Jobsworth to scrutinize the stains on his Skoda. We rejoin the back of the pack just as the last remnants cross the road by the pub. They begin to jog in loose order back up the pathways to the gates. We let them go. Safdar and Michael trudge up the hill well behind them.

"Sir... you never axed if anyone had my soxes!"

"Oh, Ali... I'm sorry about that. Come on, I'll get you some football socks."

I lead him towards the laundry as Howard begins to shout at the next group of swimmers, the other half of the Year 7 boys.

"Everybody line up in twos by the fence, no talking... you two stop chasing and come over here – NOW! Right, today it's your last swimming lesson before the Christmas holiday so we are going to have a little distance test..."

Chapter Six

WRESTLING WITH RAZOUK
(1987)

I THINK it is correct to say that I have known only one Iraqi and one wrestler. They were both combined in the formidable form of Mr. Razouk. His first name was Morfuk, but I only heard that informality conferred upon him once, by his Head of Department, and Mr. Razouk was not present at the time. The title of Mister fitted him perfectly. How else could one suitably address a 6' 2" Iraqi wrestler for whom the word "solid" seemed to have been created. "Solid", meaning firm, stable in shape, of strong material and construction, most certainly not hollow. A good scientific description for a capable no-nonsense Science teacher.

He was a large presence in the staffroom. A gentleman, with the emphasis on gentle. His regular appearance on the orange cushioned chairs of this staff sanctuary was unusual in itself. The Science department rarely ventured into this communal area during the working day, preferring their own "bolt-hole" of the prep-room, replete with its shelves of neatly ordered text books, boxes of test tubes and brown jars of seldom used chemicals. The general tone of staff opinion was that the scientists were an odd lot, being too detached, formal and objective to play much of a part in staff social circles. Mr. Razouk, filling the cushioned chair and half the one next to it, refused to fit this mould and his quiet wry humour at break and lunch times belied his almost military bearing and lesson organisation.

He would occupy the same space every lunchtime, his back to the radiator beneath the vertical blinds which shielded the staffroom from the view from the street. He could be found sitting there most days, in his blue blazer, grey flannels and co-ordinated shirt and tie, devouring amazing quantities of sandwiches while occasionally refilling a cup from his flask of strong tea.

Mr. Razouk was happy to engage anyone in conversation who happened to wedge in alongside him or take residence in the seats opposite, across the low coffee-stained table.

A frequent neighbour during the lunch hour had been Paddy, the head of the art department. Paddy was a lively outgoing personality, always ready to challenge life's injustices. She was a stimulating lunchtime companion, not least for being a reliable informant on scandal, gossip or the misfortunes involving staff in school. Paddy was an entertaining and informative friend to the likes of myself, stranded in the lost empire of the P.E. department where lines of communication were very stretched when it came to news of staff or pupil indiscretions.

Paddy had confided in me that Mr. Razouk had once asked her out. She was a buxom and attractive divorcée in her mid-40s and Mr. Razouk's invitation had seemed a reasonable one to me. Paddy, out of curiosity, had accepted. The invitation had been quite simply a lunchtime rendezvous away from the regular confines of the staffroom. Paddy, a woman of the world, with three grown-up children, had been a little nonplussed on arrival at the venue for their lunchtime tête-à-tête. It turned out to be a strip club down a rather seedy side street not far from Birmingham City Centre. In providing a contrast to a morning's lessons and a means of diverting thoughts of those to follow in the afternoon, the club might have had no equal. Paddy had been astonished. She had also added that the food had been disgusting with the soft lighting from the gyrations on the stage making the inedible also indiscernible.

Paddy's good humour had prevailed but the possibilities of a developing relationship with Mr. Razouk had not been enhanced. They had been reduced to zero, in fact. Some weeks later, Paddy, with a mixture of incredulity and irritation, had made the discovery that Mr. Razouk had made a similar tactical approach to Meyra, the other mature, well endowed and outgoing half of the Art Department, with a similar singular lack of success. Perhaps Mr. Razouk's method of courtship had secured him some advancement in the past, but in these two instances the strip club scenario had proven a miserable failure. This judgement, on my part, seemed to be well supported by the subsequent staffroom seating arrangements which saw Paddy and Meyra nowhere in proximity to the luckless Mr. Razouk.

His misjudgement in this matter may have been partly understood and forgiven for he had previously revealed himself to me as an admirer of "belly dancing". This form of Eastern exotic and erotic movement was denied him in the West Midlands and perhaps the charms of the side street club were the nearest he could get in replicating this method of getting the "sap to rise". Paddy and Meyra, however, had definitely not risen.

Mr. Razouk had several interesting sources of conversation topics over and above the mundane everyday events of school. In his gentle, prepossessing way he would describe the skill, subtlety and eroticism of the Levantine art of the belly dancer. In a similar manner, he would give those who cared to listen an insight into the growing nightmare and insufferability of life in Iraq under the dictatorship of Saddam Hussein; the daily denunciations to the security police, the dictates and corrupt self-aggrandisement of Saddam and his immediate family and the way the country was being led to isolation and disaster by a ruthless leader. Mr. Razouk made the assertion,

"Saddam Hussein... a very bad man."

There was no benefit of hindsight in this statement for he had made it in the Holte staffroom years before the Iraqi invasion of Kuwait. It was at the time of the Iran–Iraq conflict which subsequently revealed the West, and Britain in particular, secretly supplying ordnance to the latter and its dangerous dictator. At the time we had just taken Mr. Razouk's word for it as we knew little or nothing of Iraq, and after all, he had been born and brought up there.

Mr. Razouk's reasons for leaving his homeland always remained unsaid. He had hinted at various problems and conflicts but would not go into detail. The impression I gained was that he had left quickly before he was likely to be prevented from doing so, with serious consequences for himself. He admitted to having upset important people and took the opportunity to leave while he could still do so. He recounted several unpleasant experiences with security police that held everyone's rapt attention in his small circle in the smoky staffroom.

He had fled Iraq, with no chance of returning, and embarked upon a science teaching career in England, leaving his life and wrestling potential in Iraq forever.

"Wrestling," he would say, "it is about balance, grip and using a man's gravity and momentum against himself."

Under his blue blazer, the heart of a wrestler beat strongly. Mr. Razouk's sleepy dark brown eyes would brighten and a hint of a smile would be revealed beneath his thin black moustache as he remembered his abilities as a wrestler in his youth. He was rarely beaten. He had always felt he could have had a future in wrestling, but it had not been possible because of his unspoken situation in Iraq. He believed that he still had the strength and feeling for the moves. He no longer practised as there was little or no opportunity. He was a science teacher;

"I am now retired from the wrestling."

Or so he thought, until he achieved the status of a "Legend" at Holte School.

A few weeks later during the summer term, the annual day trip had seen several coachloads of fourth and fiftth year boys and girls depart for Blackpool. Mr. Razouk had been one of the many staff on board looking forward to the adventures of the day.

Upon arrival at the coach park, warnings had been made, safety procedures outlined and irrelevant encouragement to enjoyment given by the organiser, me.

The Holte hordes disappeared into the extensive acres of Pleasure Beach while I, feeling that my immediate duty was done, decided upon a solitary stroll along the promenade of the Golden Mile with its abundant eye-catching attractions. This decision denied me the opportunity to witness Mr. Razouk's moment of glory and immortality in the Holte "Hall of Fame".

I was to hear much about it.

"He just took him out, Sir!"

"He was really bad!"

"Mr. Razouk... he was fantastic."

These were some of the comments and exclamations of hero-worship, from adolescents wearing "Kiss Me Kwik" hats and sucking on teeth-rotting sticky toffee apples, that echoed round the coach on the long journey back to Birmingham. It had been Mr. Razouk's finest hour.

I was able to construct the story myself from the repeated, detailed information I had received, both in the coach park and on the journey home. The kids were full of it and the story was embellished with each telling.

"And he got the twenty quid!"

Reducing the rhetoric and gleaning out facts from exaggeration, I was able to establish the following train of events culminating in the Legend of Mr. Razouk.

In the funfair there had been a wrestling booth. The purpose of it was to offer "all-comers" the chance to challenge the host man-mountain of a wrestler, "Mad Mick". The task of any challenger was to avoid being pinned, or to remove the above wrestler from his feet and make him fall to the mat. The reward for achieving either of these two feats was a prize of £20. Once a challenger had been found to attempt the task, the booth would be filled with sufficient spectators paying more than enough to cover the costs of an unlikely defeat for the battle-hardened grappler inside. Mr. Razouk had been gently teased then strongly encouraged to have a crack at this by several pupils whom he had had the misfortune to encounter near the booth. Howard had been among the one or two other staff present and of course had egged on the pupils with some relevant information concerning Mr. Razouk's wrestling experience in a previous life.

This mixture of encouragement and temptation had proven too much for Mr. Razouk to resist. The entry fee had been paid and with the vociferous backing of his staff and pupil entourage he had entered Mad Mick's den. Several minutes had elapsed to enable enough spectator custom to be drummed up by the man in the kiosk who would also double up as Mad Mick's manager and referee of the bout. There had been two rows of banked seating on three sides of the shabby arena, which enclosed the ring formed by two ropes and a tatty blue mat approximately eight metres square.

Mr. Razouk, to the delight of his supporters, had removed his blazer, shirt, tie and shoes then separated the two ropes in order to squeeze through into the ring. Sporting a white string vest, grey flannels and ankle socks he had limbered up by performing a few perfunctory stretches and moves. The growing crowd had bayed their support for the challenger.

The wrestler-in-residence, Mad Mick, had then appeared, a grizzly, battle-hardened, though flabby, red-haired heavyweight. Howard had reported that of the two, Mr. Razouk was heavier and clearly in better shape. Mad Mick had probably been accustomed to a series of far from demanding challengers ranging from jokers, those suffering from a dose of bravado and too much alcohol, to the physically strong who fancied their chances but lacked the technique to overcome a skilled wrestler, albeit one gone to seed.

I was told that he had hauled himself through the ropes following a tinny fanfare from the P.A. system, and begun to showboat around the ring. He had circled Mr. Razouk, hamming it up and attempting to raise the ire of the audience. I imagined the antics of Jackie Pallo and Mick McManus, those TV wrestling pioneers of my schooldays. They had been the inspiration for many a two falls or two submissions bout on the living room carpet with my pre-teen friends.

The villain in the ring had been described to me as wearing similar tights and one piece costume that I could recall from those monochrome TV days.

"... and he'd got one of those thick leather belts round his stomach... Mr. Razouk had grabbed it straight away."

The reports on the fight had come thick and fast without much prompting from me. The referee-manager-kiosk man had brought the two wrestlers together in the centre of the ring to shake hands. After some posing and manoeuvring, both men had grappled and mauled each other in order to secure a firm and decisive hold. Mr. Razouk had grabbed the wrestler's belt, overbalanced and in falling had toppled his opponent. Through dragging his opponent over with him, Mr. Razouk had managed to position himself firmly across the body of the prostrate wrestler. Mad Mick had lived up to his name and struggled to free himself for a few seconds, but Mr. Razouk's bulk held him down comfortably. The wrestler had rapped loudly on the mat with his free forearm to indicate acceptance of the fall... and defeat.

The bout had apparently lasted less than a minute but the crowd had been ecstatic at the turn of events in Mr. Razouk's favour. He had regained his feet and the picture I formed was one of him shaking hands with his chastened opponent, sharing the brotherhood that only true fighters understand. Mr. Razouk had collected his £20 and I am certain his supporters would have carried him along the promenade shoulder high in triumph, had they possessed the strength and courage to do so.

The trip to Blackpool would remain a memorable one. It was the day "Mad Mick" met his match in the "Irate Iraqi".

Mr. Razouk's path and my own would rarely cross, other than in the lunch hour. My P.E. commitments all took place a good distance from the routines of the science department on the second floor. I was head of the second year in addition to being head of P.E. and I was rarely called to science lessons to help with problems or disciplinary matters. The formal nature of the lessons and the methodical, stern nature of the science teachers left me largely unemployed in this area of the school, a situation I was happy to see continue. There were always plenty of crisis calls elsewhere. I would receive an occasional memo asking me to lend moral support and another voice in pursuit of science homework defaulters, but the need to help in chastising poor behaviour hardly ever arose.

One wet and windy Wednesday, after lunch, I had been sitting in my head of year office enjoying the luxury of a non-contact afternoon. Two lessons with no classes to teach and no sign of a cover slip for an absent member of staff. I had just come from a frantic basketball club in the gym and was savouring this oasis of peace, the door firmly closed against the rumble and shouts of surrounding classrooms. I was faced with plenty of choice as to how to use the two hours productively. My warm comfortable office had an ambient array of greenery; rubber plants, ferns, cheese plants and an assortment of variegated species, all of which seemed to be thriving in the soft light from the one high window and the heat of the radiator below it.

I could have left this warm fug to visit a second year French class just down the corridor. Even with my door shut I could hear the noise rising from that location. The class were slipping into their normal Wednesday afternoon mode; that of tormenting unmercifully the hapless teacher, known to the kids as "Jesus". He had a mane of fly-away hair, and a short, straggly beard below a thin, pale face – hence the nickname. The staff surreptitiously felt it was appropriate too, on account of his being "crucified" every lesson. I did not really feel like paying a visit and having a meaningful glower in that classroom yet, so I had decided to see if they would settle down. I did not hold out much hope for that prospect.

I could have made several phone calls to parents enquiring after unexplained pupil absence. That procedure would be bound to be a painful one. In most cases, the telephone would be answered by someone not speaking English, I would be left hanging on the line with a "one minute... one minute... no English."

I would be able to hear background sounds of dogs barking, animated conversations or shouting, TV in the background and would be on the verge of putting down the receiver when a clear, articulate voice would query,

"Yes, who is that?"

It would turn out to be the absent pupil's younger brother or sister aged five or six who would then tell me,

"Oh yes, Sir... she's here."

I would wait another few minutes listening to shouts echo down the line requesting the subject's presence at the telephone. Eventually, just before I lost all hope, a hesitant though polite voice would arrive on the line.

"Yes, Sir... it's me, Rina. I've not been well... I'll be back tomorrow."

The telephone would then click and there would be silence. Ten minutes of my life would have passed in futility, though I had achieved the promise of a pupil's return. I had decided I could not face the telephone.

I could have attempted some statistical returns on my year group's attendance figures for the term. My computer screen stood reproachfully silent and blank on the corner of my non-executive desk.

There was an assembly to prepare for the following day; the head of year's weekly address. I had looked at the "Theme for the Week" on the schedule of assemblies on the pin board above the desk. It was Guru Nanak. The list was full of various Jewish, Catholic, Muslim, Buddhist and other multi-faith themes. I rarely attempted them as I felt a total phoney in attempting to promote these, to me, alien concepts. I preferred story telling with a moral theme or word of wisdom. I had decided that "Iron Head and The Greatest Army in the World" would suit me better as I knew it virtually off by heart; sorry, Guru.

I had also been requested to write a report on a pupil who had been excluded which was top of my list of 'To Dos' on the notice board in front of me. The list looked unexciting.

- Phone EWO (Educational Welfare Officer) re. John 8S
- Homework diaries – check 8S, 8T, 8W
- Write merit certificates – Bronze/Silver
- Prepare Agenda for Year Team Meeting – Monday

- Letter in registers re Christmas Hamper
- Write report on Rachel – behaviour and truancy
- Water plants

My eyes had scanned the list and I had decided to water the plants, then write a report. I had given the greenery a drink then opened my pencil case to extract three coloured felt-tipped pens. I had begun to write the report with a thick purple one on the pre-printed format A4 piece of paper. I wrote in large capital letters.

HOLTE HAMMER HAMSTEAD IN TOP OF LEAGUE CLASH. I had decided to write the football report, on last night's match, for the P.E. notice board. I had just begun to write the players' names with their "star ratings", out of 10, when there had been a gentle knock at the door.

"Come in...!"

There had been another rap on the door, a little louder.

"Who is it? Come in!"

The door had not been opened so I had hauled myself irritably from my chair to find a quiet girl, Amanda, on the other side. She had been clutching a science memo. I had taken it from her and looked at the scrawled message:

> *Mr. B*
> *Carla has run out of the lesson – 1.50 pm.*
> *M Razouk*

I had sighed and asked Amanda what had happened. She had reported that Carla had been laughing and would not stop talking so Mr. Razouk had told her to go into the science office to do her work and that was all she had known about it.

I had told Amanda to go back and tell Mr. Razouk that I would be along in a few minutes, and as I repacked my pencil case I felt my tranquillity shattered irretrievably.

The noise from Jesus's classroom was louder than I had thought now that my door was open. I knew a surprise visit there would now definitely be needed too. I had stuck the match report in the desk drawer, locked my office and set off with a heavy heart down the corridor to the science department.

The science area, with its perspex covered display boards, was full of mildly pungent smells. The somnolent drone of teachers from the open laboratory classroom doors, laboured scientific theory with drowsy classes. I had knocked on Mr. Razouk's door, the only one to be closed to the corridor.

I had entered hesitantly; a room that seemed a perfect model of silent scientific endeavour. The whole class appeared to be working on individual sheets using their textbooks. There had not been a whisper, though all eyes had been fixed on me as I had scanned the class on entering.

"We have a little problem, Mr. Boothroyd. This group of girls here think it is correct to laugh and joke in science lessons."

Mr. Razouk had indicated the table at which were seated three Afro-Caribbean girls and one empty chair.

"I give them warnings... still they talk and laugh."

I had known the girls as lively and chatty but no serious problem to anyone generally.

"Carla was the worst and to me was preventing everyone from working. I tell her to pick up her book and go into the science preparation room and I will deal with her in there."

Mr. Razouk had pointed over to the door in the corner.

"When I go in preparation room... I have strong words with Carla about her poor attitude... she throws book on floor and runs out of the office door and away down the corridor... It is not good."

My knowledge of Carla was one of a cheerful friendly girl but with a tendency to lose her temper quickly when confronted by critical teachers, particularly male. It was not good. I had asked Mr. Razouk to step into the corridor so that the class, who were all ears to every word of our conversation, would not be able to hear our discussion of the situation.

"Did she say where she was going?"

It was a silly question but I was puzzled over where to start in dealing with the disappearance.

"She says she's going home to get father, I think."

This was definitely not good.

"Why would she..."

My next question had been interrupted by a crash of the door at the end of the corridor. I had turned to see the swinging fire-doors pushed open and a tall, well-built, pale Afro-Caribbean man striding purposefully in our direction. A few strides behind him had trailed the tearful Carla. He came to an angry halt a few feet in front of us.

"Which one is it... baby?"

Carla had pointed. It had looked like the finger had been pointed at me.

"Him Daddy!"

Daddy had reached into his jacket pocket. The next thing I was seeing was a cut-throat razor being flicked open and held menacingly with intent to use... on me.

I had been given no time to react before Carla had shrieked: "No, Daddy... him!" (Thank you, Carla.)

I recall that in that split second of his advance upon me there had been a sudden change of direction. Carla's Daddy had raised the razor threateningly to match the abuse he was now raining upon Mr. Razouk. As quickly as the razor had been raised by the flexed arm, Mr. Razouk had grasped Daddy's wrist and pinned it against the wall. The instant reaction of raising his other arm had seen that similarly held in a vice-like grip.

"Daddy! Daddy!" Carla had screamed.

"Calm down... stop it!... calm it, come on!" I had urged to no one in particular as Mr. Razouk's whole body had seemed to be pressing Carla's powerful parent against the perspex in such a way that there had been little space to lever the kicks or butts he was attempting to inflict upon the teacher. This maul against the wall had seemed to be heading for stalemate until the pressure of Mr. Razouk's grip had forced the razor to be released. It fell to the floor. Carla had been still wailing hysterically as I had picked it up.

Another member of staff's face had appeared at a classroom door further down the corridor and I had urged this teacher to get help. He had hurtled through the fire-doors and down the stairs in the direction of the administration block. I remember feeling helpless and not knowing how to begin to physically intervene in the struggle. Carla's Daddy had been cursing between gasps for breath as Mr. Razouk was quietly urging him to quit.

"Calm down... come on... if you stop this I will stop too... calm down... please... please."

I had turned to Carla and pleaded with her to calm her father down and she had gradually recovered some composure as the violence of the struggle had seemed to be subsiding.

"Daddy, Daddy... stop it."

I had slipped the razor in my tracksuit pocket and began to pat Daddy gently on the shoulder.

"Come on, mate... let's try and sort this out. We don't need all this... come on."

I had heard the flurry of footsteps behind me and the science teacher who had gone to get help had now returned, accompanied by the Deputy Head and a senior woman teacher. They were soon adding their soothing voices to the situation. The whole atmosphere of threat and violence had seemed to dissipate in the face of our calming chorus. The man's body, beneath the weight of Mr. Razouk, seemed to deflate like a punctured airbed and his struggling had ended.

Carla's father had been led away by the woman teacher with a comforting arm around him. Carla had linked on to his other arm as they disappeared down the stairwell. The deputy head had followed, having first told Mr. Razouk that he needed him to come down to the office at the completion of the lesson. Mr. Razouk and I had been left in the now silent corridor. I held out the razor in the palm of my hand and both of us had looked at it and begun to realise the implications of what might have happened had it not been for Mr. Razouk's quick reactions.

"Are you O.K., Mr. Razouk? Do you want to have a breather in the staff-room while I keep an eye on your class for a bit?"

It had seemed the least I could have offered at that moment.

"Of course not... it is all very unfortunate. It is no problem. Thank you for your help."

He had straightened his tie, hitched up his trousers and gone back into the room where his class had remained throughout the pandemonium outside. There had been plenty of animated discussion but everyone had appeared not to have left their seats. The last I had heard him say was: "Everyone now be silent. There was a problem but it is now finished. Get on with your work."

I had closed the door. My sweaty palms and racing heartbeat still bore testimony to the skirmish I had witnessed as I opened and closed the razor in my hand. I had walked down the stairs unsteadily. On reaching the Deputy Head's office I had seen the door ajar and the sight of Carla and her father sat side by side in comfortable armchairs. Daddy had been crying and was still dabbing his eyes with a tissue. The woman senior teacher edged past me carrying cups of tea: "Now Mr. Strickland, here's a cup of tea... let's try and sort this out."

He had accepted the proffered cup.

"No one locks my baby in a cupboard..."

I had gently closed the door on the scene.

Going back to my office I had paused outside the French classroom. The sound of missiles and accompanying cheers assaulted my hearing. I could hear Jesus's shrill voice being totally ignored. I had gritted my teeth, taken a deep breath and thought "Sod that!"

I had walked into my room, locked myself in and taken out the football match report.

Chapter Seven

OUTDOOR PURSUIT
(June 1976)

THE MOUNTAINS of the Island of Arran rise majestically. Their mauve tinge contrasts perfectly with the low level greenery that skirts their feet. Approaching by ferry into the heart of Brodick Bay, the towering peaks of Goat Fell, Caisteal Abhail and Beinn Tarsuinn in the northern half of the island provide a stunning backcloth to the lush woods along the coast which are emblazoned with magenta, purple and ultramarine rhododendron in flower. The more rounded, rolling mountains to the south, fronted by extensive pine forests, have visible waterfalls and provide a gentle counterpoint to the threatening giants of the northern triumvirate of peaks.

This stunning vista was to be denied us for another 24 hours as I sat disconsolate on the grass verge of the slip road off the M6 motorway, two miles north of the Hilton Park Services. The school minibus, heavily laden with camping equipment and provisions, stood obstinately on the hard shoulder, its bonnet open at 90 degrees. The endless stream of heavy lorries and commuter traffic roared by 30 feet below along the busiest stretch of motorway in Britain. The attendant exhaust fumes were becoming overpowering and added to my frustration. At least someone seemed to be making the most of this unforeseen interlude, as I heard the laughs behind me.

Malcolm, my number two in the P.E. department, was engaged in a 3 v 1 wrestling match with the three third year boys who were journeying with us to the western Scottish isle. We were the advanced party for a camping/walking outdoor pursuits holiday of 10 days' duration, jointly organised with the neighbouring Hodge Hill School. Our gallant band of five had the task of transporting tents, cooking equipment and food from Birmingham to the Isle of Arran while the remaining 11 boys and girls from Holte, and the 16 strong Hodge Hill expedition made the journey by train from Birmingham New Street to the Ardrossan ferry via Glasgow 16 hours later. Our task, quite simply, was to transport the equipment there safely, find the camping site overlooking Brodick Bay and pitch the tents in readiness for the main party's arrival and occupancy. And so far – so bad.

We had loaded the minibus to the roof the previous evening. The roof rack holding the packs of the Stormhaven tents was neatly covered in black tarpaulin and secured tightly with a criss-cross of ropes. We had set off in good spirits eager to be on the road after the early-morning rush hour. The three "bearers" – Tuzzio with his shoulder length, straw-coloured hair and flattened nose, Muzalfar, sporting an almost perfect Beatle haircut, and John, the virtual skinhead – look an incongruous trio, singing: "Here we go, here we go, here we go!" as we had pulled out of the school gates with Malcolm at the wheel. We had covered exactly nine-and-a-half miles of our testing journey of more than 400 when the temperature gauge had begun flashing a warning red. Malcolm had pulled the minibus off the motorway at the A5 exit and onto the relative safety of the slip road. Bonnet up, we had established immediately the reason for the warning – a broken fan belt. With no spare and no means of repairing it we had sat there for the best part of an hour after calling the AA rescue from the SOS telephone box 200 yards away.

The three boys had Malcolm pinned to the ground as he tried to wriggle his lean, six foot frame from their tangle of bodies. I glanced up from my newspaper, to see the winking orange lights of the AA van approaching us up the slip road. Malcolm and the boys disentangled themselves as the van pulled in behind the minibus. A brown and yellow uniformed figure eased himself out.

"Are ye going far then fellas?" came the Scottish accent.

"Only as far as the Isle of Arran."

"Aye... it's a beautiful place yer heading for, I knae it well. You've nae far to go then... ha! ha!"

Not being in the mood for irony I fired back,

"Oh Yeah... we've managed all of 10 miles so far... we're well pissed off... it's the fan belt."

His head went under the bonnet and after a return to the yellow van for a couple of tools and a fan belt, it took only five minutes of tinkering, one groan and two curses before the Fourth Emergency Service had delivered the necessary repair.

"There ye go then... the Isle of Arran awaits ye... hope ye have a good journey with nae more problems."

Malcolm and I thanked him as he returned to the van; I tipped him a quid after I signed his chitty. The three boys wedged themselves back into the double seat behind Malcolm and I belted myself into the other front seat. As Malcolm negotiated the roundabout and steered us back towards the three lanes of solid traffic on the motorway I uttered the optimistic words, "Oh well, let's hope that's the end of our troubles... that Scots guy might have been a lucky omen."

We alternated the driving over the length of the tedious motorway journey, the heavily laden minibus barely able to exceed 50 mph in its relentless chug. Our three assistants in the back switched from sporadic chat and occasional horseplay to snoozing as our journey in the slow lane ground endlessly onwards. At last we encountered a change of scenery and rhythm as we left the soulless three lanes of the motorway and headed along the road for Dumfries. I took the wheel for the first stage of the journey northwards as a pinkish sunset formed over the Glenkens to the west. The headlights rose and fell over the undulating country road that traversed the drumlins through Sanquhar, New Cumnock and Kirkconnel. We were all in a state of deep mesmerisation as we approached the neon-lit outskirts of Kilmarnock. The bright lights dazzled our tired eyes after the unbroken darkness of the switchback country road. We exchanged seats for a final time and it was Malcolm who had the honour of pulling on the handbrake and shutting off the engine after driving the last stage to Ardrossan.

It was 2.30 in the morning. It had taken us 16-and-a-half hours including toilet stops and AA rescue. It was pitch dark in the ferry car park and we felt disoriented, drained and bedraggled.

The 7.30am ferry pulled away from the dock and was soon slicing its way through a millpond smooth stretch of water on the hour long voyage between the mainland and the promised land of Arran, resplendent in the distance on a calm, sunny morning. We had all slept fitfully, cramped and uncomfortable across the seats of the minibus. Coffee and cooked breakfast at the greasy café on the harbour front had revived us, but seeing my 24-hour facial growth in the toilet mirror reminded me we would have to pay at a later time for the rigours of the previous day.

Malcolm and I leaned over the guard rail, the cool morning air brushing our faces as the purple shaded mountains became more visible. We took in the approaching beautiful spectacle in silence. Muz, Tuzzio and John were being similarly enthralled – by two games machines in a small room adjoining the bar, where they were frantically pressing buttons and loudly encouraging each other above the sound of bells and beeps. I shut out the irritating sounds in the background and the monotony and staleness of the journey began to subside from my consciousness as the majestic splendour of Arran became more apparent as the boat made its approach to Brodick Harbour.

Malcolm eased the minibus down the ramp of the ferry as I gave him the directions for the short run to the campsite. We pulled out of Brodick, heading south, following the circular road that rings the whole island, rarely more than a few yards from the rocky shore with small, sheltered bays of silvery sand. After ten minutes' cautious driving, a combination of admiring the view and following instructions, Malcolm turned the minibus down a cart track. And there it was, our home for the next ten days; a gently sloping field attached to a dairy farm, bordered by neat hedgerows and overlooking the whole vista of Brodick Bay. It was idyllic.

The boys were quickly out of the doors, Tuzzio football in hand. The ball was kicked skywards and within seconds was being passed between the three of them in the sheer joy at being free of the confines of the minibus until: "Sir... there's shit all over this field!"

I shouted back.

"Well it's hardly surprising, Tuz... it is a cow field!"

The three of them continued to hoof the ball around but in a less enthusiastic and far more circumspect manner. I noticed John sniffing his hand and looking anxiously at the soles of his white trainers.

Malcolm and I allowed them the luxury of some free-time frolicking in the field while we surveyed the site for suitable locations for tent pitching. We agreed upon four areas of site planning. The Hodge Hill encampment would be to the north side of the field alongside the hedge, which would involve us erecting six Vango Force-Ten tents. Their two staff, Glyn and Chris were bringing their own and would erect them on arrival. The Holte company would be located 100 yards away on a flat plateau towards the bottom southern corner of the field. They would be accommodated by two six-berth Stormhaven tents with a three-man tent for the footballers who had stopped the game and were now eating berries from the hedge-row.

"What are those you're picking, lads?"

"Dunno... but they taste great," said Muz, popping one in his mouth.

"Hang on lads... let's have a look at those."

I took a couple from Muzalfar's hand and after scrutinizing them decided they looked sufficiently like blackberries not to present any danger of a slow and painful death.

"They look O.K... but I wouldn't eat them like that... they're probably full of worms and bugs, lads."

John immediately spat out his blackberry while the other two cast a wary eye over the berries on their palms. It was only a matter of seconds before all interest in eating them was replaced by blackberry throwing... at each other.

"Come on boys... pack it in! We have a lot to do before everyone gets here."

They continued throwing and ducking until the supply of ammunition ran out.

Our third area of operations would be the pitching of the latrine tents. We decided that we would tuck them away in the bottom left hand corner of the field, to minimise noise and embarrassment, close to the hedge. We were of one mind in agreeing that the fourth area, the staff and cooking tents, would be best situated at a mid-point along the bottom perimeter of the field, equidistant between the Holte and Hodge Hill encampments and the latrines.

In the remaining six hours, before the two hired minibuses arrived with the rest of the party and staff, Malcolm and I, with our not-so-helpful team of footballing fruit-pickers had the challenging task of creating a camp ready for residence.

I started to untie the ropes securing the tarpaulins covering the tents on the minibus roof rack as Malcolm reached in through the rear doors and produced two spades and a bundle of wooden pegs.

"Right lads, follow me...you can start by digging the latrines"

"What are latrines, Sir?"

Already they were getting an education in excrement.

"Those latrines are a bit close to the hedge, aren't they?"

(Well thank you very much for driving 400 miles, suffering a breakdown, having no sleep for 24 hours and pitching all the tents while we enjoyed our journey with British Rail.) Those were the first words Ann offered us as she jumped down from the front passenger seat of the hired minibus. She had surveyed the immaculately constructed encampments of green and orange tents now situated in tidy rows in different portions of the field. The rest of the minibus passengers began to spill from the side and back doors. Ann was one of our P.E. staff, the wife of Glyn, the Hodge Hill Outdoor Pursuits Leader. She was short, chunky, though attractive, with long nut-brown hair. Her blue-grey eyes in a pleasantly freckled face reflected her amiable personality that gave an aura of "cuddlability". Her occasional proneness to lack of tact quickly transformed this into "stranglability", a feeling more in keeping with mine and Malcolm's mood at that moment.

"Here... we 'aven't bloody stopped for 36 hours!"

Malcolm was not very good at dealing with implied criticism and was immediately protective of his well dug latrines. He was not in the mood for toilet design modification talks and strode off to his tent in a huff, as the Hodge

Hill minibus pulled up alongside. Again, boys and girls leapt excitedly out of every exit door, began to mingle and explore the site. Glyn and his assistant Chris walked over.

"Hey, Gary... you fellas have done a great job here!" (Thanks Glyn!)

"... though I think I'd have had those latrine tents further away from the hedge."

I let this go, though was quietly relieved Malcolm was sulking in his tent and not around to hear this.

I explained our logic for the site and who was situated where, also taking the chance to summarise our journey and early mishap. Glyn was all sympathy.

"It's a great site, Glyn... what fantastic views."

"Yes... we used this a couple of years ago with a Duke of Edinburgh Gold Award group."

Glyn was an outdoor pursuits fanatic and looked the part. He wore checked, lumberjack-style woolly shirts, cord or canvas trousers, thick, woollen socks and had feet encased in heavy well-worn walking boots – and that was just for shopping in Tescos. He was wearing similar garb at that moment with the exception of the trousers which had been replaced by baggy, green shorts. A fashion icon he was not. His face had that weather-beaten, leathery look of having been exposed to too many force ten gales. His hands were brown and gnarled from a lifetime of knot-tying, canoeing and hanging by precarious finger holds on precipitous rock faces. He was totally at home in the open air, preferably with wind and rain battering his eroded features.

It began to rain at that moment. Just a few hesitant spots at first. It would rain more or less solidly for the next five days.

Our encampment was subjected to rain of all kinds; drenching drizzle, stair-rodding torrents and teasing trickles, but it just would not stop. Everyone seemed to be attired permanently in bright orange, yellow or red kagoules. Footwear and socks became impossible to dry. We arrived at the point where we had to issue plastic sandwich bags to put on feet inside boots to delay trench foot, and keep some socks dry.

All cooking and eating in the Holte party had to be done in the staff tent, my own personal eight-berth Cabanon frame tent with a large awning and transparent windows on three sides. It had been intended as a haven from the kids, but during the downpours in the evening and early morning became a communal social area.

Thankfully, the tents stood up to the water test sufficiently well having been well erected, "though too close to the hedge". They remained more or less waterproof, though we had to give constant reminders to the occupants not to lean against the inside walls and make sure items were not pressing the inner canvas against the outside fly-sheet or leaks would be sure to occur. I had intended to run the camp along the semi-military lines of my boy scouting days with an early morning reveille, bedding out and tents brailed up for airing with personal kit laid out for inspection. The rain denied me the chance to impose some good old Baden-Powell discipline on these inner city "recruits". Instead the rain allowed late lie-ins with mid-morning breakfasts as even the leader (me) proved reluctant to make an early foray into the monsoon outside the musty warmth of the tent. The kids' morale remained good, despite the conditions, although the same could not be said for the staff as the rain continued to fall hour after unforgiving hour.

The first night, after a quickly made meal of sausages and beans, with rice pudding to follow then various field games in the drizzle, had not been a comfortable one. Neither party of campers would go to sleep and their voices travelled uninterruptedly across the field in the silent countryside. There had been a chorus of singing and raucous laughter from the Stormhaven housing the six girls. The three Afro-Caribbean girls among them, Pauline, Sonia and Trudy, were a tuneful trio and had been giving soulful renditions of some recent Top of The Pops hits. My appreciation of their talent was diluted by the grope for my watch that revealed it was 2.33am. I must admit to a liking for the Three Degrees but not at that time or in those circumstances. Any reluctance I had about scrambling out into the rain and quietening them had been overcome when it had also become apparent that some of the boys were outside the tents and up to no good. I had pulled on my damp boots with a curse and had peered out of the zip front of the tent to see Owen, Keith and Lloyd poking the side of the girls' tent with sticks causing none too convincing screams from inside. I had stumbled over, chastised them angrily and had forbidden them to leave their tents again until morning, upon threat of death. I had then told the Three Degrees to quieten down and try to sleep – some hopes! They had remained quiet for the whole of the 60 seconds it took me to get back to my tent and zipped into my still warm sleeping bag, then the talking had begun again.

The boys followed my instructions to the letter, they did not emerge again until daylight as my fitful restless night was brought to an end by the sounds of Holte youth playing football. It was light and it was 5.17am.

Noah had been able to build an ark in the face of his watery challenge. We had no such provision. He also did not have to arrange expeditions, walks, sightseeing and games for his ship's company. We cooked in the rain, ate in the rain, walked in the rain, played football, rounders, cricket and tag games in the rain. We explored sea shores in showers, walked through woods in the wet and made rendezvous by rivulets in the rain. The children of the Holte party remained ebullient in their outdoor surroundings. However, they were never so enthusiastic as on the occasions we came across a shop, where they would fall upon the sweet counter like a swarm of locusts on foliage, stocking up on chocolate and gruesome teeth-rotting goodies to supplement their carefully planned, wholly boring, packed lunches. They were indifferent to the natural wonders around them, but shops provoked intense interest.

They were unanimous in their dislike of the camp menu, yet all the food seemed to disappear quickly from their plates. They dragged their feet over every campsite chore on the duty rota and seemed at their happiest when settled in the warm damp confines of the large green tents where music, card games and gossip held sway. Finally their ecstasy knew no bounds when the increasingly pungent latrines were finally abandoned due to flooding. The underfoot conditions around them would have rivalled the Somme. Ann had successfully pleaded with the farmer to allow our party to have the use of his outside toilet adjacent to the barn. He had readily agreed providing the children kept to the path, made no noise and brought their own toilet paper. We had laid down these conditions at the evening briefing. Sitting on a toilet seat as opposed to squatting over a foul smelling pit in a mud-spattered tent in torrential rain was to prove a new prominent item on "life's list of luxuries", though I was sure Glyn was not entirely convinced.

While the two school parties organised their day separately, we merged for an evening game or activity. The Hodge Hill group were working towards achieving Duke of Edinburgh Awards while the Holte aim was to gain outdoor experience. Four days on, the weather had been so adverse that we had been forced to limit our ambitions to walking and low level visits, with no opportunity to venture onto the mountains and attempt climbing or canoeing, some planned activities. The rain just had to stop some time.

The children's spirits had not noticeably dropped, they seemed to find amusement easily, but the nightly staff gathering had become increasingly gloomy with each passing rain-laden day. Expedition Choler was setting in. This phenomenon can arise on any long group excursion, for instance trans polar expeditions, jungle treks in untrodden tracts of Amazonian rainforest or in mountain exploration parties in the isolation of far-flung regions of the Himalayas. This syndrome reveals itself when members of an expedition, being stuck with each other for long periods in testing morale-sapping conditions, begin to start being irritable with each other. Small annoying habits or mannerisms become magnified. Individuals start to show signs of instability and begin to eye up knives and harpoon guns as tensions surface. Our growing irritation with each other made me begin to understand why Ranulph

Fiennes preferred to tackle the icy wastes alone, or why, perhaps, Oates had said he might be gone for some time on that ill-fated Scott expedition. Perhaps he had tired of the inescapable question: "What shall we do tomorrow?", though he did not have to contend with 14 exuberant adolescents in incessant rain. To combat our evening ennui, the staff resorted to that tried and tested solution – alcohol.

It was agreed that we would permit ourselves a two hour break at the local pub each evening, which would be taken on a rota basis in pairs. Later that evening, sitting in the warmth of the inn, having drunk a pint and a half of amber nectar and having devoured a crusty cheese and onion roll I was suitably philosophical with regard to the progress of our expedition, thus far, to observe to Malcolm,

"These five days have gone well, really, considering. The kids have come through it with no problems... the weather's bound to get better."

Malcolm nodded agreement while tucking into his fourth Scotch egg.

It did. The rain stopped, the sun came out for the first time since our arrival on the campsite and the peaks to the north were again visible against a clear blue horizon. The entire vista of Brodick Bay shimmered in a morning clarity previously denied us.

All was well with the world. We took the party to the beach and frolicked on the sand as well as having our planned afternoon of sea-canoeing. It meant getting wet again, but at least we chose to do so. The kids lapped it up, paddling their kayaks through the shallow surf under Malcolm's expert tuition. Ann organised a girls versus boys rounders match which resulted in a poorly accepted defeat for the latter. Tuzzio, Lloyd and John wanted to retain face by a rematch at football but the jubilant girls would have none of it, prancing up and down the beach taunting them unmercifully. The resulting arguments turned to threats of reprisal until the boys were offered the chance of revenge in the Night Game that had been scheduled for later that evening.

After dark, Glyn had set up two circles of 20 yards diameter marked by lamps. In the centre were several small flags. The circles were situated in two fields adjacent to the campsite with hedges, bushes and scrubby woodland separating the two marked areas. The purpose of the game was for each of the two teams to send out invaders to try and penetrate their opponents' circle and capture as many flags as possible. To ensure fair play and verify the captures, staff would act as observers in each circle. The target area would be guarded by no more than two defenders while the rest of the team went off stealthily into the dark to attempt to capture an opponents' flag. Each player had a torch, but the key to the game was not to be seen. If "spotted" by a member of the other team, either a guard or passing attacker, the "caught" invader had to return to base, report to the staff, then start out again from their own circle. We had offered to mix the teams but the girls were adamant in their desire to add to their rounders victory. Malcolm, Chris and I were to act as observers in the fields, while Ann stayed at the girls' base and Glyn sat watch by the boys' home flags.

It was a clear night, but with no moon it remained pitch dark away from the lamp-lit circles. The whole game lasted for two hours and was played with the intensity of SAS manoeuvres. The only breaks in the silence were the muffled whispers of the combatants in the dark, crawling through undergrowth, then the occasional shout of "*spotted!*" after the sudden beam of a torch light.

There was the inevitable cheating when someone would refuse to acknowledge having been spotted. The culprit would run off into the darkness followed by shouts of complaint from the spotter. Otherwise fair play was generally maintained. Even my heart pumped with adrenalin as various bodies scuttled and crawled silently past me in the dark, and shouts went up for me to verify a capture as a torch flickered on suddenly.

It was midnight when the game was ended and everyone called in. Glyn announced the results as we all sat by the glowing campfire clutching tea or orange juice and eating handfuls of biscuits from the huge catering-sized box.

"Girls, four flag captures and 23 spotted... at 10 points for a flag and minus one point for being spotted, that adds up to 17 points."

Whoops and cheers went up from the girls' contingent.

"Boys... six flag captures and 41 spotted... that adds up to 19 points – the boys win by two points!"

A bigger cheer rose from the assembled males together with much punching of the air.

"Tuzzio... I saw you but you ran off and never gave yourself up, you cheater!"

Pauline pointed a vigorous finger in Tuzzio's direction.

"Get lost... you didn't!"

"Some of the girls never even bothered to move so how could we spot 'em!" Owen chimed up in support.

The howls of protest and counter-accusation began to escalate and, to avoid having to call in U.N. peacekeepers, the evening was brought to a close by the campfire being doused and all parties being directed back to their respective tented encampments.

The arguments and recriminations continued for some time afterwards, even as I went round the tents checking guy-ropes, tent zips and fly-sheets for the night. Twenty minutes later, insults were still being hurled from one tent in the direction of another.

"Eeeeeek!"

A piercing scream rang out from the girls' tent as I was just about to return to my own. The front flap of the girls' Stormhaven was thrown open and out leapt six bodies, one after the other in various nightwear.

"Lord, Lord... it was 'orrible... it was on my sleeping bag!"

Sonia, one of the Afro-Caribbean girls, was still wailing in terror outside the tent as I came back over.

"What is it? What is it?"

I shone my torch on the six huddled, distressed figures.

"I dunno, I dunno... it was black and it was massive... it was crawling... 'orrible!"

The Three Degrees were hugging each other in a combination of tracksuits and jumpers, a mixture of fear and the cold night air. I opened the tent flap and shone my torch along the walls and ceiling and then I saw it move in the corner, over a towel.

It was the biggest black beetle I had ever seen in my life. I bit my lip to prevent myself from screaming and running out to join the comforting cuddle outside.

I crawled over in its direction, keeping the monster in the searchlight beam. It died a violent death under a hail of blows from a rounders bat. I squeamishly scraped up the crushed, lifeless body with several sheets of toilet paper and crawled back out of the tent holding the wad of tissue in my hand.

"Did you kill it?... is it dead?"

Sonia refused to return to the tent and her sleeping bag until I had convinced her that the beetle was in the crumpled tissue and that I was going to deposit it in the rubbish container. They all reluctantly went back into the tent but I could see six flashlight beams combing the inside of the girls' Stormhaven, silhouetting the nervous crouching figures inside, as I trod wearily back to the staff quarters.

I must admit to having inspected the inside of my sleeping bag with much torchlit scrutiny before I zipped it up under my chin, ten minutes later.

"I've got one... I've got one!"

Pauline's exclamation was a mixture of joy, surprise and terror as her orange nylon twine tightened unmistakably away from the boat. We were engaged in a morning of mackerel fishing in the bay. We had hired three rowing boats from the harbour, together with the necessary eight inch square frames with lines to make our catch. Ann, Malcolm and I had assumed responsibility for captaincy of each boat as well as steering and rowing, while the four or five Holte anglers set about catching our supper. My crew consisted of the Three Degrees, John and Owen and it was Sonia who had got the first "bite".

"What do I do, Sir, Sir... it's pulling!"

"Wind it in round the frame."

"I don't want to... it's scary."

Before I could relinquish my oars to help, Malcolm's boat, which was only a few yards away, pulled alongside.

"Here... pass the line to me."

Pauline, with some relief, passed the spool over to Malcolm in the other boat. He had his sun-hat pulled down over his eyes and, sporting several days of stubble on his face, was beginning to look more and more like his hero, Clint Eastwood, the outdoor life and deprivation honing his features into a look-alike for the outlaw Josey Wales. Chewing intently on his gum, Josey wound in the orange line, his steely blue eyes on the surface of the water. Ann had also rowed her boat to within a few yards to witness the impending catch and the contents of all three boats raised a unified cheer as the glittering silver fish broke the surface of the water and Malcolm hauled it out and into the bottom of our wooden rowing boat.

There were more screams from Sonia and Pauline as the fish flapped frantically at their feet. They both jumped over the wooden bench in the middle of the boat to get away from it. Malcolm leaned over the side of his boat.

"Do you want to take the hook out of its mouth, Sonia... one of you hold it down!"

"No way... I can't touch that t'ing!"

"It's only a fish, Sonia."

"Me hate fish!"

Everyone, in all three boats, was laughing now, but I had a sneaking sympathy for Sonia. It was also in my rowing boat and I was hoping Malcolm was not expecting me to deal with it as I was no angler. To my own and Sonia's relief, Malcolm lifted the mackerel back into his own boat and gripped the foot long fish by its middle. He carefully removed the hook from its lower mouth then suddenly banged its head twice on the side of the boat.

"Here you are... it's all yours."

He lobbed the now limp fish back into the bottom of our boat, bringing on more shrieks from Pauline, Sonia and Trudy. Owen and John crouched over its lifeless silver and black mottled form.

"Is it dead, Sir?"

I leaned over my oars to look at it.

"No... it's just resting."

Malcolm and Ann pulled their boats away as we all focused on the fish on the wooden slats.

"It's quite a big one... we can have that for supper girls, they're very tasty, mackerel."

"Me no eatin' no fish... me hate fish!"

Any wistful thoughts I might have had of beautiful Caribbean girls eating fresh barbecued fish on a white palm-fronded beach were somewhat shattered by this distaste for that night's potential delicacy. They would have all probably preferred a double cheeseburger over filet-o'-fish at the local Wimpy in Birmingham had they been there, so far were they distanced from their ethnic nutritional roots.

"Well I'm looking forward to having grilled mackerel tonight, girls."

"You can have it."

We all returned our attention to our slack lines as the three rowing boats floated within twenty yards of each other. The girls in my boat quickly lost interest but John and Owen continued to tug hopefully on the nylon lines at short intervals, without success.

"How long we going to be out here for? It's boring."

This came from Pauline, sitting in the bows with her chin on her hands.

"Come on, Pauline, we're going back at twelve... we've got another hour to go yet. Have another go on your line."

Pauline slumped back with her hands thrust in her anorak pockets unwilling to take any further part in the fishing. I continued to row the boat intermittently in the hope of securing another catch, but as the minutes went by it seemed more and more likely that Sonia's was to be the only success. Tedium was beginning to settle upon the three crews.

Then we saw them. The unmistakable black, sinister fins – sharks. Ann had pointed them out first and everyone in the bobbing boats had followed the direction of her arm to a distance half a mile away on the calm flat surface of the water. The two fins seemed to be circling but not getting any nearer, perhaps because I was subconsciously paddling my oars in the direction of the harbour. The initial curiosity turned to nervous giggles and quickly to anxiety.

"We want to go back... we don't like it, Sir."

Apart from Clint, who insisted they were only basking sharks, which he had heard were quite common in the area, everyone seemed to sympathise with Pauline's appeal for a return to port. I had difficulty allaying her fears as I had a few of my own.

"It's all right Pauline, they're quite a way off... they won't come near us."

At the same time I rowed with more conviction towards the harbour, 400 yards away.

"I think it's time we went back in anyway... we're not going to catch anything else."

The previous year, *Jaws* had been a cinema sensation and the scene in which the fishing boat had been engulfed amidships by the huge set of teeth still lingered in my memory. The rowing boat was a good deal smaller and images of bitten-off limbs and blood-clouded water must have been creeping into everyone's mind. Well, mine anyway. I had not swum more than 20 yards from the shore in the Aegean on my Greek island holiday the previous summer as visions of disintegrating lilos still filled my mind from having seen the film.

The three rowing boats all headed back to the harbour with Tuzzio and Muz, who were rowing Ann's, trying to wind up the girls by shouting, "They're coming! They're coming! They're after us!"

This proved entirely effective as the Three Degrees in my boat began to shriek.

"Oh no... we're gonna die."

"Sonia, be quiet... don't be so pathetic, they're only basking sharks... they're harmless."

Malcolm's reassurance from the boat alongside had little effect, as the two sharks who had now finished "basking" came after us in hot pursuit.

Well, perhaps I am exaggerating. The two sharks just continued their circling and if anything seemed to be heading further out into the bay.

Ten minutes later we were tying the boats up at the low jetty and handing over our fishing lines to the "old salt" on the ramp. I told him of our encounter with the two cold-blooded ocean predators and how we had survived. He laughed, telling us they were regulars who never bothered any boat as they only ate plankton, probably had no teeth and the worst they could do was give someone a nasty suck. As our intrepid anglers headed purposefully for the harbour café-shop I saw Malcolm holding up our solitary mackerel for inspection. I could not help thinking that even Jesus would have struggled to stretch that among us for that night's supper.

On the last full day on Arran, we teamed up with the Hodge Hill party for Expedition Day. The boys and girls from their group were all close to achieving their Duke of Edinburgh award and Glyn had planned that they would fulfil their personal challenge element by completing an unsupervised expedition towards the end of this trip. Glyn and Chris had been coaching them all towards this throughout the second week once the weather had improved. Their youngsters had been put through a series of walking, map-reading and mountaineering exercises while the Holte contingent under our close supervision had stuck to low level wooded walks, waterfall visits and coastal excursions. We had only diced with death in shark encounters.

There had been a hint of friction at the informal staff get-together the night before the anticipated expedition. Malcolm and I felt the Holte pupils should have the chance to gain similar experience of a walking challenge. Glyn was of the firm opinion that the Hodge Hill pioneers were well prepared and ready for the task but that the Holte "irregulars" should follow a less demanding route. Pressing our case, Malcolm and I insisted our group were well capable of reading the map and following a route as we had taught map-reading exercises before the trip to Arran and issued maps on all our walks, helping the boys and girls to follow them as we rambled each day.

We also knew that our kids were keen to have a go and not be outfaced by the Hodge Hill group. Over the course of the stay on Arran, the relationships between the two parties had remained good, socially, but with a definite air of superiority in outdoor pursuits in favour of the Hodge Hill battalion. However, pride demanded that we gave our group an equal opportunity in pressing for Holte participation. We won our case with some help from Ann who put aside matrimonial allegiance to take our side. Glyn irritably conceded but I felt Ann would be facing a separate sleeping bag that night.

Glyn placed a condition on his agreement; that the Hodge Hill party should set off a respectable period of time ahead of our group in order that they would not be interfered with by the novices to the rear. It was agreed that both expeditions would follow the same route and that, as added security, Malcolm and I would follow on behind to make sure any chances for disaster were minimised.

It was with these conditions in mind that we had an after-breakfast briefing with our intrepid explorers. Every boy and girl had been issued with their own map as I slowly and carefully outlined the route, starting from the drop-off point.

"Right, everyone... the path starts here."

We were all sat inside the staff tent awning identifying the direction of travel.

"Do you see the red dotted line... running alongside the blue stream... got it?"

"Sir, do we have to go? Can't we just stay here on the camp?"

"Emma, we're all going to do it. It's our last day and it's a matter of regimental honour. We're going to show we can *all* do it. Look at the map. We follow the stream up the valley... be sure to keep the stream on your right. The path may be hard to see at times but as long as the stream's on your right it's O.K. When you get to this point here... there are some woods... see them?"

I pointed to the small green area on the map.

"Follow round to the left side of the woods... *don't* follow the stream any more. At the end of the line of woods you will take the path to the *left* up the hillside. This is the most important point… you must go left here."

Ann and Malcolm moved around the seated group indicating the crucial junction.

"The path leads up a very steep slope and over the side of a ridge then down into another valley. The path is clearly marked as it goes through a pine forest plantation… you know, trees like big Christmas trees. You come out of the woods here… then join a track which follows another stream coming down the valley… can you see the thin blue wavy line?"

There was a general nodding of heads.

"From then on, the path follows a gentle slope over fields and stiles. There is no need to climb walls or gates, so make sure you don't do that. You'll be able to see the coast road running along the bottom of the hill. Mrs Roberts and Glyn will be waiting for you with the minibus… here."

Everyone was helped to identify the point at which the path met the road to the south of the island.

The whole walk amounted to between nine and ten miles with the first half an uphill haul. It was anticipated it would take four-and-a-half to five hours of steady walking with rests. I did not tell them Malcolm and I would be keeping an eye on them in the rear. They folded their maps with the route showing through the transparent map wallets and headed off excitedly to collect their gear from the tents.

We stood at the gate looking up the valley. Malcolm watched through his binoculars as the Hodge Hill party proceeded at a brisk pace, approaching the woods. The Holte expedition had set off two minutes previously, 20 behind the rival party, who were now a mile-and-a-half ahead. I leaned on the gate, watching the Holte group in their multi-coloured anoraks and rucksacks become smaller as they climbed a stile and began to walk alongside the stream. After 400 yards there were already some stragglers, noticeably Emma and Tracey. A vanguard of four or five boys were striding out in front. We had stressed that the group should stick together and not get strung out. We had insisted that the leaders stop at regular intervals to allow those at the rear to catch up.

We had decided to give them 20 minutes start in order that our following them would not quickly become apparent. I took the binoculars. Balancing on the middle rung of the metal-barred gate, I could just see the Hodge Hill back-marker disappearing around the side of the wood, halfway up the valley ascent. I slowly drew my focus down the valley to the line of Holte figures.

"They've stopped! What are they doing?"

Malcolm relieved me of the binoculars and climbed on to the stone wall to get a better view of the distant group.

"They've stopped... someone sat down... they seem to be playing in the stream."

"I don't believe it... they've only been going 20 minutes!"

We opened the gate and set off after having observed the spectacle for a few minutes and decided that our walkers had definitely ceased to walk. Our intention of following at a safe distance in order that the expedition could complete the route unaided had already been frustrated.

"What are you all doing?"

I stood on a pile of rocks looking down on a grassy bank where a gentle curve in the pebbly stream had created a perfect picnic spot. The kids had seen this too and that was what they were doing, picnicking. Tuzzio and John were paddling barefoot with trousers rolled up above their knees while Lloyd and Muz were treading across a line of stepping stones lower down. The rest of the party were sat on the bank tucking into their packed lunches of sandwiches, fruit and Kit-Kats.

"We thought we'd stop for a rest, Sir."

"Trudy... it's only 11.30... you've not even covered a mile yet. You were meant to have your lunch when you got over the hill and into the next valley. I don't believe you lot... come on, get your stuff together and let's get going. The Hodge Hill kids are miles ahead by now... Tuzzio, get yourself out of there – *now*!"

It took five minutes for trekking order to be restored and the whole party to be ushered off along the upward sloping path in the direction of the woods. The "Three Degrees", Pauline, Trudy and Sonia, were bringing up the rear with a rendering of "When Will I See you Again?" in tuneful harmony. The Duke of Edinburgh would not have been happy had they been seeking his award. Malcolm and I gave them another ten minutes start before we again set off following in their footsteps.

Another half an hour further on we came clear of the woods and turned to look up the steep slope to our left, expecting to see a line of coloured dots scaling the incline. Nothing. Malcolm scoured the mountainside with the binoculars but there was no sign of them.

It seemed impossible as our pace of walking meant we would have been catching the group up and there was no chance that they could have already scaled the difficult slope and disappeared over the top and out of sight in such a short period of time. My puzzlement soon ended for I saw them without the help of binoculars. The coloured anoraks could be seen off to our right on the opposite slope to that intended for climbing. They were heading towards the mountains and oblivion.

I jogged up the incline and when I got within distance shouted.

"Stop... you lot... stop... come back!"

My voice echoed around the silent hillside. The message reached them and the party hesitated. Gradually, one by one they began to turn back. The leaders, John, Tuzzio and Muzalfar were the last do so as those in the rear shouted after them.

They were all gathered by the wall at the edge of the wood when I laced into them.

"I can't believe what you did... you stop after twenty minutes for lunch... and then you go in exactly the opposite direction to which we talked about!"

I threw my map on the floor for emphasis.

"It was Tuzzio's fault... he said that was the way..."

"Then why didn't you put him right, Emma? You all know the route... you didn't have to follow him if you knew better... did you?"

"We just followed him."

"You might just as well have followed those flippin' sheep!"

I pointed at the chewing "woollybacks" that seemed to have come closer to listen to this interesting exchange as a diversion from their normally mundane existence.

There was a general air of sheepishness as we all set off again up the correct incline with Malcolm at the front.

"Hodge Hill will probably be back at camp by now, having their tea," was the last comment in my tirade as I brought up the rear, chivvying along the whingeing Emma and Tracey.

The minibuses could be seen parked alongside the road that ran close to the edge of the bay. There were some weary legs among our band as we straggled down the last hillside and two of them were mine. It had proven quite a demanding route and the Holte pupils had probably walked further in one day than they had ever done before.

"Me foots are killin' me... me's never doing this again in me life... no Sir!"

"Come on Sonia, we're nearly there. Admit it, you've enjoyed every minute... wait 'til you're telling all your pals at school what you did."

"Me's never going to walk again... never!"

The three black girls staggered along with me at the back as Malcolm could be seen athletically climbing the stile that led to the road, half a mile ahead. I could also see Ann at the open side door of the Holte minibus.

"What a day we've had... but at least we've made it. Glyn was right about it being too much for our kids on their own," were the first comments I made to her as I levered myself over the stile. She had a distinctly anxious look and I noticed Glyn himself walking towards us from further down the road, at the same time scanning the hillsides.

"The Hodge Hill kids haven't got back yet."

Ann and I peered hopefully back up the slope which we had just descended but there was nothing to be seen.

"I just can't believe it... they were well ahead of us. We never saw them again from the moment they disappeared into the trees when our lot had a picnic."

"We just can't understand it... we went over the route with them, Glyn can't believe they could've got it wrong."

Glyn and Chris had gone further along the coast road to see if the Hodge Hill party had come down at a different point, but had drawn a blank. Disquiet had changed to anxiety and panic was not far behind. The Holte kids had dropped in a heap in and around the minibus and there were constant appeals to return to camp and comfort. We agreed that we could achieve little by remaining so I decided to transport them back while Malcolm, Chris and Glyn retraced the route back up to the ridge. Ann would stay with the minibus.

"Do you think they're lost, Sir?"

Tuzzio, my front seat passenger as I drove along the winding coast road, could identify with that concept quite readily as he had almost led our group to just that fate.

"It looks like they've taken a wrong turn somewhere, that's for sure."

I brought the minibus to a halt in the middle of the campsite and the kids dragged themselves out wearily, disappearing into their tents, with the exception of two reluctant helpers whose task it was to help me prepare the evening meal. During the next few hours I anticipated the sound of the returning minibus at any moment, but it did not materialise. The only distinct sound we did hear was that of a helicopter passing in the distance as we ate supper in the fading light.

We had been back at the campsite for more than three hours, it was getting dark and there was still no sign of our fellow campers from the northern edge of the field. Visions of front page headlines, recriminations and unthinkable griefs were beginning to form in my mind. Mountain disasters, canoeing tragedies and similar school party misadventures were not commonplace, but, when they did happen, every schoolteacher who has ever led or taken part in outdoor trips would read about them with a sinking heart and the thought, "There but for the Grace of God..." I was beginning to anticipate that reality and offered up silent prayers when the beams of headlights lit up the gates at the top end of the field. The minibus pulled up by the Hodge Hill tents and the sound of children's voices travelled down in our direction.

I jogged up the field to witness the dishevelled and chastened Hodge Hill party departing for their tents. No one was missing.

All staff heartbeats had returned to normal resting rates as we sat around the embers of the campfire later that night, clutching our cans of lager. We had enjoyed the final night communal sing-song including "Ging-gang gooly, gooly, gooly, gooly watcha, ging gang goo, ging gang goo..." which had been my contribution from Boy Scout days. The Three Degrees greeted this with wild derision but they still joined in with a soulful, sweet rendition of the chorus; "Hayla, hayla, shayla, hayla, hayla, hayla ho"; which might have earned them a recording contract had it been heard by an RCA talent scout. Everyone had eaten their baked potatoes, nicely burnt, as a last supper treat and spirits had been totally revived as the day's mishaps had retreated into history. Morale was at its highest. After all we were going home tomorrow and we had all survived... just.

The helicopter had been called out after Mountain Rescue had been informed of the party's disappearance. Glyn had acted quickly, realising darkness had been only a couple of hours distant, after he, Malcolm and Chris had not been able to locate the group. It turned out they had done a "half-Tuzzio", going neither right nor left after the woods, and instead more or less continuing their ascent straight up the valley. They had gone over the wrong ridge and ended up two to three miles further north in the mountains. To their credit, they had eventually realised the extent of the mistake and were in the process of retracing their steps when the helicopter had spotted them.

The tired and footsore expedition had been guided back to the safety of the junction where they had made the error and Glyn had welcomed them in the way of an angry, though anxious, parent. I can imagine the exchange of words that might have taken place and could not help but think that had it been Tuzzio on the receiving end, the response would probably have been,

"Sir... have I passed?"

Chapter Eight

ENGLAND'S YOUTH
(May 1998)

IT WAS not the best choice of evenings to have organised a cricket match. England were playing Italy in a crucial World Cup qualifier and the nation would be tuned in to their TV sets by 7.30 that night. The entire Holte Under-13 cricket team were also looking forward to watching the match and for once their enthusiasm for a game of cricket was not all it should have been.

"Why've you fixed the game up for tonight, Sir? It's the England game on TV", was one voice reflecting the general tone as they had straggled into the changing room after school.

"Because it's the cricket season now, that's why! We're also a week over the deadline for playing this cup match and if we don't play it by tomorrow it's likely we'll be kicked out of the competition," was my unsympathetic reply.

"And anyway... we should be back in time for the kick-off if we play well."

The whole team were fanatical in their enthusiasm for cricket and were keen to play any time or anywhere, and it was really no contest where their loyalties lay when it came to a choice of watching England play football on television or the chance to play in a school cricket match. Cricket won hands down. My squad rotation system brought the inevitable looks of disappointment as I announced the team.

"Yasser, captain, Nasair, Irfan, Qasam, Raswan, Sikander, Koheleth, Dean, Mohammed, Mohbur, Imran, 12th man Saheedur, and Ramzan and Adnan reserves. I want the 12th man to come but the reserves can decide if they want to come or go home to watch the football... it's up to you."

"Sir, I don't think I'll be able to play."

It was Dean. "I have to be at Birchfield for athletics training at half past six."

Dean was a well-developed, muscular Afro-Caribbean boy who was also a temperamental opening bowler, fast but erratic. He was also a big-hitting late order batsman, a useful slogger in fact, and it was a big loss him not being able to play. However, he was likely to have more of a future in athletics than he ever would in cricket so I was not going to lean on him in this instance.

"O.K. Dean, it's a pity about that... don't forget there's a game on Monday. Saheedur... that means you're in."

Dean grabbed his bag and walked out of the door just as Koheleth came in.

"I'm not bothered about playing tonight, Sir, someone else can play instead of me."

Noble sentiments indeed, but coming from Koheleth I felt there were less than altruistic ulterior motives.

"I think I'd rather watch the England game... and my knee's been hurting me anyway."

Koheleth was not a cricketer but he always wanted to be involved when it came to sporting activities; football, basketball, badminton, athletics, table tennis, tennis and the rest. He was a naturally talented all-rounder. He was also fiercely competitive. When it came to cricket he was decidedly average, but at various times would want to open the bowling, try being a spinner, bat at number three or field anywhere other than the position the captain, Yasser, had placed him. He was also experiencing the early symptoms of Osgood-Schlatters condition in his knee, not helped by his constant involvement from a very early age in football, the sport for which he had most potential.

"Alright, Koheleth... it'll give Ramzan a game. Don't forget we have another match next Monday."

Koheleth followed Dean out of the door as the two reserves' disappointment had been quickly transformed. I could feel the glow of anticipation coming from their corner of the changing room as they both began to get changed briskly.

"No shouting out of the windows and make sure your seat-belts are all fastened!"

These were my last instructions as I reversed the 16-seater minibus through the obstacle course of haphazardly parked cars. There was some kind of function taking place at the adjoining Lozells Primary School, whose minibus I was now manoeuvring. We hired their bus at £10 per journey, as Holte did not have its own. This proved a mutually satisfactory arrangement as they needed the finance and we needed the transport – frequently.

The minibus's reversing "bleepers" were finally silenced as I crunched into first gear, squeezing the bus between two rows of vehicles and onto the main school driveway. Heads were already sticking out of the sliding windows as the team shouted to their friends, apparently just released from detentions.

"Hey Jagdish!... Rakab... your mum!"

"Get your heads in and close the windows now!"

I nudged the minibus slowly over the speed ramps and past a group of girls by the main gate. There was more cheering from inside the bus as arms were extended through the windows to "high-five" the girls as we paused, waiting for a gap in the traffic.

At last we were away and the boys in their cricket whites settled down in their seats, the excitement over.

"How far is it, Sir?"

"Who are we playing, Sir?"

There are always plenty of questions, many previously answered, but I restricted my replies to a minimum. After a full day of teaching, driving a minibus full of lively 13-year-olds in heavy city traffic demands a total change of concentration.

"We're playing Shenley Court in the cup and it'll take us about 30 minutes to get there" was all the information I was prepared to give as I negotiated the speeding traffic on the inner ring road. We were playing a team from one of the largest comprehensive schools in Birmingham with an outstanding sporting reputation. However, in cricket, they were unlikely to prove a match for the Holte teams. It was probable that their team would be predominantly composed of white boys who would have neither the skills nor tactical know-how in the business of winning cricket matches. My quiet confidence was based upon my experience of cricket in the inner city where the boys from the Asian sub-culture lived, breathed and slept cricket. The Holte team was filled with them; they were all mad about cricket. That is when they were not being mad about football. I foolishly mentioned the England match.

"Who do you think's going to win the big match tonight, lads?"

"Engerland!... Engerland!... Engerland!"

The chants from the cricket team echoed round the bus and as we pulled up at traffic lights I had to turn round to quieten them down.

"It's nice to know you're all so patriotic, lads"... and why should they not have been? After all, they were all English, every man-jack of them. Although from Pakistani and Muslim backgrounds they had the right to that identity and a right to a passport to match, should they need one.

The Conservative politician Norman Tebbit once suggested that our "coloured brethren" should take a cricket loyalty test in order to ascertain if they were English or not. I do not know if the intention was to suggest they be sent "home" if they failed to show the requisite allegiance to St. George. Had the "test" been applied for the contents of this minibus, the "failures" would not have had far to go, for Handsworth, Birmingham, was their home, and many of them had never ventured very far from it. Yes, they would have been rooting for Pakistan in a Test Match, but even I was struggling to find much enthusiasm for supporting England at cricket, they were that bad. And I was not English either. I was from Yorkshire.

At this moment, Mr. Tebbit, they were all unashamedly English.

"England! England! England!"

"All right... that's enough boys, quieten it down!"

I was beginning to wish I had not opened my mouth as the noise level in the back continued to distract me as I accelerated the minibus up the Middleway.

Gradually, the team fell into a gentle stupor as the bus plodded its way through the leafier Birmingham suburbs, the silence only interrupted by, "Wow, look at that house!... is it a mansion, Sir?" or "A Ferrari... wicked!"

The outskirts of Harborne represented a different planet from Lozells. We entered the more functional surroundings of the estates beyond, which provided Shenley with the majority of its pupils. Finally, 35 minutes after we had departed from the Holte school gates, I completed a left turn onto the Shenley Court site and the minibus climbed the long straight driveway which led to the Leisure Centre, that stood apart from the main school campus. I knew where the cricket pitch was from previous visits so I parked the bus at the side of the building.

The boys prised themselves out stiffly from the sliding side door.

"Right, boys. 12th man and Adnan carry the bag... we go round the front of the Leisure Centre and the pitch is over through the hedge on the other side."

I locked the doors, having grabbed my white umpiring jacket, scorebook and shooting stick, then followed the excited group in cricket whites in the direction of the pitch.

Mr. _____ shook my hand. He was a young NQT (Newly Qualified Teacher) and seemed nervous about the procedures to be followed, admitting it was his and the Shenley team's first game of the season. He had a firm handshake and an affable manner that made me warm to him immediately. His team was practising at the side of the pitch. A couple of boys had bats and were hitting tennis balls skywards for the rest of the team to catch. It was noticeable several were going to ground.

Their captain, a ginger haired boy, was wearing full whites and cricket boots together with sweat bands and floppy hat. He looked professionalism personified. In stark contrast the rest of his team, as I expected, were white boys but were attired in trainers, grey school trousers and white uniform shirts with one or two T-shirts providing exceptions. Upon seeing the mini-Pakistan Test team approaching I could see the little confidence the Shenley boys had quickly beginning to evaporate as they stopped their practice to weigh up their opposition.

"The boys are very keen, but they haven't played much I'm afraid. We should have had two games but both were cancelled because of the weather. I'm sure you're going to be too good for us... is it O.K. if we bat first so you don't score hundreds and discourage them too much? I think they're also a bit worried they're going to miss the England match tonight."

I readily accepted Mr. _____'s logic as we had not played much either, but we had still squeezed in three matches, all won comfortably. I agreed that we would field if we won the toss and they would bat if they called correctly. I told Yasser this.

"Oh, Sir... can't we bat first?"

Being the captain and opening batsman, he could quickly recognise a fifty when it was there for the taking. Yasser had run his expert eye over the Shenley boys in the way a tiger would eye a tethered goat for dinner, with the thought, "Now where shall I start?"

"No, Yass... we're going to field first... these haven't played much before."

Yasser trudged out to the middle with the immaculate Shenley captain, a totally unwilling participant in the toss-up charade. Yasser "lost" the toss and Shenley decided to bat. The decision was met with universal groans from the Holte team wielding bats in anticipation of a run-feast.

Shenley did not do too badly – and I am not being patronising. I was able to protect my suspect back by perching comfortably on my shooting stick at square leg during alternate overs, keeping score and observing Yasser masterfully throttle the opposition's batsmen. I liked to keep score meticulously with my fine-line pen, giving only the occasional encouraging comment between overs and a whisper to Yasser.

"Make sure Saheedur gets a bowl."

Which he chose to ignore until the last man was in.

The ginger haired captain fought a gallant lone battle as wickets tumbled at regular intervals at the other end. He scored a creditable 22 from a total of 42 all out in the 17 overs bowled of the 20 overs per side agreed before the match. He tried his best to defend stoutly, farm the strike and protect the procession of "rabbits" accompanying him. His sweat bands were dark with persperation by the end, from wiping his brow, and striding off each time a wicket fell to give advice to the next hapless batsman. He was unluckily next to last out when he chopped an attempted cut onto his stumps. The Holte team gave him a sincere clap as he dragged his bat back to the boundary as he departed.

Yasser, with my insistence beforehand, had used all seven bowlers. I had also told him not to take off his wicketkeeping pads and bowl himself. The last time he had done that he had taken a hat-trick and spoiled the game. (I believe Alec Stewart has yet to achieve this feat.) Yasser was an amazingly talented cricketer.

When the last wicket fell, both teams clapped each other from the pitch and I could not help feeling things were going according to plan with regard to time calculations. Between innings, I outlined the batting order as the boys stretched out on the grass behind the boundary line.

"Mohbur, Number 1, Izzy 2, Ramzan 3, Irfan 4 and after that we'll see how it goes, Yasser... it's up to you."

There were moans from Yasser and Nasair, the two regular openers but it was a good opportunity to give boys who had not bowled and did not often get a meaningful bat to have the chance to do so. Yasser and Nasair, in their normal form, would probably have passed the Shenley total in four or five overs. They could improve their batting averages another day.

Mohbur and "Izzy" (Mohammed) strode out to the wicket. Mohbur, a quiet exemplary boy, was an outstanding fielder who rarely got the chance to bat in a match. He was a plodder whose "correctness" made him a bit of a liability in the 20 or 25 over matches that provide the format for the majority of state school cricket. True to type, he played back a maiden to a nondescript first over, two full tosses and three long hops included. Izzy, a bit of a hitter with a good eye for the ball, could have ended the match very quickly had he got going. The Shenley captain marked out his run up as Izzy took guard. The ginger haired lad hit a good length and uprooted Izzy's middle stump first ball. Nought for one! The Shenley team surrounded their ginger haired hero in a back-slapping huddle as Izzy trooped off chin on chest to face a mixture of mockery and sympathy in the Holte camp.

In came Ramzan. We now had a batting combination ideally unsuited to limited overs cricket or any moderate run chase. It was an example of poor tactical consideration and game management – by me. I should have left it to Yasser. Ramzan could not hit the ball off the square. He had no strength and needed pace on the ball.

The pitch had proved slow and the grassy outfield denied any hope of a scoring shot unless a great amount of effort was put into the stroke. Mohbur, at the other end, was playing the innings of his life. He was like Chris Tavare settling himself in for a three day occupation of the crease. After eight overs we had lost no further wickets and the score had rattled along to 6 for 1 (4 wides, 1 bye and a solitary single to Ramzan who snicked a ball past a slip fielder who was five yards too close).

"Slog out, Mohbur!"

No, that was not me. That was the loud prompting from the rest of the Holte team as Mohbur prodded another full toss straight back to the bowler.

"Come on Mohbur... let's try and get on with it. Tell Ramzan we need runs now... there's only 12 overs left."

I whispered this through gritted teeth between overs. The play had become completely soporific as Shenley did not seem to realise that they were in with a serious chance of winning if this run rate was maintained for much longer.

During the next over, Ramzan threw his bat at every ball. He missed everything including a wide which added one more miserable run to the total, 9 for 1 from nine overs. The first ball of the 10th over, Mohbur was struck on the front leg in a perfect forward defensive position. The half-hearted appeal, "OWZAT!" that followed, was rewarded with the slow raising of the umpire's finger... mine. I just had to give him. The Holte team on the distant boundary erupted with a wholehearted cheer. Mohbur turned, disappointed, and made his way back to the boundary where he was berated loudly by his team mates. Passing him on the way out to the middle, striding purposefully, was Yasser. Now that was initiative.

He took guard in a businesslike manner, modelled on hours of Sky TV Test Match viewing. Yasser then stood back and with an air of malevolence, noted the gaps in the ragged circle of Shenley fielders, all the time spinning the bat in his hands. The first ball he received was a juicy long-hop which he prodded confidently into the offside field.

"Yes!" he called.

"No... go back!"

He changed his instruction just as Ramzan reached mid-pitch. Yasser turned quickly and trotted back to the safety of his crease as poor Ramzan floundered on the uncertainty. He made a determined effort to regain his ground but failed to beat the gentle underarm lob back to the bowler, being run out by a clear two yards.

Yasser leaned on his bat with a look of sorrow that could have been mistaken for satisfaction at a job well done. Ramzan trudged past him muttering "first language" swear words that, as yet, I understand the gist of but not the meaning. Next in came Nasair. Irfan was still leaning on his bat on the boundary edge, ready to make his appearance... a redundant no. 4.

Eight for 3 in the 9th over became 44 for 3 by the 15th – game over!

"Well done, boys... a good game, Shenley."

I rose from my shooting stick, closed my scorebook and extended my handshake to Mr. _____.

"I thought we had you in a bit of trouble there."

"You certainly did... Mr. _____, I thought your boys did very well." (and they did!)

The two teams shook hands as the Shenley Court team reached the boundary edge as we walked in behind them, wickets under our arms.

"Thanks for coming all this way over... our boys have really enjoyed the game. You've got a good team there, they're going to take some beating. Best of luck for the next round."

Mr. _____, a really decent chap, led his team away along the path and through the bushes as I sat the Holte team down for a few minutes of post-match de-briefing.

"Right, well done boys... a good win. I thought we bowled and fielded well. Izzy... you don't play that kind of shot first ball, do you? Think about it, Izzy... you missed your chance to play a proper innings today. Mohbur, Ramzan... well played... excellent defence... excellent, but remember you've got to keep the score ticking along.

"We'd only got eight runs from nine overs – at that rate we'd have lost. You don't have to slog out... it's no good shouting that out boys, it just puts more pressure on the batsmen. What you need to do in that situation is keep backing up and push the singles. Put the pressure on the fielders by playing 'tip and run' if you have to... but you must keep the score moving. Do you understand that?"

Mohbur and Ramzan nodded in unison, the rest were impatient to be away.

"I'm sorry you didn't get a bat, Irfan... I think Yasser did the right thing in the situation we were in. Well done Yass... and you too Nass. Irfan, you're number three in Monday's game... O.K.?"

Irfan shrugged with equanimity at Yasser's having pulled rank on him. He was a good, solid batsman who would have his own successful days, many times.

"Let's get going or we'll be late for the England game."

The boys trotted ahead down the path and through the gap in the bushes. I followed on behind, with Saheedur and Mohbur carrying the heavy team bag. Stepping out of the foliage and onto the pavement that crossed the front of the Leisure Centre entrance, I could see our advanced party had come to a halt in front of a group of older youths, who seemed to be physically barring the pathway. There were seven or eight of them. I heard a voice quite clearly.

"What're you fuckin' Pakis doing here?"

The Holte boys were hesitant to push through the youths to reach the minibus round the corner.

"We've been playing a game of cricket and now we're going home... all right lads?" I said, with a hint of hopeful affability, as I came within a few yards of them.

"... and who are you... Paki lover?"

This came from a stocky white youth sporting a baseball cap with ENG-LAND lettering on the front above the peak.

"I'm their teacher... go through to the bus, boys... go on."

I kept us moving, edging my way forward, giving a gentle push to the two bag carriers that forced the group of youths to part and allow us space to move through.

"How can you take Pakis? Don't the smell put you off?"

I counted seven of them. A far from magnificent seven. This offering came from a tall youth with crew cut, earring and red England football shirt – three lions on his chest. They were all white except for one, who I guessed was of mixed race. I calculated all of them as being 15 or 16 years old.

I ignored the previous comment and shepherded the team along the pavement and round to the area where the minibus was parked. None of the Holte boys were saying anything as they huddled by the side of the minibus. I turned the key in the sliding side door and a football thudded into the window next to my head.

I turned sharply to see the rebound kicked hard and rebound off the hunched shoulders of the cricketers as they began to stumble in an anxious rush to get into the bus.

"Just get in boys... take it easy... don't rush!"

In a matter of seconds they were all inside and I heaved the cricket bag into the space left. I slid the door closed and turned holding my shooting stick loosely at my side.

"Look lads... we've just come for a game of cricket... we've played it... just leave us alone... we're going home."

I tried to sound matter-of-fact and unperturbed but I sounded pleading and pathetic.

"Leave you alone... are you going to fuckin' make us then?"

This was baseball cap again, clearly the leader-cum-spokesman. The rest laughed or smirked. One youth, wearing a T-shirt sporting "England 3 Germany 0" on the front and "Two World Wars and One World Cup" on the back, kept the football up two or three times on his foot and thigh then volleyed it against the rear side of the minibus. I could see the pale faces inside flinch back as the ball struck with a loud reverberation on the metallic panel.

I glanced around for any sign of Mr. _____, or any other likely source of moral or, more pessimistically, physical support. There was none. My heart was beginning to thump as the adrenalin rush of "flight or fight" kicked in. I definitely preferred the thought of flight.

"Look, lads, don't make trouble... I'm getting in the minibus and we're going."

"We're not making trouble... are we lads... we just hate the sight of fuckin' Pakis!"

Baseball cap took one menacing step forward to spit a gobbet of phlegm that splattered on a side window.

Had it been possible to have one wish granted at that moment, it would have been to have traded my MCC Cricket Coaching Award for an (Advanced) Black Belt at Karate, as it appeared that my efforts at appeasement were not succeeding. Again the ball whacked against the side of the minibus. (What is it they say? In a fight always strike the first blow... as hard and as dirty as possible, taking out the leader... it discourages the rest.) I had my shooting stick grasped tightly in my sweating right palm. If it came to it, I was beginning to wonder what amount of damage the sharp pointed end might do to Baseball Cap's testicles. All I knew was that mine were definitely contracting!

I had a fleeting thought of wishing that I'd brought Koheleth and Dean along with us – not to provide a couple of pairs of fists, but to add a more comprehensive racial balance and perhaps win over the mixed-race youth in the group confronting us. Throughout the whole exchange he had not opened his mouth.

I backed off round the front of the minibus.

"We're going."

I jumped into the driver's seat and turned sideways to take in the wide-eyed faces cowering in the back.

"Boys... don't say anything... ignore them... make sure all the windows are shut."

The minibus failed to start. It fired into life at the second attempt. (Thank you, Lord!). I put it into reverse and managed a laboured three-point turn, not assisted by sweating palms. The group of youths stepped back to avoid crushed feet. Two explosions of spittle hit the windscreen. I flicked on the wipers as the liquid began to trickle its way down the glass in front of my eyes. I turned the wheel quickly and as I pulled slowly away along the narrow road the tense silence inside the minibus was contrasted by the loud jeers from the youths now trotting alongside and making obscene gestures.

The chant rose up from all of them:

"Engerland... Engerland... Engerland!"

The minibus gathered speed and we began to descend the long straight driveway to the main gates, 150 metres away. Thankfully there were no speed ramps to slow us. Halfway down, the entire contents of the bus, me included, jumped as the sound of the football hitting the rear doors exploded in our ears. I stopped at the main gate to see if it was safe to pull out.

The football rolled past and across the road. It came to rest in the gutter directly in front of us. I glanced in the rear view mirror.

"Imran... quick... jump out and get that ball."

There was a collective whisper of glee from all round me as Imran leapt from the front passenger side door, sprinted across the road and quickly picked up the ball.

Another look into the mirror revealed the sight of the group of youths with "England 3-0" T-shirt in the lead, sprinting headlong down the drive-way. They had 50 metres to cover to reach the minibus.

Imran jumped back into the front seat, clutching the ball into his lap. Another look rearwards... one or two of the less athletic youths had stopped and were now hurling stones in our direction, over the head of the now-labouring sprinters. A pebble hit the roof as I wound down the side window. I leaned out from the waist, turned towards the now gasping runners and raised two fingers in their direction.

A reverberating cheer went up as I made the sharp right turn into the road and accelerated away. The four youths who had reached the gate shook fists and mouthed inaudible "goodbyes" as their figures became smaller in the rear-view mirror of the minibus. From each open window protruded a brown arm at the end of which was being signalled a frantically eloquent "V".

A happy mood pervaded the minibus as it made the return journey to Lozells. It was that glow of camaraderie peculiar to a well-earned, shared team victory. The football was a good quality Mitre matchball, which everyone signed, including me. I heaved the kitbag onto the Holte car park and Nasair and I carried it to the top of the steps leading to the changing rooms.

"Sir, they were racists, weren't they?"

"Nass... they were scum."

I watched the game on TV that night, stretched out on the sofa, working my way steadily through a pack of Budweisers. Mr. Tebbit, I was definitely rooting for Italy.

Chapter Nine

WHY THE GERMANS WILL NEVER TAKE UP CRICKET
(July 1992)

IT IS a bright summer morning with hazy sunshine accompanied by a slight breeze blowing in from the Aston Expressway End. The pitch, a lightly sanded Astroturf, definitely favours the batsman, though the orange wind-ball could cause difficulties in the hands of a spinner. The pop-up stumps are still where I carefully positioned them before break-time and the coloured marker discs form a neat straight boundary along the halfway line of the football pitch. There is tension in the air, for today I had promised them a game. The tension is all mine.

"They", are a Year 9 C group and they can be seen crowding round the doorway of the Sports Hall at this moment. The skill of lining up is well beyond them.

"Right, everybody... line up along the Sports Hall wall. We're not going in to get changed until everyone is quiet and ready!"

"Sir... can we have a match today?"

"Sir... I've forgotten my trainers..."

"Sir... Wayne and Paul have just wagged it!"

"... how do you know, Neville?"

"Sir, I saw them running out of the gate at the end of break."

This information is perfectly credible on two counts; one, the kids are more than happy to grass each other up in the matter of truanting and in this case it is Neville providing the information, a reliable source. Secondly, Wayne and Paul are always truanting. Wayne's terraced townhouse overlooks the Astroturf and often he can be seen in his pyjamas, watching my lessons from his bedroom window. (His mum goes to work, his father is rumoured to have been detained for a few years at Her Majesty's Pleasure).

"Right, Neville... thanks for the tip-off. I'll tell their Head of Year after the lesson. Now everyone, go in quietly... get changed... today we're having a game of cricket... *quietly!*"

My last few words are drowned in cheers as they stumble in through the double, metal plated doors.

I sort out one or two kit problems and, while they get changed, I glance at the register in my blue mark book. Today, there are exactly 11 of them participating. The group consists of 16, but two, Asjad and Raju, are abroad, working on their leg spin on the dry dustbowls of Karachi or Bangalore.

The fugitives, Wayne and Paul, have a dislike of cricket or, come to think of it, anything physical, except running (away) and the other missing pupil, Sarfraz, appears to be absent. Sixteen minus five leaves eleven, which is a perfect number for my purposes today, for we are indeed going out for a game of cricket. It's the first time I have allowed them outside the confines of the Sports Hall, for they qualify as an S.E.N. group (Seriously Encouraging Neuroses... in me).

I have good coaching qualifications in cricket. I have played our oldest traditional game since my dad threw a tennis ball in my direction on Bridlington beach. I have played at an acceptable club standard, even coming up against the occasional overseas professional. I have been to Test Matches, followed Yorkshire, read everything (Sir) Geoffrey Boycott has ever written on this great game and developed many a successful school team.

None of the above has prepared me sufficiently for the task of honing the cricketing skills of the Spasmodic XI, getting changed noisily in the changing room behind me. Their performance will indeed be spasmodic – i.e. functioning only in fits and starts... and once they start I have to resist having a "fit".

The girls need the Sports Hall today. They are going to practise the shot put with rubberised indoor shots. I agreed to let Julie's group have the facility so there is no escape. We have to go outside onto the wide open space of the Astroturf. The team file out and I give them final last minute encouragement.

"I'm warning you... any messing about and I'll abandon the game."

Here are their brief pen-pictures in the batting order I prepared earlier with much consideration:

1. Neville. A descendant of St. Kitts, though as yet has no representative honours. Has a tendency to sulk, refusing to move his fielding position and prone to bat-throwing when given out. Will dispute borderline decisions, for instance, all three stumps being demolished at once while batting – he will claim it was the wind. (Needs tact, sympathy and careful handling... or simpler still, ignore him when he throws a "wobbler").

2. Simon. A small boy with spiky hair, of Chinese origin, though arrived from Vietnam. His family have recently been taken under the wing of the Catholic Church. His general air of confusion extends to all ball games, owing to his apparently never having handled, thrown or caught a ball prior to his arrival at Holte a year ago. A bit of a liability in the field as he drops catches with depressing regularity. Can be prone to tearfulness when berated by teammates for above habit. (Needs constant encouragement and hiding away in the field to avoid likely contact with ball).

3. Nasser. Has an ideal temperament for the game, being good-natured, always smiling, well-liked and prepared to treat those two imposters, success and failure, just the same. The reason for this is that he does not understand either of the above nor cricket for that matter as he is a Martian. He must be, for he is the only boy of Pakistani background I have ever come across who appears not to have a glimmer of insight into the game. It does not help that he is square in every body part. He has a square head, accentuated by a no. 1 crew-cut, a square neck and square short legs. He has perfect blue chequerboard kit but on his feet sports "squarish" size two, black leather, ankle boots. His body is not designed to run or bend, though he can move slowly in a straight line. (Needs to be given an early bat then placed somewhere in the field where the ball is likely to run and hit against him).

4. Curdiva. A dynamic force in the team. A pale Afro-Caribbean boy who wants to bowl, bat, field, keep wicket but preferably all at the same time. Always claims it's his turn to bat or bowl, does not trust umpires' decisions which he believes are prejudiced against him. He can fluctuate from all-out action to total non-participation. (Be firm but fair – ignore his requests for a decision from third umpire).

5. Azim. Walks with a slight limp, not helped by frequently having his finger up his bottom. Azim is anally fixated and is constantly telling me of his bottom problems. He is late coming out of the changing room.

"I've had a bit of diarrhoea, Sir."

His awkward gait and frequent toilet calls make him unreliable as a bowler; he may need to go to the toilet halfway through an over. (Keep encouraging him in order to take his mind off bowel problems – also remember not to handle any bat that he has used).

6. Tung. Recently arrived from Vietnam with no English. He is a bit raw at cricket as Vietnam is not yet playing and beating England at Test level. He is big, strong and probably 17. He throws a cricket ball like a hand grenade and is capable of smashing the ball for miles in baseball fashion. (A definite middle-order batsman. Keep him away from bowling, but use as a distant fielder, perhaps outside the Astroturf fence).

7. Ahmed Khan. Another big, solid lad who is slow and persevering. Everything tends to bounce off him, especially the ball, as his slow reactions make fine skill co-ordination difficult. Reminds me of an armoured car. (A useful close fielder in the Brian Close mould – someone else can catch the rebounds off him. Will score all his runs in leg-byes as the ball is likely to hit his body and run away for extras. No bat required).

8. Tabassum. A huge boy, overweight and overwrought, often laughing and giggling in a quite manic way. He pretends to be frightened of the ball and is adamant he cannot play cricket. He protests his hopelessness continually. He also does this in swimming (arm-band group), hockey (will not hold the stick), gymnastics (sits like a Sumo on the mat, refusing to move), football (leans against the goalpost and talks to the goalkeeper), athletics (forget it...), table tennis (the ball hurts), basketball (ditto). He is a real captain's problem... how to involve him meaningfully in the game?

9. Martin. A pale, frail white boy of pallid complexion and straw-coloured hair, pastel blue eyes and porcelain legs. He has no strength to lift a bat of any weight. When he bowls, the ball will not cover the distance required to reach a batsman. (A handicap system needs to be introduced to cricket similar to golf – England might then start winning against Australia... must write to *The Cricketer*).

10. Anamul. A lively, energetic, aggressive Bangladeshi boy, lacking self-control and always on the brink of a punch-up. I frequently have to resist the temptation to call him "Animal". He's a definite all-rounder, batting and bowling with no technique whatsoever yet posing a threat to all around him. (Needs to be given plenty of bowling to tire him out in order that his threat with a cricket bat is reduced).

11. Ghufur. Has a perpetual smile, always seeming happy and in tune with the world (alas... not this one). He is an almost Disney-like character. He is immaculate in his blue games kit. He cannot run as he is still concentrating on walking but he *can* bowl. He has an amazing behind the head arm action resembling that of Abdul Qadir, the lethal Pakistani leg-spinner. (Ghufur is definitely going to be the first bowler as he bowls straight, but when batting will only deal in boundaries as his running limitations always results in him being run out by yards... 22 to be exact).

The Eleven emerge onto the hallowed turf (Astroturf), limping, stumbling, charging, squawking and grumbling. I follow on behind... me, I'm mumbling, "Stay cool, keep calm". You might be wondering why I am even thinking of attempting a game with this rather ill-matched assortment of characters. Yes, I know... we should practise. I have done it, I have been there, but no T-shirt has been designed to prove it. We have played in the gym with tennis balls, we have practised alone against a wall; bowling, throwing and catching. We have played in pairs (arguments), we have practised in threes (fights) and we've attempted drills in fours (abandoned).

I have demonstrated basic techniques then stood back and watched as attempts to reproduce my movements made me wish I had taken video footage to see if I had really shown them how to bat with one hand using the back of the bat. Oh... and we have used the indoor cricket nets too, but only with soft balls. Utilising hard cricket balls would have made necessary the kitting out of the group in pads, gloves, helmets and abdominal protectors. This projected vision produced images in my mind of the kind that would provide sufficient material for a whole series of *You've Been Framed*.

The net session proved a salutary experience for your Cricket Coach. The batsman in the net came to resemble a coconut on a shy as the bowlers peppered him with orange wind-balls. At first the bowlers took it in turn to bowl, but as boredom and innovation combined, two then three balls would be directed at the hapless batsman to test his reactions. The bowlers then gradually shortened their run-ups until the "target" was receiving deliveries from approximately five yards range, making hilarious direct hits on the batsman's person more likely.

Having sorted out this slight overstepping problem and persuaded the bowlers to return to 20 yards and one at a time delivery, I stood back to see the first ball land on the roof of the net. It did not take long before virtually the whole basket of balls had been hurled up in an attempt to dislodge the trapped projectile.

The session came to an end with the Cricket Coach standing precariously on a chair, arm aching from holding a badminton post, desperately trying to prod down the dozen wind-balls frustratingly just beyond reach on the roof of the net.

Please believe me, I have tried everything in an attempt to produce something that might resemble cricket, with this, my favourite "challenging" group. David Lloyd, Bobby Simpson, Duncan Fletcher, Bob Woolmer – I await your call.

My previous ventures into attempted games had been strictly limited to simple tip and run formats, where the batsman, should he hit the ball, must run. This had its problems. It takes for granted two things; one, that the bowler can bowl a ball that can be hit; two, that the batsman is capable of hitting the above ball. Neither of these two conditions were fulfilled very often, which resulted in the worst kind of stalemate. Wide unplayable ball followed high unplayable ball, followed "straightish" ball missed by batsman followed by wide unplayable ball followed by... we went back to practising.

Today, however, we would have a game. Not a game that would stand up to ICC scrutiny, but a game in the spirit and shape of cricket just the same. Not a game involving two sides with a winner, loser or equitable draw, but a game in which everyone is involved at all times. A game in which every player bats, every player bowls and one in which they are always fielding when they are not executing either of the previous two disciplines.

In my game there is no sitting out, no waiting to bat, and no dismissal to the no-man's land of the pavilion, only wholehearted, continuous participation in this most glorious of games, cricket. I have developed my hybrid form of cricket from other various formats and adaptations. It has been arrived at through trial and error, success and failure, frustration and above all the hope that cricket can be enjoyed and played by children with little interest in or talent for the game. It works – I have used it many times. I have never tried it with the Spasmodic XI.

"Now boys, today we're going to play a game. Listen carefully... here are the rules."

We have had a little warm up; shadow bowling without a ball, then in twos bowling a ball to a partner trying to pitch it so that it only bounces once. This practice lasted 10 minutes, eight of which were spent retrieving the balls from the opposite half of the Astroturf, completely disrupting the girls' rounders game. After much exhortation the bowlers finally managed to re-place the orange balls in the basket, now at my feet. The boys are all sat on the low wooden edging board which lines the inside of the high Astroturf fence. My cricketers are paying undivided attention to... the girls in their short blue skirts and aertex blouses, screaming as a batswoman runs round the posts. (Is screaming compulsory in rounders?)

"Pay attention... look at me, boys. These are the rules we are going to play and you *must* remember... listen!"

"Sir, can I bat first?"

"Curdiva, be patient... everyone will get their chance to bat and bowl, but listen to the rules first – O.K.?

• You are all playing for yourselves – so you keep your own score.

• Everyone will have a number one to 11.

• Numbers one and two will bat first.

• Number 11 will bowl first.

• When number one or two is out, number three bats next, then number four and so on.

• When number 11 has bowled his six balls, number 10 bowls six, then number 9 and so on... do you get the idea?

(Some nods, some not so sure, some totally vacant looks... already my doubts are beginning to rise).

• You keep your own score in your head. If you hit the fence it's four runs."

"Sir, what if it goes over the fence?"

"Good question, Curdiva... that's six runs."

"And are you out, Sir?"

"No, it's a six and you keep batting... you just add it onto your score – O.K?

• If you hit it, you *don't* have to run, we're not playing tip and run today. If you hit it and run, it's the person who hit the ball who gets the run on his total... have you got it?"

"Sir, if you hit it, do you have to run?"

"Azim, what did I just say?... If you hit it you don't have to run, unless you think there is a run... then you do run... do you understand? (This is very worrying).

• Everyone else is fielding, except when it's their turn to bat or bowl, but remember... if you get anyone out you add 10 runs onto your score. How many runs do you get when you get someone out, Ahmed?"

"....." (He has not been listening).

"Tell him, Simon."

"Ten, Sir."

"If you get someone out, caught, bowled or run out, then you add 10 runs to your score. Ahmed, remember it!

•   Final rule – you bat for ten minutes and if you're not out in that time, you retire to give someone else a bat. When everyone else is out you can then come back in to bat if you retired – O.K?"

"Now, everybody... any questions on the rules?"

Curdiva immediately jumps up and grabs the nearest bat and Neville reaches into the basket for a ball.

"Sit down, you two... put the bat there, Curdiva. I haven't told you your numbers yet... now listen!"

I read out the batting order previously outlined.

"Neville one, Simon two, Nasser three..." and so on.

"... Anamul 10 and finally Ghufur 11, which means Ghufur is the first bowler."

I throw Ghufur a ball as Neville and Simon rush to grab the bats. Neville decides his bat is not to his liking so he snatches Simon's out of his grasp. I let this go as the rest of the group are milling around the stumps and Curdiva and Anamul are having a pushing match to decide who will be the wicketkeeper.

"Animal... Anamul, let Curdiva keep wicket for the first over then you can have a go, all right?"

He grudgingly concedes to this instruction but stands only one metre to the side of Curdiva who is now crouching down in wicketkeeping fashion behind the stumps.

"Now everyone spread out... no, not you Ghufur, you're the bowler, go to the bowler's end over there."

I direct the remaining fielders to positions that arrange them in a balanced formation, three on the onside, three on the offside in an approximate circle 10 to 15 yards from the pitch. I have to direct Tung by sign language to push into the expanse of space behind the bowler. In cricket parlance this position might be described as "long on" you could rename it "deep far-out and fetch it" in our case.

I assume the umpire's position behind the non-striker's wicket, satisfied that everyone is in position and the game is ready to commence.

"Right, Ghufur – bowl!"

Ghufur comes in off three clumsy strides and with his behind-the-head action, eyes turned groundwards, he produces a straight full-toss that Neville swings at and misses. The ball shatters Neville's stumps.

"Yes, yes, yes... Out! Out! Out!" Curdiva erupts from behind the stumps as Neville throws down his bat in anger.

"Neville, don't do that... hang on, Ghufur. I think Neville wasn't ready, we'll start again. Neville, pick up your bat, we'll give you another chance. Goof, bowl again... and this time, *Nev be ready!*"

Neville picks up his bat and adopts a severely intense pose of concentration. The rest of the fielders seem indifferent to Neville having gained an undeserved life, though Curdiva is sucking his teeth profusely and uttering the occasional "Tcha, Tcha" and "Rasclat", an Afro-Caribbean swearword that is extremely offensive yet has failed to register its severity on my ears the way Anglo-Saxon oaths always do.

"Curdiva, keep quiet."

In comes Ghufur again. This time he bowls a wide that slams into the fence a few feet behind Curdiva.

"Wide ball... that's one run to you, Neville."

Neville holds his bat aloft to acknowledge his "success" and assumes his correct stance again. (I taught him that!)

Ghufur's next ball is a beauty, on a length, moving slightly off the pitch and clipping the top of off stump.

"Yes, yes, yes, *out!*"

Curdiva jumps for joy and races round from behind the wickets and tries to tug the bat from Neville. Neville holds on to the bat and a tug-of-war ensues.

"That wasn't out, it never hit."

"Yes I'm afraid it did, Neville, it touched the top of the wicket. Come on, you're out for 1 run. You might get to bat again later. Come on, give Curdiva the bat."

Neville tugs the bat free of Curdiva's grasp, then throws it to the floor.

"Neville! Go and field over there. Hang on, Curdiva, you're not number three."

"I am."

"No you're not, Nasser's number three, give him the bat... come on Nasser. Curdiva, you're next in at number four."

There are more "Tchas" through sucked teeth as Nasser waddles up and takes possession of the bat which Curdiva thrusts at him with definite ill-intent. While all this is going on, Anamul has taken the opportunity to seize the wicketkeeping position again. Another pushing match takes place between him and Curdiva.

"Anamul, let Curdiva stay as wicketkeeper, it's still the first over." (Time is positively rushing by).

"Right, Goof – bowl again... by the way, everyone, Ghufur got 10 runs for bowling Neville out, remember that. *Bowl*, Ghufur!"

Ghufur bowls the remaining three balls of his over, all of which miss the stumps by inches as Nasser survives.

"Well bowled, Ghufur... batsmen change ends, it's you to face, Simon. Next bowler is number 10."

Nobody has moved except Tabassum who has edged nearer and nearer to the fence and now sat down.

"Tabassum, get up! Go and field over there or you won't get a bat when it's your turn."

"Suuuuur... I can't field, my legs are aching."

"Tabassum, go back over there and field, don't be lazy... come on."

He pushes himself up from the low ledge below the fence, walks slowly back to his fielding position (squareish leg) and stands arms folded, legs crossed and then starts to emit high-pitched "eeking" noises.

"Tabassum, stop that... *now*! Who's number 10?"

There's no response so I look at the list on my card and ascertain that it is Anamul.

"Anamul, it's you – you're number 10 – remember your number, please..."

I throw Anamul the ball as Ghufur limps off to take his place in the field. Anamul walks back 20 yards to take his run-up to bowl.

"Anamul, there's no need to take such a long run-up, come closer."

He ignores my instruction and begins his charge up to the wicket. He delivers the ball at least two yards closer than the crease allows, releasing a beamer that hits Simon on the upper arm with some force, as he ducks to take evasive action. There is uproarious laughter from all the fielders as Simon goes down as if poleaxed. He rolls around the floor clutching his arm and moans loudly. Tabassum is clapping his hands in sheer joy at this spectacle. I jog over to the prone Simon and, crouching over him, rub his arm briskly.

"Come on, stop crying, Simon, it's only a wind-ball, it'll soon stop hurting."

I help him up from the floor and guide him over to the fence.

"Come on, sit over here until you're recovered... you're going to be all right... come on, dry your eyes."

Simon is still sobbing on the sidelines as Anamul, in true fast bowler style, comes pounding in again, this time in the direction of Curdiva, who is swinging the bat in baseball fashion. The ball arrives well out of Curdiva's reach, a wide.

"Slow down, Animal... one run to Curdiva."

Let us recap the state of the game so far; we have had one wicket, one injury, three misses, two wides, two tugs-of-war, and one sulk – Neville has wandered off and is now pointedly leaning against a football goalpost upright, his back to the action. I ignore him. We will return to the game. Over to you John Arlott:

"And Anamul's third delivery is clipped away with the exquisite timing and wristy technique of the Caribbean batsman at his best. The ball is dismissed disdainfully from his presence with an arrogance reminiscent of Vivian Richards at his supreme best..."

Back to me:

"A fine shot indeed, though somewhat assisted on its route to the boundary by its having gone directly to Tabassum, who, seeing the ball rolling threateningly towards him, had run out of the way and allowed the ball to hit the fence unhindered."

It was still a good shot by Curdiva.

"Tabassum, get down and stop the ball... four runs to Curdiva – good shot!"

"Sir, the ball hurts... I can't field!"

"Tabassum...!"

Tung has by now run from deep far off to fetch it, and hurls the ball back to the bowler, just missing my head as I am berating Tabassum. The ball rolls onwards for 50 yards in the direction of the rounders game.

None of the girls makes an effort to stop it or retrieve it as it rolls past them.

"Martin... go and get it please." (Bad decision).

Martin jogs off on his thin pasty legs and has to run the gauntlet of the girls' taunts and wicked comments as he retrieves the ball from the furthest corner of the Astroturf. He attempts to throw the ball back and it travels all of 10 yards so he has to run forward, pick it up again and repeat the process. He does this twice before he realises the futility of his efforts. Instead he picks up the ball and runs with it all the way back to the bowler. I begin to feel my life ebbing away.

"Right... well done, Martin. Anamul, bowl again... but please... slow down. Are you ready, Curdiva?"

This time Curdiva hits the ball straight to Tung who has stayed close in on the onside. Curdiva sets off running and Nasser begins to waddle from the non-striker's end in response. Unfortunately, Nasser on his little "square" legs has no chance of completing a run as Tung picks up the ball, then runs up to the wickets that Curdiva has just departed. Tung knocks over the stumps before Nasser reaches even halfway in his waddling sprint to safety.

"Curdiva, that was a terrible run... poor Nasser had no chance. Sorry, Nass but you're out. Well done, Tung... 10 runs to you for the run-out.

Tung knows he has done something right and beams as he picks up the ball and throws it again against the wickets.

"No Tung... stop, stop. He's already out, you don't have to do it again!"

I motion vigorously to him with my arms to stop demolishing the wicket as he is enjoying seeing the spring-up wickets bounce up and down. At last we can continue as Azim picks up the bat and takes his position at the crease.

Anamul completes his over with one wide and two balls missed by Azim. It is Martin's turn to bowl next. His over consists of six balls all delivered in a reasonable style, but which fall short by approximately 10 yards. The result of this discrepancy in distance means that Curdiva, who is now on strike, is left with what amounts to be the difficult task of striking a slowly rolling orange.

The lack of pace in the wind-ball added to the violence of his blows can be compared to that of someone trying to flatten a sponge with a fence post. A lot of effort for little tangible reward. I witness a maiden over in which the ball takes a horrific battering. I pick it up and am amazed it is not split and unusable.

It is now noticeable that the ring of fielders has crept in, with the result that all of them seem to be within 10 yards of the wicket. Ghufur, Tabassum and Ahmed are all within touching distance of each other on the leg side and there are no fielders at all on the offside. Azim is batting, Simon is sobbing,

Neville is still sulking and Martin, having finished his over, continues to stand just behind me.

"Come on Simon, you're all right now. Neville, come over here and field – it's your turn to bowl in a minute. Listen everybody, I'll be an extra fielder on this side. Come on, Tabassum, it's your turn to bowl."

"I can't bowl, Sir... I don't want to!"

"Come on, Tabassum, yes you can... have a go."

I give him the ball. Azim's on strike now and he holds his bat at 45 degrees in his crouching gait. Tabassum throws the ball rather than bowls it, in a deliberately effeminate way. He can bowl in the correct manner, I have seen him do it. They can all do it, we have practised, endlessly. Azim misses the ball. Tung, who has now taken over the wicketkeeping position, also misses the ball. It hits the fence behind him and he retrieves it, then throws the ball with some accuracy back to Tabassum... who runs out of the way. The ball proceeds on its travels at some pace towards the distant rounders match. Martin runs off in hot pursuit.

"Nooooooo... Martin, don't bother, I'll fetch it!" (I need the exercise).

I jog after the ball and collect it, demonstrating a perfect one handed pick-up. I decide against throwing it back to Tabassum who is standing by the wickets making them spring up and down by pulling them back and releasing them.

"Tabassum, leave the wickets alone. Tell you what, go back and field... I'll have a bowl."

I turn my arm over a couple of times to loosen up.

"Sir, that's not fair."

Curdiva complains from the non-striker's end and sucks his teeth.

I run in exaggeratedly fast then bowl a deliberate slow long-hop with a gentle bounce to Azim, who amazingly hits the ball. It rolls between Ahmed and Anamul and reaches the fence at midwicket.

"Well done, Azim, brilliant shot – four runs."

"That was an easy one for him... it's not fair. I bet you don't bowl me an easy one like that."

(I certainly will not, Curdiva!)

My next ball is a beauty. It is an inswinging yorker that Gough, Waqar or McGrath would have been proud of delivering. Azim's middle stump is knocked back and I follow through down the pitch first finger held aloft in triumph.

"That's out. Bad luck Azim... it was a great ball. That's what happens if you hit me for four – the bowler's revenge!"

Azim accepts his dismissal in a sporting manner without complaint.

"I'm not bothered... I need to go to the toilet anyway... I'm desperate."

I agree to let him toddle off to the toilet in the sports hall, which he does, clutching his bottom for emphasis.

The field now looks pretty thin as we appear to be running short of fielders once Tung takes his place at the wicket. He stands waiting for my next delivery, holding his bat out baseball fashion. I bowl, he swings and misses, head, body and arms all rotating in one movement. The ball hits Ahmed, the wicketkeeper, in the midriff.

"Tung... watch the ball."

I point to my eyes, then to the ball to indicate what he must do to make contact between bat and ball. This proves to be a good teaching point. My coaching skills are reaffirmed as my next ball is met with a vicious baseball swing that together with a still head and eye on the ball combines to allow perfect contact, sending an orange missile over the 12 foot high fence behind the square leg, Nasser. Tung proceeds to run up and down the pitch, touching his bat down at each end while Curdiva stands and watches him bemused at the non-striker's end.

"No Tung, no... six runs... no need to run, stop!"

I have to physically restrain him as he turns back from my end to complete his fifth run. I reach in and get another ball from the basket after guiding Tung, by the arm, back to the striker's end.

"We'll get that ball back later... well done, Tung, six runs."

Anamul attempts to grab the ball out of my hand.

"No, Anamul, you've had your turn – it's number seven next... it's you, Ahmed."

I look at my watch, hoping there will be be time for them all to have a bat.

"Tell you what, Ahmed... you have a bat. Curdiva, you can retire as you've had well over ten minutes. You're not out, Curdiva – 10 extra runs on your score. Give the bat to Ahmed."

"I haven't had 10 minutes – no way... tcha!"

"Curdiva you've had 14 minutes... I've kept the watch on it. Come on... give Ahmed the bat."

Curdiva, drops the bat at Ahmed's feet (it would have been on Ahmed's feet but he showed good anticipation and reflexes in jumping back just at the right time). Curdiva stomps off to stand, arms tightly folded across his chest, at slightly-seething silly-mid-on.

"Right... next bowler should be Ahmed, but he's batting. Number six is Tung and he's batting too, so it's number five... Azim. He's gone to the toilet so it's... number four... Curdiva!" (sigh!)

Curdiva struts over slowly and stops his seething to take the ball. He runs in aggressively and bowls to Ahmed.

"A wide... bad luck, Curdiva."

"That wasn't a wide... he never even moved."

There was some truth in this observation; it was a wide but Ahmed had not moved. Movement was not Ahmed's strongpoint. The next five deliveries hit the solid, stationary body of Ahmed on arm, stomach, chest, ankle and "privates" respectively. Each one elicited an LBW appeal from the frustrated bowler. Each appeal was turned down by the totally unmoved umpire – me. The final blow to Ahmed's more tender regions saw Ahmed flinch for the first time and bend double as well as bringing hoots of laughter from Nasser, Ghufur, Anamul and Martin, the only fielders now taking any remaining interest in the game. Tabassum had wandered off to talk to Neville by the goalposts. Simon was still sat down at the side holding his arm, so was unable to bowl, leaving me with no alternative but to give the ball to Nasser. It would have to be the last as time was running out and the group would need at least 15 minutes to change back into school uniform. I could not help feeling this was a pity as the game was just beginning to take on its own rhythm in the way only cricket can do.

I throw the ball gently underarm to Nasser, who drops it. In trying to pick the ball up, his stubby little body does not have sufficient flexibility to permit him to reach the ball and he inadvertently kicks the ball, which rolls away. He attempts to pick the ball up again with the same outcome. The ball rolls inexorably away as he "toddles" after it. The ball remains teasingly out of reach. My hand goes to my forehead as I watch this spectacle of ball and boy, beguiled. The ball finally comes to a halt at the boundary fence, where Nasser manages to crouch and pick up the pursued object. He trundles back to the wicket.

Hours have passed, seasons have come and gone. He reaches the wicket, his arm comes up to bowl... and he drops the ball. He makes as if to pick it up but I get to it before he does and place the ball in his hands, deliberately closing my palm around it.

"Right... Nass... bowl!"

Nasser somehow gets his arm over from a standing start by the wicket and the ball is straight enough to trap Ahmed LBW on the second bounce.

"Sorry, Ahmed... that's out LBW. Well done, Nasser, 10 to you."

Ahmed puts the bat down and hobbles gingerly away massaging his groin area. Martin takes up position at the crease and gamely tries to lift the bat above knee height. Nasser bowls him a straight "grub-hunter". The ball bounces once, then trickles along the ground. Martin, in struggling to lift the bat (it is the lightest one we have), is too slow to swing it and the ball hits the bottom of the off stump.

"Oh bad luck, Martin... another superb delivery from Nasser. Nass, you've got 20 from two wickets in two balls, brilliant. Hat-trick ball and it's Anamul to bat."

Nasser is beaming at his success, a mixture of happiness and disbelief. The happiness is all his, the disbelief mostly mine. I collect the ball and give it to him again as Anamul takes up the batsman's position in front of the stumps. His eyes are screwed up in a rictus of aggressive intensity as he holds the bat out at a right angle to his muscle-flexing body. He wishes to impose maximum force to the orange ball bouncing invitingly towards him after Nasser has propelled another gentle delivery. Anamul becomes a blur of flailing arms and torso as he succeeds in smashing the ball over the distant goalposts against which Tabassum and Neville are now both leaning. They pay only token attention to the ball as it flies over them and the fence and disappears into the bushes by the burnt-out car wreck.

I move my arms upwards above my head to signal six as Anamul continues his follow through and completely demolishes the stumps with his bat. He's out, hit wicket.

"Nasser... a hat-trick! Never mind, Anamul, I'll give you the six for such a good hit but I'm afraid that's out."

Anamul looks at the shattered wickets. One of the steel uprights has become completely detached from its spring-held base. The wickets are broken. I feel it is a good time to call a halt to the day's play.

"Right, boys... we've run out of time. I'm sorry Ghufur, you'll have to be number 1 batsman next week, sorry you didn't get a bat."

He smiles in his permanent good-humoured way.

"Right everyone... over to the fence and sit down."

I have managed to round them all up and they are all sitting on the low fence. I ask them for their scores. I have made a note on my card in my pocket as the game went on, just in case their numeracy skills were found wanting.

The Scorecard

1	Neville	1	(Disqualified for sulking)
2	Simon	0	(Retired hurt)
3	Nasser	30	(Run out 0 + 3 wickets)
4	Curdiva	32	(Not out)
5	Azim	5	(Has not returned from toilet)
6	Tung	21	(Not out)
7	Ahmed	5	(All leg-byes, body then fence)

8	Tabassum	0	(Did not want to bat)
9	Martin	0	(Bowled, will open batting next time)
10	Anamul	16	(A six + one wicket)
11	Ghufur	10	(One wicket – no time left to bat, will open next time with Martin)

Only Ghufur and Nasser knew their scores. Curdiva claimed 50. We have managed to bowl nine overs in 40 minutes, one of which was delivered by the umpire. We would run the risk of a big fine by the ECB for slow over rates.

"Right, everyone... well done. I think that next week we'll have our game back in the Sports Hall. Neville, I'm very disappointed with you – see me afterwards. Curdiva, you had the top score, but you don't need to cheat, you didn't score 50 and you know it. Tung, Tung... well done. Simon... come on, stop whimpering, your arm's not that badly hurt. Sorry you didn't get to bat Goof – next time you will, I promise."

I give them all individual, personal coaching feedback as we straggle back to the changing room. Anamul is dragging the broken wickets behind him.

"Well bowled, Nass... good hits Tung. Tabassum... you're such a lazy boy."

The ten German exchange students who had been observing through the fence during the preceding 35 minutes began to disperse in the direction of the main school building.

Chapter Ten

LOCAL HERO?
(September 1992)

I WAS there. Millions of TV viewers had witnessed an incredible missed "sitter" by Ronny Rosenthal on *Match of The Day* late one Saturday night in September. The ball had been laid across the face of the Villa goalmouth and from all of three yards out, with the sheer impossibility of missing, Rosenthal had somehow managed to blast the ball upwards against the crossbar and out, for the Aston Villa defence to scramble gratefully away.

I was six rows back, just to the right of the Villa goal on the heaving Holte end of the ground, one of a 37,863 full house. The collective groan from our ranks as Rosenthal shaped to hit the ball into the vacant Villa net changed into a roar of unrestrained delight as the ball ricocheted from the quivering crossbar and back over reckless Ronny's head to keep the score at 0-0. The Villa fans' joy inspired yet another vindictive chorus to bait the unpopular visitors:

"In your Liverpool homes,
In your Liverpool homes...
You look in a dustbin for something to eat,
You find a dead dog and you think it's a treat,
In your Liverpool homes."

This had been a repeated refrain throughout a first half largely dominated by the slick passing and movement of the green-shirted Liverpool. Their left-winger had been a major factor in this domination for he had constantly teased the right side of the Villa defence and had given Earl Barrett, the number two, a particularly torrid, head-spinning 40 minutes.

The Liverpool player's mesmerising body-swerves, trademark "step-overs" and out-swinging left foot crosses had instigated frequent panic in the claret and blue defence and square-jawed Nigel Spink in the Villa goal.

At times it also appeared that the Villa defenders were taking it in turn to dish out a bruising to the elegant Liverpool player who was tormenting them. Half-time was approaching as he went down under one particularly meaty and unforgiving challenge from the stocky light-heavyweight defender Shaun Teale, who had been comprehensively bamboozled by the winger's jink and sudden change of pace. The Holte-Enders gave vent to a unanimous howl of hatred in the direction of the black Liverpool player as he lay motionless on the pristine turf. He was clearly hurt by the Villa player's hack.

"Same old Scousers – always cheating
Same old Scousers – always cheating!"

came the chiming, rhythmic chant from the crowd around me.

The player lay prone 15 yards away, just outside the penalty area. The physio had made the head-down gallop to his assistance and with a mixture of chilling spray, wet sponge and sympathy gently hauled the injured player into a sitting position. The grimace on his face suggested no feigning of injury, the sweat beading on his forehead, below a neat tight Afro hairstyle, trickled into his eyes. The physio mopped his face with the sponge and the Villa centre-half Paul McGrath sidled over, appeared to offer a few condolences, then offering a hand helped to haul the winger to his feet. There were no similar sympathies being expressed from the banks of seating behind me.

"Get the fucker off!"

"I hope 'is leg's broken!"

"Tealy... finish the bastard off next time!"

and from a previously subdued gentleman in the seat to my left,

"You scouse get...fuck off back to Liverpool!"

The player in question, Mark Walters, tentatively stretched his assaulted leg and began to jog gingerly towards the jostling players in the penalty area, finally taking a position near the six yard box as Don Hutchinson prepared to take the free kick. The crowd, again still standing, directed their venomous shouts of hate in his direction. The spite was palpable. His sole focus, under this verbal barrage, was on the anticipated incoming cross and he showed not a glimmer of recognition of the bile directed at him with such frenzy from a few yards away.

I could not see clearly what happened next. The ball came in, there was a scramble in the goalmouth and a green and white left leg hooked the ball past Spink into the corner of the net. A strange, breath-holding silence enveloped the ground. The vacuum was suddenly filled by the eruption of sound from the banks of Liverpool supporters leaping in a frenzy of celebration. Walters ran off in the direction of this multitude to my right with his teammates in elated pursuit. He was caught in a mass embrace, swallowed up by the front row of Liverpool supporters and the leaping pile-up of green shirts from behind.

Drowning out the jubilation, the Villa fans around me screamed their frustration. The sheer unbridled enmity for the scorer, Mark Walters, at that moment reached a new peak and had he continued his celebratory run in the direction of his "Liverpool home" in search of sanctuary, he would not have had far to go. You could have seen the roof of his mum's house just half a mile distant, beyond the Aston Expressway, one of the many on the modern functional housing estate surrounding Manor Park Junior School where he had first learned to kick a football.

Far from being a Scouser, Mark Walters could claim to be more local, more Brummie, and definitely more Aston Villa than anyone berating him for putting Liverpool ahead.

I was absolutely delighted for him. My heart applauded though my hands could not. He was my local boy made good.

In a school with 10 football teams the imminent arrival of a promising first year with a Primary School reputation was nothing new. Holte's teams in the 1970's were predominantly black, aggressive and successful. A notable percentage of new arrivals who had been regular members of their primary school teams found it difficult to earn a place in the A or B teams, such was the array and quantity of talent and potential available among the boys keen to play football. Everyone "in the know" had been insisting that this kid was really something special, though in the P.E. Department we were always determined to keep pupils' egos in check and adhered to constructive positive criticism rather than unstinting adoration and "king-making". The P.E. staff jury would remain out on "superstar" talents.

Mark Walters' brother, Michael, had preceded him by a year in arriving from Manor Park. Michael was a genial, even-tempered character with a ready smile and good all round athleticism. He had dependable, average football skills that enabled him to become a solid, though unremarkable, central defender. Michael was easy-going with a completely non-aggressive personality. Though he was a good sporting all-rounder, being a regular member of athletics, cricket and basketball teams, he clearly lacked the edge to take him beyond the comfortable social scene of school teams. When I came across him a decade later on the Lozells Road he had grown into the man he always seemed destined to become, a gentle, genial Rastafarian making a life and living from herbal remedies and culture. Michael, in his first year, had been naturally approachable and likeable, capable but certainly no sporting prodigy. The arrival of his precocious footballing younger brother seemed nothing to become particularly excited about... but sometimes a genius is placed among us.

Mark was always quiet from the start. He had an inner, intelligent, intensity about him. He laughed with the rest of his peers, he was always one of the gang. When he played he did so without malice or ego and he was unreasonably fair and even-tempered in the usual rough and tumble of school life and sport. When playing football he had a lightness and an aura about him. A quiet, self-contained certainty permeated his positive disposition and character when he pulled on football kit. Here was a future football star. He was only 11.

In a football world driven by ambition, false agendas, greed, money, mean motivations and blinkered selfishness, pure innocent skill can still stand apart untainted. Mark's talent and attitude shone beacon clear. Everyone who saw him play recognised his special abilities and qualities with the occasional exception of an opposing myopic parent pacing the touchline in exhortation of their own offspring. There was grudging admiration from rival one-eyed P.E. teachers attempting to referee the games while organising their own team's offside trap. And, of course, there were always the shifty-eyed part-time club talent scouts that came by the dozen to watch the showcase Inter-District matches in which players of Mark's level went through their competitive rites of passage. They had all "discovered" him and to secure his signature would prove a significant coup.

Neutral observers were virtually unanimous in acknowledging his talent and potential although it was a period when the doubting of the black players' "bottle" was still being widely voiced. The usual rhetorical question; "Yes they've got the skill, the speed but... can they handle the rough stuff, the pressure, and when the snow's on the ground they don't want to know?" I am not certain but I am sure Viv Anderson, the first black footballer to play for England, was not excused duty in Poland or Russia in February – though I might stand correction.

A glance at Premiership teamsheets in 2002 provides adequate rebuttal of this 1970s attitude. A recurring comment from opposing ranks would be "We should have won, he was the only difference between the two sides. You're lucky – without him you'd have no chance".

One might have had some sympathy for this point of view but it was not entirely true. The teams that Mark played in and against, be they School, District or County, were all composed of above average, often outstanding, players, most of them holding the belief that they had what it took to attain the

Holy Grail of future professional football. However, Mark stood out even in the most talented of these aspiring ranks. He scored goals.

A common trait in Yorkshiremen is one of being naturally pessimistic, ready to anticipate the worst in situations and, above all, qualifying praise at all times. It provides a certain insurance against inevitable disappointment. In his early school matches for Holte, I discounted Mark's five goals in a 7-6 win as beginner's luck. His seven goals in a 10-0 win was clearly the result of the opposing team's defensive frailties and the three consecutive hat-tricks in the following games being handed to him by the fact that Holte had a physically strong side in which Mark could indulge himself with goals against softened-up opponents. This feeling on my part did not stand close scrutiny for the standard of football in Aston at that time must have been as high as any in the country, Liverpool, Manchester or the North-East included. There were no easy games or potential walk-overs. Every school had its ultra-competitive P.E. teacher driving their teams for a win, a league championship or a prestigious cup final at Villa Park or St. Andrews.

Most school teams at that time, before Sunday boys' club football took a hold, were sprinkled with players who would subsequently play for Football League clubs or one of the abundant semi-professional clubs around the West Midlands. There should have been no easy games; 10-0, 12-1, 12-3, 11-1, these were scores that were totally unusual. Mark's tally of 243 goals was the undeniable factor, a total made more remarkable by the fact that once he reached 15 years of age, he was frequently unable to play for school teams as he was constantly required to represent the Aston District, West Midlands County, England... and Aston Villa. It was hardly surprising the demand for his services was so comprehensive for it was difficult to lose if a player could be worth a three goal start.

At this juncture I must state that I taught Mark Walters everything he knew; about wearing shin pads, making sure his boots were tied up correctly and not arriving late for the minibus. In every other respect he appeared self-taught and I stood back and watched in admiration. He taught me that pure, natural, sporting genius cannot be taught and that as a P.E. teacher one should only protect, cherish and encourage it by providing a safe and healthy outlet. It had to be left to the professionals to knock genius into shape, to bend it to their tactical will, shoe it into a strategic master plan of negativity, offside traps, winding down the clock, tackling back, work rate and "knocking it long".

Outstanding talent in a youngster is a joy to behold. It is the "journeymen" among us who constantly desire and strive to make it conform. Of course, football is a team game. It requires team strategy, working for others in a tactical plan taking into account an opposing team's strengths and weaknesses. Football teams do need "water-carriers'", tacklers and grafters. Above all, every team needs goals. Mark Walters delivered goals, both for himself and for teammates, usually on a plate with a hint of garnish.

Two hundred and forty three goals in four seasons is a lot and I have trouble remembering any of them – except one. He was in the Under-13 team. Not being the team manager, I was a spectator on the touchline with several others. Holte were leading by five or six goals early in the second half and the opposing team had long since given up hope of a fightback. Their teacher/referee had reorganised his team into an eight man defence and blown for offside at every opportunity in an attempt to staunch the flow of goals against. Brian, the young P.E. teacher in charge of the team, had signalled to Mark that his time was up and a substitute was warming up to take his place. The opposing centre half, a very big boy for his age, prepared to take yet another goal kick. His howitzer kicks, which were almost reaching the halfway line, were providing a useful respite from the constant Holte attacks. His hapless goalkeeper, who looked totally dejected, clearly suffering from goal concession concussion, stood forlorn in the mud on his goal line. The big lad took his well delayed run up and launched the ball some 30 to 35 yards in the direction of the centre circle.

Mark, who was midway between the circle and our opponents' penalty area, controlled the ball on his chest, let it bounce once on his thigh and proceeded to volley it left-footed back over the groping goalkeeper's head. At no point, from the moment the centre half dispatched the ball into the atmosphere to the point where it hit the roof of the net, did the ball touch the ground. Mark was 12 and I was in awe, begrudging Yorkshireman notwithstanding.

Holte did lose with him in the team. I recall a defeat in the City-wide Villa cup quarter-final to a school from Chelmsley Wood by three goals to one. The opposing teacher had brashly claimed to know how to restrict Mark's scoring habit. Amazingly he proved correct, hence the defeat. The solution involved playing on the muddiest, narrowest pitch available, conveniently avoiding much grassier, larger ones adjacent to it, then assigning two close marking defenders to accompany Mark throughout the game. One would delay him while the other kicked him, often without penalty. There was also the novel introduction to shirt pulling and unpunished tackles from behind. "Welcome to the world of 'professionalism'!" The advantage of the opposition manager having possession of the referee's whistle should never be underestimated. (Alex Ferguson and Arsène Wenger, eat your hearts out.) Mark was mildly complaining on the minibus journey back, the rest of the team were far more unreserved in their expressions of perceived injustice. Mark had shown no dissent or dirty deeds of retaliation on the pitch – a hallmark that remained with him until he had to be more 'nasty' playing for Rangers under Graeme Souness, where he achieved a couple of respectable sendings-off. (I often felt his heart was not really in it... being nasty.) I saw one of these dismissals in an televised European match. He was sent off for a bad tackle. Tackle! Expecting Mark to tackle always seemed a little demeaning.

Holte also lost 8-6 to Thomas Telford School in an English Schools Shield match. He scored four goals, one more than there were inches of snow on the pitch. Mark could take losing. He did not sulk, berate the referee, blame his teammates or kick the opposition. Why should he when he was a winner in the truest sense. To play with his talent, belief and joy in football – he could never lose.

Mark even won when he was not playing, or at least was not strictly meant to be. I had been manager for the Aston District Under-14 team in which Mark's brother made a few appearances when the better players from Handsworth Grammar School, Great Barr Comprehensive and St. Philip's R.C. Grammar School were not available. On one such Saturday of una-vailabilities I was faced with the daunting journey to Coventry for a West Midlands Cup match.

Friday evening cry-offs, injuries and various misplaced alternative priori-ties had eventually left only 11 bodies assembled on the Crown and Cushion public house car park at Perry Barr for a seeming "Mission Impossible". One of those in that number was me, the manager-coach-physio-minibus driver. I would have liked to have played but being thirty-something I was slightly over-age. We were faced with a ten-man trek to certain defeat, probably a very heavy one too.

Michael made the suggestion of driving over to Aston to call for his brother with a view to asking him if he wanted to play. I was sincerely re-luctant to do this as we were heading for a hiding and did not want Mark to take part in a futile exercise. However, the clamour from the rest of the players in the minibus made me realise that to decline to do this would have plunged this skeleton squad's morale even lower than it already was. I drove over to Aston.

Mark was still half-asleep as I opened the side door of the minibus to let him in. I drove up the M6 in the direction of Coventry with a sense of fore-boding. I need not have. Of course, we won. It was 3-2 and Mark scored all three. Our defensive display bore resemblance to that of Custer's Last Stand as Mark's precious goalscoring gave the team the injection of adrenalin, hope then belief to hold off the siege. What a win!

Mark gave me so much joy (restrained, of course). He also secured me a seat in the Royal Box at Wembley – well not far from it, anyway.

He had brought his letter into school. The headed notepaper looked official and important with the unmistakeable three lions crest. Mark had achieved the seemingly unachievable; he'd been selected for England at Under-15 level. I struggled to find suitable words of congratulation, for too often I had seen talent evaporate, become jaundiced, misdirected or rejected. In the inner city where talent is in abundance in every conceivable field of interest, it is only matched by its degree of disadvantage, distraction and, in most cases, inevitable denial and disappearance. Mark had risen above it. He had been selected from all the hopefuls, from Liverpool to Leicester, from Bradford to Berkshire. He had risen as cream rises and been drawn into the elite.

I said, "Well done, Mark". I did not have a clue where we went from there. It was out of my league – England!

Well, we went to Carlisle first. Mark had been selected for the England Schoolboy squad, managed by Jim Morrow, the Walter Winterbottom of English Schools' football. The first competitive match was to take place at Brunton Park, Carlisle against Northern Ireland. I admit that it was not exactly the centre of the footballing universe; in fact, it was definitely an outpost. Perhaps it had been selected for its proximity to Northern Ireland and the need to reduce travelling expenses. However, it was a big stage, an international match. To be within the circle of "greatness" means an occasional perk comes one's way. Mine was to be offered the chance to accompany Mark to some international games, together with travel expenses and directors' box seat, courtesy of the English Schools' Football Association. An all-expenses paid trip to Carlisle was not to be sniffed at.

We caught the early Saturday morning Birmingham to Glasgow express from New Street station, myself, Mark's mum and Michael. Mark was already with the England squad in Carlisle. It was easy to deduce from where Mark had inherited his personality and character. His mum was a quietly spoken and friendly person who seemed to have no strong opinions about Mark's progress or future possibilities. She certainly declared no ambition to drive Mark on to a future in professional football. I had never seen her at a school game and though she admitted to be pleased with Mark's footballing prowess she seemed a little bewildered by Mark's success up to this point. Michael also showed no hint of jealousy or grievance at Mark's step into the spotlight. The two of them were low-key, yet supportive, of Mark's steady rise to prominence. They appeared the direct antithesis of the pushy parent syndrome, where vicarious aspiration puts unnecessary pressure on a talented child in the hope of a future sporting Eldorado. Neither of them indulged Mark or sought reflected glory in any guise. Our trip on the train involved no over-excitement, after all it was only Carlisle.

We sat together in the stand adjacent to the directors' box. The two teams walked out then formed up in line for the playing of the National Anthem over the less than impressive P.A. system. The 16 England players in their immaculate white shirts and navy shorts stood to attention directly below us, with manager Jim, in his blue England blazer, at the end of the file next to Mark. Of that class of '79 stumbling nervously over the words of "God Save The Queen" that afternoon, several were to achieve fame and future fortune as professional footballers; Paul Rideout, Trevor Steven, Andy May, Mark Hutchinson and Darren Wood. In that season's series of internationals the team turned out to be a fairly average one in terms of both performances and results. The only star to shine was Mark.

The game at Carlisle was uninspiring in the extreme. A 0-0 draw between two obviously nervous, physically strong, functional and heavy-legged sides. It was a depressing mirror to the nature of much of professional football at that time in the late 1970s. Only Mark's flowing footwork and occasional flash of subtlety and inspiration shone through a gloomy game on a dull cloudy day in Carlisle. Even the sheep behind the goal at one end had disappeared before the end.

My reflections on the team and Mark's stature within it were echoed by an expert commentator, excusing me of being guilty of blinkered bias in my assessment. Two games later, England met West Germany at Wembley and I watched the game which, amazingly, was shown on television. Ian St. John, the ex-Liverpool and Scotland international, was the match commentator in his newly achieved, but short-lived, role.

Although England were beaten by a well-organised and technically superior German team, St. John singled out Mark as the best player on the pitch and a certain future professional. His skill, trickery and ability to beat his marker stood out, as always, for all to see.

I observed it from the excellent viewing position of the Royal Box (well five rows back from it to be perfectly exact) at Wembley against Wales a couple of weeks after the match at Carlisle. One or two changes had been made to the side that had been so uninspiring against Northern Ireland but Mark, quite deservedly, had kept his place. To be 15 and to play at Wembley... the highlight of my footballing career was a last minute winner in the Gloucester County Junior Cup Final at Cheltenham Town's Whaddon Road.

Mark rose to the occasion. He always did. If he was able to handle the intense nerve-jangling pressure of an Aston Cup semi-final against local deadly rivals St. George's Comprehensive with their fanatical, chain-smoking, P.E.

veteran Glyn Edwards prowling the left-side touchline in his weather-beaten greasy mac, exhorting his catenaccio defence to close down Mark, then the Holte left winger could certainly cope with Wembley and a 30,000 crowd.

Mark teased the Wales defence continuously. He hit a post with a 25 yard free kick and executed a superb dummy to create England's equalising goal in a 1-1 draw. It proved to be another uneventful, disappointing match which placed Mark's talents in even sharper favourable perspective against such a prosaic 80 minutes. If these young boys were England's selected top 16, Mark was clearly number one, certainly in the attacking sense, and there would be no doubt that the professional clubs would be knocking on his mum's door to try to secure his signature on an apprentice's contract.

In actuality they did not. There were rumours of approaches from a couple of the big Northern clubs with accompanying substantial "sweeteners" and financial inducements, but Aston Villa already had that signature in principle. Mark and his mum had indicated their decision to stay with the local club that had nurtured him. If Mark and his family had been approached with better, under-the-table offers they did not disclose them to me. It is hard to believe that the titans of Manchester, Leeds, Liverpool and London did not make approaches for Mark and if they had done they were rejected. Mark chose to begin his career with mighty Villa in the pre-"Deadly" Doug Ellis days, with its century of tradition, redbrick Victorian frontage and not-so-magnificent Second Division status.

Aston Villa did make a big effort to demonstrate that it valued youth. I and several other Aston P.E. teachers had some months earlier spent a day with Villa, the invitation being aimed at showing us the integrity of their youth set up and provision, from training facilities, coaching and diet to hostel accommodation and pastoral care. It appeared well-organised, coherent and genuine in its desire to develop not only the football skills and professional potential of its young players but to balance that with interest in and care for non-football, personal issues. Perhaps they were ahead of their time. The access we were given seemed well-judged as a P.R. exercise towards local, enthusiastic, physical educationists with its further possible intention of encouraging us to direct any future discovered young talent in the direction of Aston Villa. Half-an-hour with the dour Villa manager of that time Ron Saunders might have diluted our uncritical admiration a little. He was gruff, monosyllabic and made us feel like the football world "no-hopers" which we were. He gave us a real whiff of the pragmatism, ruthlessness and mental hardness of football behind the scenes. Even the look in his eye as he fielded questions spoke volumes as to how he regarded tracksuited amateurs. We departed a little cowed but clutching our glossy brochure issued to Villa's potential youth captures; "An Introduction to a Career in Professional Football with a Great Club". I had glanced at the back cover and it read:

"Now you know what we have to offer, what we are and what we can do. Above all we offer honesty, hard work – and opportunity. By all means look at other clubs. Listen to what they say. Then come to us, hear us and see what we provide. We will be content to let you make up your mind. But before you take the decision that could make your life, remember...

> Be Prepared
> (Aston Villa motto)

Mark signed for Aston Villa in July 1980. He left Holte as a football legend, with a couple of unremarkable GCE passes and everyone's good wishes. He disappeared into the relative obscurity of a footballing apprenticeship and the underbelly of the glamorous life; a day-to-day drudgery of toilet cleaning, boot scrubbing, tea fetching and an occasional appearance in the public arena of a Youth Team match. We hear it often – "Learning the Trade". The professional gates of Bodymoor Heath training ground slammed shut behind him, leaving us wistful amateurs to ponder a couple of enigmatic questions; how would his football education continue and that other constant all-embracing one, would he make it?

I watched Villa in an early season game in late August 1980 against Coventry City. A mediocre match resulting in a 1-0 win for Villa remains in the memory for only two reasons; one, Gary Shaw, a local boy, scored the winning goal – his career had a meteoric rise and an equally fast plummeting fall following a desperately serious injury, and, two, a photograph in the match programme. The photograph in question shows nine fresh faced, clean-cut, optimistic boys looking into the camera with the pitch and Villa's imposing North Stand in the background.

The caption read; "New apprentices making the official start to their Villa Park careers." They were Martin McKenzie, Tony Rees, Kevin Rogers, Ray Walker, Mark Hutchinson, Jonathan Hill, Dean Glover, Brian McClair and Mark Walters. Of these nine, perhaps all had meaningful fulfilling football careers, though only Mark and a certain Brian McClair (Celtic, Manchester United and Scotland) became household names on top salaries. Another demonstration of how the weeding out, falls from grace, injury or disillusionment continuously filters out the hopefuls from reaching the upper echelons of the professional game.

Mark was to step out onto Villa Park as a professional for the first time as a 17-year-old apprentice in April 1982 against Leeds United. I was away on holiday and was not there to see it.

I was there, however, that earlier April afternoon in 1978, the first time Mark ran out onto that same patch of grass as a 13-year-old. I was sat on the bench in the Villa dug-out. Yes, it is a source of great pride that I can boast that my bum has occupied the same plank of wood as such luminaries of the game as Billy McNeill, Graham Taylor, Dr. Joseph Venglos, "Big Ron" Atkinson and Ron Saunders.

It was the Aston Villa Trevor Gill Trophy Final for Birmingham Schools in the Under-14 age group. Holte were playing Shenley Court Comprehensive and the upper tier of the Trinity Road stand was full of the rival schools' supporters who had been bussed in for the afternoon. Holte's path to this prestigious final had been a struggle; Wheeler's Lane 11-1, Broadway 12-3, Ladywood 9-0, St. Philips 4-1 and a nervous 11-0 win against Maypole in the semi-final. Mark had managed to score a few goals along the way.

On the huge Villa Park pitch, goals were not so easy to come by. After taking an early lead, Holte began to tire and a physically stronger Shenley team dominated the wide open acres as the game progressed.

Mark's threat seemed to be nullified and a 3-1 deficit with a few minutes left was proving to be a true reflection of the game. The Holte team's legs were "gone", and the large, silver, trophy was already set up on the table at the side of the pitch. The light blue ribbons of Shenley Court were being made ready for attachment to its handles.

The trophy was shared. Going it alone, Mark was twice brought down by fouls in the dying minutes. Both resultant free kicks, one from 25 yards, the other from nearer 30 yards, hit the back of the net having been struck sweetly by Mark's left foot. It had been truly astonishing.

Following that first appearance against Leeds United, Mark played 224 times for Villa, scoring 48 goals. He became fondly known as "Wally". In his Aston Villa "obituary" upon his departure to Glasgow Rangers an article in a match programme reminisced,

"He is probably best remembered for an astonishing individual goal against Spartak in Moscow in a UEFA cup-tie in 1983".

I saw that goal on TV – it was nothing compared to the amazing dribble past four defenders and a left foot curling shot against Warren Farm Secondary at Burford Road, Kingstanding in 1975!

Mark's Villa record of 48 goals was disappointing. From my regular seat in the Trinity Road Paddock I would often see the reason why. I would watch Mark "plying his professional trade" and observe the coach or manager screaming at him from the pitchside area. The need to double-up on marking, cover for the hopeless Villa left back when he went on one of his headless-chicken overlapping runs, the requirement to take up a defensive near post position on opposing corner kicks, the exhortations from the bench to "give it and go", knock it down the channels, "get rid!" and other heated instructions all having one thing in common – do not retain the ball for too long.

Whereas Mark always treated the football like a friend to be welcomed and embraced, now it appeared to have been transformed into a suspicious character to be passed on and treated as circumspectly as possible. Yes, the professionals did their job, though, of course, Mark occasionally forgot his lines and demonstrated the genius that was always within him. He remembered the joy of football, did his remarkable thing and scored astonishing goals – even in Moscow.

Having left Aston Villa, Mark played for Rangers, Liverpool, and then on to Stoke City, Swindon Town, Southampton, Wolverhampton Wanderers and, finally, Bristol Rovers as age inevitably took its toll on his flowing athleticism. He gained one full England international cap under Graham Taylor. He should have been born a Brazilian.

I was a spectator when Mark played his last game for Villa and I was not cheering for him at all on that occasion. It was at Huddersfield Town's Leeds Road ground on a cold December afternoon, three days after Christmas. The score was 1-1 and we did a good job of subduing him, though perhaps his mind was elsewhere as he produced a very reticent display. Mark signed for Glasgow Rangers four days later. I had thought about hanging around outside the players' entrance to have a word with him after the match, but a family dinner was waiting so I decided against it and left with the rest of the Town grumblers.

The next and last time I ever saw him play "live" was against the same opposition.

It was a 7.45 kick off and I happened to have a "free" lesson last period on a Wednesday afternoon. I had deliberately kept my diary clear of extra-curricular commitments as I had planned to disappear early for the trip to Wiltshire. It was with a keen feeling of anticipation that I drove out of the Holte School gates and headed for Swindon on that afternoon in October 1996. Huddersfield were in a good patch of form under Brian Horton and were not far from the play-off positions. Swindon were a few points below us and playing uninspiringly. A promising double was in prospect; a chance to see Mark play again and a possible away victory.

On a cold, clear night, I and the Huddersfield travelling army (112 to be precise) huddled together for warmth on the open and totally inhospitable Stratton Park end. We cheered our team in the pre-match kickabout, clapped in unison to the chant of "Huddersfield, Huddersfield, Huddersfield" and gave a heartfelt rendition of our signature tunes:

"And it's Huddersfield Town
Huddersfield Town F.C.
We're the greatest team in football
The world has ever seen!"
and:
"Those were the days my friends
We'd thought they'd never end,
We won the League three times in a row.
We won the F.A. Cup
And now we're going up,
We are the Town!
Oh yes we are the Town!"

When you are playing away, optimism and wishful thinking are important parts of a supporter's psychological state.

I also watched Mark, in the distance, during the pre-match warm ups, having not seen him for some time in the flesh. He had definitely filled out physically and in football terms looked a little middle-aged. He looked as balanced, complete and composed as ever as he stroked the practice balls around in the various warm up drills. The aura was still there.

The score was 5-0 at half-time. No, not Holte versus Perry Beeches School, a familiar half-time scoreline, though with similar familiar thoughts on my part concerning the brilliant stylish left-sided player. Yes, it was Swindon 5 Huddersfield Town 0 and I was in shock, along with 111 others. Mark had only scored once but had been instrumental in creating the other four goals.

Our defence had been bewildered by his pace, skill, trickery and intelligence. I showed remarkable sangfroid in resisting the temptation to mention to my neighbouring fellow Huddersfield sufferers that the black guy giving us an evening of torture was one of my ex-pupils.

The half-time plastic cup of Bovril was not enjoyable at all as the Swindon fans provided the choral accompaniment of:

"Can we play you every week?!"

and:

"Are you Oxford in disguise?!"

Our loyal band of Huddersfield supporters cheered ironically as our lads jogged out sheepishly for the second half. Brian Horton, the manager, had made three tactical substitutions, either that or three of the first half participants had failed to come out of the toilets owing to diarrhoea. Within three minutes it was 6-0 and for once Mark was not directly involved. The score remained the same as Swindon became complacement, then bored. Mark was substituted to give someone else a chance. Even Steve McMahon, that archetypal hard-knock professional, had a P.E. teacher's heart beating under that Swindon manager's jacket.

I should have waited to speak to him but I did not. The debacle of Huddersfield's defeat was beginning to sink into my soul as we filed out of the exit. I faced a long drive home which would take me well beyond midnight. My admiration for Mark was undiminished but I had nothing to say. I was hurting. It would be the last time I would see Mark playing other than on the brief late-night Nationwide League highlights programme.

Mark's career continued but, predictably, in the manner of all professionals, once their peak has been reached and passed the acceleration disappears, the skill is still there but more youthful opponents close it down quickly.

The brain is as alert as ever but the limbs betray it more frequently. "An experienced old head"; could this be the epithet I heard a commentator ascribe to Mark after he had scored from a left-foot curling free-kick for Bristol Rovers on the Nationwide League highlights previously mentioned? It was a piece of artistry which earned Rovers a precious point against mediocre opponents in a Division Two relegation battle in 2002.

How could a football career be born, grow, flourish and begin to wither so quickly? The bright eyes, full of optimism and promise still look out to me in that Aston Villa programme from August 1980.

Liverpool were still psychologically celebrating Mark's goal in front of a chastened Holte End. Villa kicked off and in a flurry of movement a claret and blue shirt broke clear of the Liverpool defence. The goalkeeper advanced, the ball was tucked beyond him, neatly into the corner of the net. Silence, unbelieving then... pandemonium. Dean Saunders had equalised for Villa. It was half-time almost immediately and as the players trooped off, the ground hummed with excitement, exhilaration, discussion, elation and wonderment.

McGrath, the Aston Villa centre half, put his arm around "Wally" and gripped him in a friendly head lock, ruffling his hair. He broke free and they both laughed. I brushed a tear away from my eye. Football!

Mark Everton Walters Playing Record		
Club	Appearances	Goals
Aston Villa	224	48
Rangers	106	32
Liverpool	94	14
Stoke City	9	2
Swindon Town	112	25

	Appearances	Goals
Wolverhampton Wanderers	11	3
Southampton	5	0
Bristol Rovers	82	13
Total	643	137
England	1	0

(Also played Schoolboy, Youth, Under-21 and B'Internationals)

	Appearances	Goals
Holte School	85	243

Chapter Eleven

TIME FOR SOMETHING DRASTIC – IT'S GYMNASTICS
(February, late 1990s)

"I DON'T like gym... I wish we were doing football."

No, that is not another whingeing pupil, it is the thought passing through my mind as I stand there at the top of the six steps that lead down to the gymnasium door. The 25, A group, Year Eight, pupils are tightly pressed, quiet but fidgeting, in line against the wall and up the steps adjacent to the door.

It is the second time we have had to go through this process. I had made them go back down to the changing room after their first attempt to present themselves as being ready for the discipline of a gymnastics lesson. They had failed to make the journey from the subterranean depths of the changing room along the bottom corridor and up the three flights of steps to their present position, in any reasonable kind of order. Having taken a register, my usual instructions,

"Right boys, everyone up to the gym, quietly, no noise and no running,"

had fallen on deaf ears. Of course, they had run all the way and the noise of their excited shouts and horseplay could probably have been heard in the nearby administration block where the Head was meeting with the school governors.

I had sent them back down and once they were seated in the changing room, heads down sheepishly, I had given them my evil eye, and a threat to go with it.

"Right you lot. What did I say? No noise, no running. So what do you do? You charge out of here like maniacs then shout and yell all the way up to the gym. It's not good enough and it'd better improve right now. We're going to go up there again and I warn you... if there's one 'peep' from anyone's mouth when I get up there then that's it. We'll come down and you'll have no gym lesson. We'll just sit here in silence in the changing room and look at each other. Understand?... Now go up there again and do it properly."

They had filed out and gone up to the gym in a deliberate fast walk. As I had followed them out I could feel their need to burst up the steps again. It was just all that latent energy desperate for an outlet. I had kept a respectable distance behind to allow them to settle in their line outside the gym door and I could hear the whispers and giggles as I reached the top flight of stairs.

"Even now there's people who can't stop talking – after all I've said. Damien, stand still... Ian and Shaun, get your hands off each other – show some self-control!"

That is the trouble with gymnastics; it demands so much self-control, particularly with apparatus to provide distraction. Why is it that gym makes me feel so close to the edge of inadequacy? Here I am, the apparent model of a Physical Education teacher. My trainers are immaculately white, my tracksuit bottoms with their white stripe co-ordinate perfectly with my Persil-white Fred Perry sports shirt; I look like a gym teacher. At training college we were completely brainwashed into the importance of "looking the part", whether we were about to teach rugby, cricket, athletics or gym. (I still feel an irritable mood descend upon me when I come across a student teacher casually arriving for a gym lesson wearing an All-Black rugby shirt, shorts and designer basketball boots). Why do I feel so insecure at the entrance to the gymnasium, with its perfectly sprung varnished wooden floor, its carefully ordered apparatus store and fully functioning wall equipment? I look into my heart, and that need for perfection, so much a part of gymnastics and its original Spartan ethos, always defeats me. We have not even got through the door and I am already irritable and "failing".

I have stood here many times, at the top of these steps, waiting for silence. On one occasion it was the first time I was observed as a fully-fledged teacher in my probationary year back in 1973. Mr. Bailey, the Birmingham P.E. Advisor, came to watch one of my lessons. Of course, it had to be gymnastics. The class I was taking were second years like this one in front of me now. They were totally "yampy" (noisy, undisciplined and hyperactive). I thought he and I would have to spend the whole lesson just waiting for some form of recognition that we were there, as the group jostled and chattered outside the gymnasium. We did eventually have a gym lesson and it was a success insomuch as there was plenty of activity and no ambulance was required.

I was young, inexperienced but enthusiastic and well organised and, though the class were lively and a total handful, I somehow managed to get through a warm up, floorwork, apparatus groups and closing activity. I half-believed it might not have looked too bad to an observer.

After the class had disappeared, noisily in the direction of the changing rooms, Mr. Bailey tucked his clipboard under his arm and spoke to me at the top of the stairs. My back was wet with perspiration. He said,

"That wasn't too good, was it? You've certainly got your work cut out here, haven't you? Never mind... I think you've got what it takes."

And that was all, no advice or any offer to demonstrate how to achieve perfection with such a class. He never returned and I passed.

Perhaps my antipathy to gymnastics goes further back to my own school days, where the gym was always associated with cold and austerity. A gymnastics lesson was one where you stripped virtually naked except for micro-shorts. Bare feet and no singlet, it was the nearest one could come to experiencing "Naturism". It often proved to be 40 minutes of hurting feet, sore knees and elbows and permanently erect nipples. I was never much use at being upside down either. Anything involving rotation and I seemed to lose all my spatial bearings. (I could never master a tumble-turn in swimming.) I could manage the basics; headstands, handstands and forward rolls to some degree but I shied away from any of the more adventurous movements such as handsprings or vaults over equipment. I tended to hide at the rear of the line and only performed an attempt at the required movement when the P.E. teacher beckoned and gave me physical support from take-off to landing. I was fit, athletic, a good games player but no gymnast. Perhaps it is the reason I feel I will never be a gym teacher either.

My heart always sinks a little as I head up to the gym. There are so many variables and potential mishaps. On one winter morning I had gone up to check the temperature in the gymnasium as we had been having problems with the hot air blowers, as usual. I had turned the corner at the top of the stairs to find Howard lying flat on his back by the gym door. I had said,

"Come on, Howard, what are you doing? Stop pratting about."

Howard had not replied as he was unconscious. I had leant over him to make sure he was not winding me up. I discovered he was still breathing and as he came round groggily I noticed a four-inch long welt across his forehead. It turned out that the P.E. telephone, which was situated in the broom cupboard next to the gym door, had begun to ring. This demanded that whoever was in the P.E. office, 20 yards away down the corridor, had to grab the telephone room key from its wall-hook, then sprint to open the door and pick up the receiver before the caller hung up; a commonly frustrating occurrence. Howard, in attempting to reach the telephone in the requisite 20 to 30 seconds advisable, had attempted to jump down the six steps. Being 6ft 2ins tall and gaining extra inches in take-off he had smashed his forehead on the low, staggered ceiling. Fortunately, Howard had come to no serious harm. I had felt immediate concern for him but my sympathy soon dissipated when I had to cover his first lesson as he had felt too light-headed to face it. It was a gym lesson.

If injuries of this kind are rare outside the gym, it is important to understand that the potential for injury inside its confines is a constant factor for concern. The opportunities for pupils to perform in a variety of ways are limitless. The permutations of movements, sequences and originality of ideas can be a joy to behold... equally the scope for misadventure can cause the blood to drain from a P.E. teacher's face, very quickly.

My first instruction issued to any class before entering the gymnasium is always:

"Right, everyone. When you get inside, find a space away from everyone else and sit down, crossed legs, arms folded."

Having given this clear, concise instruction I hold the door open and allow this Year Eight group to pass through in single file. I immediately notice the air inside is particularly chilly. For the past 20 years the hot air blowers, set into the walls, have either malfunctioned by blowing out cold air or have been so weak as to give only a hint of a warm breeze into a facility often having the ambience of a cold store for frozen meat. On this February morning I can see my breath as I watch the shivering boys in their blue shirts, shorts and bare feet seat themselves reluctantly on the cold shiny wooden floor.

Ian, a pale, white boy, and his friend Shaun, a chubby Afro-Caribbean boy, have huddled together in front of one of the above-mentioned blower grills. I also notice that most of the class have sat themselves within a few feet of the other blowers, leaving an empty unoccupied expanse in the centre of the floor.

"Ian, Shaun come away from there – find a space. Everyone come away from the walls – it's not *that* cold!"

I place my hand surreptitiously in front of the nearest blower grill. There is definitely a perceptible hint of warmth emanating from it but it is clearly insufficient to have much effect on the atmosphere this early in the morning.

(I am reminded of that lesson on a similar cold morning when John Gateley had insisted on coming up to the gym wearing his thick, tweedy overcoat over shorts and bare top. He was definitely one of a kind, as in a previous hockey lesson he had spent half-an-hour poking the shaft of his hockey stick into an ants' nest that he had discovered. I had left him to it as he was very volatile when distracted from tasks suited to his interests. Anyway, I digress. He had insisted that he would take off his overcoat once he got up to the gym, and, of course, I had fallen for it. Once I had unlocked the gym door, he had darted in and immediately run to the climbing ladder that ascends to the ceiling at one end of the gym. My threats, then pleading failed to coax him down and he spent the duration of the lesson at the top of the ladder curled up inside his overcoat. The rest of the class were remarkably unconcerned after the initial novelty of having this non-participant near the ceiling. They paid no attention to him at all for the rest of the lesson.

John did not stay with us long at Holte. The last time I saw him, a few months later, he was striding purposefully across the tennis courts followed faithfully by a pack of local stray dogs).

I clap my hands together and raise my voice in business like enthusiasm for the cause, in the way of a Gymnastic Evangelist.

"Right boys... let's get warmed up – it is a bit 'nippy' in here. Up on your feet... *don't* start talking! Now I want you to run lightly around the gym, on your toes... and when I say '*stop!*', I want you to 'freeze'. (all right they're already freezing) – *go!*"

The boys run around, grateful for movement and a chance to expend the energy I have been restraining until now.

"*Stop!*"

Most of them stop instantly with control, but one or two fall to the floor, possibly intentionally.

"Now Dwayne, and you too Abdul... there's no need to collapse in a heap on the floor. Remember gymnastics is all about control and balance. When you stop at the end of a gymnastics movement what do you do?"

Several hands are raised.

"Yes, Patrick."

"You bend your knees, throw up your arms and move your hips forward to stop yourself falling."

"Exactly... Dwayne, Abdul, remember that next time – well done, Patrick."

Patrick is a good gymnast with exactly the right build and upper body strength for his age. I can always use Patrick for the demonstrations I could never give.

"Right, off we go again... remember, when I say '*stop*'- jump and land like gymnasts."

We go through this routine a few times and already the air temperature seems to have risen a little, it must be 40°F by now. They are all travelling and stopping well, though I have noticed Ian and Shaun playing "tig and tag" under the pretence of following the task. I point my finger meaningfully in their direction and mouth silently, "You two – watch it!"

Warm-up completed, they all sit cross-legged around the gym. One or two try to sit on the benches that line the side walls but I quickly disabuse them of this sloppy intention. I unlock the apparatus store cupboard which houses our precious, recently serviced equipment. It contains: two boxes, two trampettes, a horse (not Shergar) of the pommel variety, a buck, three agility mattresses ("crash" mats), two beat boards and a trolley on which sits a neat stack of 6ft x 4ft mats for floorwork. I pull the trolley out myself. To invite the pupils to haul it out is to offer them the temptation to push, then dive on the trolley as it freewheels across the frictionless gymnasium floor, a temptation to which they always succumb.

"Now everyone, choose a partner and sit in twos along this line."

They rush to form pairs and there is a scramble to be first in the line. Damien, a mixed race boy, and Kurt, a large somewhat overweight white boy, sit alone having not been selected for partnership. Kurt is a pleasant lad who is quite a good all-round sports player, though needs to shed his early adolescent puppy-fat. Damien is not so affectionately known as "The Omen" by me and Howard; a tribute to his malevolent tendencies. I have placed him in the A group quite recently in an attempt to neutralise his frequent bullying and incitement of weaker students to do his bidding. He tends to be isolated in the stronger A group and this is now reflected by his absence of a partner for the next activity.

"O.K., Kurt... you join up with Damien for now and we'll see how it goes."

Neither of them seem very much enamoured at having to maintain close proximity to each other, so they sit well apart at the back of the double file formed between the white badminton court markings.

"Right boys, let me remind you. When you get a mat from the trolley – *do not drag it*! Carry it in twos into a space, then practise your floorwork sequence you started last week."

I stand over them as they get up in their pairs to lift a mat from the trolley and transport it into spaces around the floor. Dwayne and Joseph, two Afro-Caribbean boys, do not like the look of the next mat on top of the pile as it is a little frayed at the edges. They try to pull out a much newer one from underneath.

"Take the top one Dwayne, Joseph – they're all the same you know."

They are clearly not convinced but reluctantly lift off the top one then proceed to drag it across the floor as they both hold the same side of the mat.

"Don't drag it, boys! Joseph, take hold of it on the other side."

By the time I have said this they have reached their destination so they just drop it to the floor and flop down on the mat, two feet away from a blower.

"Joseph, Dwayne, pull the mat away from the wall... and don't just lie on it, let's start practising our sequences."

Dwayne and Joseph are both promising athletes, good basketball players and school football team regulars – they hate gymnastics. I think I know where they are coming from. I stand over them.

"Come on, lads... you're good at this, remember what you did last week; starting positions, balance, weight transfer, roll and finishing position."

I step back and watch as the group begin to involve themselves in the floorwork task. Some sequences appear to be developing. Patrick and his partner John are models of gymnastic correctness, style and experimentation. They stand side by side, arms held high, then move into parallel cartwheels together across the blue mat. They turn to execute perfect backward rolls with a straight push up to feet. They hand walk side by side then collapse with control into forward rolls before emerging erect in a perfect finishing position, hips thrust forward, arms apart and aloft.

Damien, meanwhile, has pulled the mat up around himself and is giving the impression of being in a canoe, rocking side to side negotiating rapids. His partner Kurt sits on a bench at the side, chin on hands.

"Damien! Don't bend the mat up like that, you'll damage it... Come on you two, try and work together. Kurt, have a go."

Damien stands to one side and as I watch, Kurt attempts a forward roll. He ends up in a heap of flesh after straying off the mat. He rubs his shoulder, being in genuine pain, having made thudding contact with the hard wooden floor.

"Never mind, Kurt... give it a rub. When you've recovered have another try at it. Look, try to tuck your head right under and go off your shoulders evenly... Damien, you give him a demonstration. Try to work together."

I wander off, not optimistic that this combination is going to come up with a sequence that will earn them a perfect "10". I cast a wandering eye over the various efforts at sequences and partner work when I feel a sharp tap on my shoulder.

"Sir, Sir, watch me... see what I can do!"

It is Boota. His name is Irfan but we always think of him as Boota (Don't ask... these things happen). I watch him, he is hopeless, but likes attention. He executes a perfect sausage roll (rolling sideways, body semi-straight), he then staggers to his feet and attempts a handstand which results in him collapsing flat on his back with such force that it even knocks the wind out of me. He scrambles back onto his feet and demonstrates a perfect finishing position as previously described for Patrick and John.

Nothing he has done could be generously accredited as controlled or gymnastic with the exception of his immaculate finishing position. In truth I am just amazed nothing is fractured.

"Boota, brilliant! Keep practising that with just a little more control... and I'll let the rest of the class watch you in a minute."

His partner, "Fish", has stood to one side to allow Boota space to perform this exercise. "Fish", otherwise known as Ali, is new to gymnastics, in fact he is new to England. He is a big, strong boy, a very amiable character who will run about tirelessly and is capable of kicking a football with the force of a cannonball. His limited English language skills mean he has great difficulty understanding instructions. I have to mime a lot and speak slowly. In this instance I point to one or two good examples of sequences on view, indicating that he should have a try too. He understands my meaning but shakes his head and smiles, suggesting that he does not fancy it at all. He sits on a side bench and tucks his knees up under his chin. (Shall I count that as a sequence?) Ali is known as "Fish" following one of Andrew's recent history lessons. For some reason Andrew had made reference to "fish" in an historical context. Ali, who up to that point had failed to grasp much of the lesson's theme, "The Medieval Way of Life", suddenly took a liking to this new word, so much so that he had spent the rest of the lesson trying the word for size as he doodled on his exercise book:

"Fish... feeesh... fisssh... fish."

Andrew had recounted this at breaktime in the P.E. office and after much laughter I could never now think of Ali as anyone other than "Fish".

"Right boys, everyone stop and sit down on your mats."

I am beginning to notice that a lot of pairs have given in to fatigue and apathy and there is too much slumping on mats in various postures of repose. It is definitely time to call a halt and remind us all of our shared lesson objectives.

"Right boys, well done – some excellent work there. Remember, the idea and the task is to form a sequence together. It doesn't have to be at the same time, but you should work as a pair. Remember, I'm looking for a good starting position, control, good body shape and style. Some form of balance – we've practised these... then getting across the mat by taking your weight on your hands. I want to see a roll of some kind and a proper gymnastics finish. I think most of you are getting there but let's watch John and Patrick as a good example."

The two gymnasts go through their frequently rehearsed routine and as they stand together, side by side, arms held high, movements complete, the rest of the class give them a round of applause. I am pleasantly surprised at the group's gymnastic appreciation.

"Yes lads – well done! Now that's the kind of standard we should be aiming for... no matter how simple your own sequences are."

We observe three other pairings selected by me, all of which make a reasonable stab at what was requested. Only Fabian, a muscular Afro-Caribbean boy who is totally fearless and reckless in equal measures, deserves mention. Fabian does not work with partners, he always operates alone. His partner, Joel, stands back self-consciously as Fabian comes charging up to his mat off a 10 metre run up. He executes a hurtling 50mph handspring with potential skull-crushing over-rotation on landing. He brings himself to a juddering stop well off the mat but thankfully on both feet before falling chest first on the floor.

"Well done, Fabian... are you all right, son?"

I offer my hand to help him up. He brushes himself off and flexes his muscles with pride. Fabian is indestructible – I hope.

It is apparatus next.

The Key Stage 3 National Curriculum Guidelines for Physical Education say that pupils should be taught to:

"Create and perform complex sequences on the floor and using apparatus; use techniques and movement combinations in different gymnastic styles and in so doing, use compositional principles when designing their sequences, for example; changing speed, level, direction and relationships with apparatus and partners."

The trouble with kids is that no matter how much you tell them that the above is what we are aiming to achieve (yes, even you, "Fish"!); when it comes to having apparatus in front of them, all they really want to do is to play about. It is my formidable task and professional duty to keep them focused on these wonderful, definitive objectives, a photocopy of which I keep in the back of my mark book.

In my heart I know I will settle for getting the apparatus out and, later in the lesson, away with some degree of efficiency, somehow keeping a basic level of control over what is going on and having no need to call for a paramedic's assistance.

This is it.

"Right boys, leave the mats where they are and sit together in your five apparatus groups."

They all scramble up and disperse to different parts of the gym, though Boota immediately begins to pull on a nylon cord which draws out the climbing ropes.

"Boota... Irfan, leave that alone, don't get anything out yet – just sit with your group."

He sits down on the bench with his group but retains his grip on the cord.

We are three lessons into this 10 week course and we spent the last lesson, more or less entirely, getting the apparatus out and putting it away correctly. This involved everyone doing a specific job, with no dragging of equipment, working as a team and sitting down on a bench or particular floor space once everything was in place.

Absolutely no one should start using apparatus until every group has completed their assemblage and I am satisfied everything is correctly in place. (School Health and Safety Risk Assessment Policy Physical Education Department, Page 10 – Gymnastics, paragraph 3, subsection ii).

Unfortunately not many of these lively lads get the chance to read this interesting tome so I have to remind them, frequently.

"Remember boys, no one is to use the apparatus until I am happy with it. Remember how we did it last week; everyone does a job... make sure all ropes are secured, benches hooked over properly and all pins are in place so everything is safe to use. Once your apparatus is out do NOT play on it. If anyone does that then they're not going to get their turn when it comes."

To help them remember the layouts, I have stuck to the walls large diagrams of the apparatus formats covered in laminate, adjacent to where they will assemble it.

"If you've forgotten anything then look at the diagram of your layout on the wall... Any questions?"

Boota's hand is raised.

"Yes, Irfan?"

"Sir, can we play on it as soon as we've got it out?"

"..."

I put both my hands on my head in mock anguish and after letting out a deep exaggerated exhalation of air,

"Irfan... think about it... Right boys, I'm watching you. It's a test of each group and how you work as a team. Go!"

They burst into action and I am nearly knocked over by the boys rushing to carry out the trampette.

"Slow down... take it steady, fellas."

I try to keep a wary eye on five different apparatus constructions at various points in the gymnasium. Everything seems to be going pleasingly well until Fabian, who has been pulling on the rope which runs out the metal upright for the beams, has pulled too hard before his assistants have been able to lift the bolts, which are released to hold the uprights into the floor. As a result one of the bolts has become jammed against the floor itself. Kurt tries to tug it out but it remains firmly stuck.

"Leave it Kurt... Fabian, don't pull on that rope any more, the bolt's jammed, you're only making it worse. All of you sit down... I'll help you in a minute."

I detest these beams. They consist of four metal uprights with pinholes at various intervals for various interlocking metal crossbeams. These are secured horizontally at different heights by curved pins which fit into the holes and lock into the beams. It requires military precision from four people working together to get them out efficiently, something along the lines of the Royal Artillery gun carriage team at the Edinburgh Tattoo. (I think even they might have trouble with our beams.) I wish we had those beautifully crafted, wooden, Swedish beams which are so straightforward to get out and secure. I think our beams come from Estonia or somewhere.

I try desperately to pull out the (damned) jammed bolt, but it refuses to budge. The other apparatus groups seem to have done well and are sitting on their benches ready for action, but then I notice the trampette group bouncing up and down on that mini-trampoline, two at a time.

"Get off that and sit down in your group!"

They all sit down on their bench and I turn to see Fabian, who has left me to his jammed upright, hanging upside down between two ropes, three feet from the ceiling.

"Fabian! What... be careful, turn over, come on, come down – now!"

He slowly rolls over while holding both ropes and then slides down one, fireman style, very quickly. Upon landing heavily on the floor he blows on both his hands. I think he's got rope burns. (good!)

I finally manage to free the offending bolt, almost inducing a hernia, as well as burst blood vessels in my face. With the help of the rest of the beam group I assemble the metal bars at appropriate heights, making sure the pins are securely inserted.

The apparatus arrangements are all safely in place. The gymnasts are ready to perform and my back and hands are really hurting from my recent exertions.

"Remember, boys, you are trying to produce a sequence on each piece of apparatus. Think about it... Start."

They are up, and begin to swarm like locusts on the feast of equipment with its multitude of possibilities. I stand back to have a mental and physical breather. I take up a position where I can see everything and everybody. What I hope to see is movement, control, originality, style and above all sequences with clear starts and finishes, demonstrating "a clear relationship with the apparatus". What I do see is this:

Apparatus Group 1

There are two angled benches hooked onto the wall climbing ladder (John

Gateley's previously mentioned temporary home), and three mats around the base for balances, rolls and landings... as well as a large one-foot thick agility ("crash") mat for flight and landings. The intention of this apparatus layout is to encourage a pathway of movement, balance, hanging, shape, flight, landing and rolls. All five members of the group have interpreted this by climbing to the halfway point of the 10 feet wide, 15 feet high ladder and then by taking it in turn to dive off chest first on to the "crash" mat below. Each pupil executes an impression of a free-fall parachutist, landing with a dull resounding thud in the middle of the suitably positioned safety mat. No one is considering any variations on this theme.

"Right boys, everyone get down."

One by one they return to the floor and stand around me except for Dwayne who lies across the "crash" mat with his hands behind his head.

"Dwayne, get up and stand here, you're not on the beach in Ibiza. Now listen all of you... we're not practising to be stuntmen. I don't want to see that happening again... no one is to dive from the ladder. If I see that again you'll all sit down and watch – I mean it. I want to see you using the benches... I want to see some hanging positions with shape... and balances. If you need to jump off as part of your sequence then I want to see a proper gymnastic landing and round off. I'm coming back to your group in a few minutes and I want to see some quality and concentration. Come on... now get on with it!"

I turn and look around towards

Apparatus Group 2

There is one beat board in front of a four-sectioned box. There are two mats beyond it then the vaulting buck with another landing mat. Two benches, turned upside down for balance walking on the narrow joist, are layered alongside the box and buck. This layout is intended to encourage bounces, flight, landing or vaults, with rolls and balance walking as the gymnasts return to their starting position, five yards in front of the beatboard. It demands a whole variety of gymnastic skills. Patrick and John demonstrate these qualities admirably as they perform consecutively two controlled and eye-catching sequences. (Where are you now, Mr. Bailey?) Damien goes next and after bouncing five or six times on the beat board, he hauls himself untidily onto the box and then lies there pretending to be asleep. The remainder of his group stand there nonplussed, unable to continue.

I stride over.

"Damien, get up... get off there. Come on, you're stopping everyone else. Don't do that again."

He jumps off the box and falls in a heap on the mat pretending he has hurt his ankle.

"Come on, Damien... get up, there's nothing wrong with you."

He struggles up with me pulling his forearm and proceeds to show an exaggerated limp, clearly for my benefit.

"All right, Damien – sit down, over there at the side until you recover... Right, carry on boys, forget about him, you were doing well."

The four remaining boys in his group continue with their sequence of movements and I am quite satisfied with what I am seeing.

"Well done, Joel... keep your legs straight, Anjad... very neat, John."

I start to move off to look at another group when I see Damien. He is just about to execute a 'swallow dive' from the climbing ladder onto the "crash" mat, 12 feet below.

"Damien...!"

Apparatus Group 3

This layout consists of a trampette with four mats beyond it. An agility mat is positioned on the nearest two which prevents it from moving when a pupil lands. Again there are two upturned benches to allow a balanced walk with a mat in between for balances and rolls. This arrangement is aimed at encouraging a two-footed bounce from the trampette, various shapes in flight such as a tuck, a straddle or a pike, followed by landing, balance walk, weight taking on hands and a roll.

Last week we concentrated on height from the trampette bounce, a good, clear shape in the air and a neat, controlled gymnastic landing. What I observe now is the spectacle of each pupil in turn charging up to the trampette and attempting a "kamikaze" somersault which results in an untidy, though safe, crash landing on their backs in the middle of the mattress. Without exception they omit to pay any attention to the balance benches or mats. Instead they jog back to the start of their lengthening run-ups to have an even faster and more reckless attempt at this manoeuvre.

"Stop! Everybody, stop!"

They form up in line against the wall beneath the basketball ring.

"Now listen, boys... the aim of this activity is to get a good bounce, show a clear shape in the air and above all... to have a good controlled landing. All I see is everybody charging up and doing somersaults with crash landings on your backs. If we didn't have the crash mat you'd all be in the hospital now. Also – not one of you is using the benches or showing me a balance or roll. Now come on, let's think about it... I want to see a complete controlled sequence from start to finish."

They set off one at a time under my steely gaze, and each one demonstrates a good bounce, shape and landing followed by the designated balance walk etc. etc. I move off to view...

Apparatus Group 4

"Sir! Look at me, watch what I can do!"

It is Boota and he is hanging upside down from the back of his knees which are hooked over one of the metal cross beams that previously, we struggled to assemble.

"Fantastic, Irfan... that's just what I want to see. Now can you move out of that by putting your hands down onto the mat and going into a roll to feet?"

He tries to follow my suggestion and places his hands on the mat, but when he releases his legs his arms are unable to take his weight and he collapses in an untidy heap, also banging the back of his head on the mat. He holds his head with both hands, clearly in some discomfort as tears well up in his eyes. I help him to his feet and also give his head a gentle rub.

"Oh bad luck, Irfan... keep rubbing it... you're not hurt."

I guide him to the bench at the side and he sits down, discouraged from taking any further part.

Apparatus Group Four consists of three horizontal metal beams held by pins at different heights with two angled benches hooked over them at each end. There are several mats beneath the beams and benches to allow for balances, landings and rolls as well as to prevent fractured skulls, e.g. Irfan. There are also two trapeze swings suspended on ropes from a metal fixture in the ceiling. There is always a battle to get to the trapeze first as swinging on these is great fun. ("Fun" – not a word found in any National Curriculum guideline). Once occupation of a trapeze is taken up it is very difficult for anyone else to remove the "swinger", so I have to limit use to one minute per gymnast in order that everyone in the group gets their turn.

On the trapeze, Joseph is swinging freely, sitting on the bar, thrusting his chest forward to maintain his momentum. At the same time, on every forward swing he emits a Tarzan-like yodel:

"Oooha, Oooha, Ooooha!"

I find unnecessary noise extremely irritating.

"Joseph!... spare us that din, there's no need for it – shut it!"

On the trapeze next to him, Fabian has managed to remove a quiet Indian boy, Satpal, by stopping him in mid-flight after grabbing the two ropes holding the bar. Satpal hopped off and did not complain as Fabian hauled himself up onto the seat bar. I watch as he begins to swing backwards and forwards alongside the now mute "Tarzan". When he has gained some height and momentum in his swing he suddenly slips backwards and I rush instinctively towards him. Fabian does not fall, but instead he hooks his legs over the bar of the trapeze and continues to swing in a 20 foot arc, completely upside down, his arms hanging loosely towards the gym floor five feet below.

My heart remains firmly in my mouth as he continues to swing backwards and forwards for a minute or more; should he lose his grip, there is no safety net and the floor is bound to be damaged. Fabian eventually tires of this mundane movement and, in the search for greater excitement, hauls himself back up onto the bar and on the next forward swing launches himself through the air and into an ankle-shuddering landing on the floor. I pat him gently on the shoulder.

"Fabian... that was very daring, but please don't do that again. If you fall off you're really going to get hurt."

He seems completely indifferent to my concern for his safety and runs off and up an angled bench onto a horizontal bar. He stops for a moment and looks about him. I can almost hear him thinking,

"Now what can I throw myself off next?"

Apparatus Group 5

The final group layout consists of a set of six ropes, suspended from ceiling fittings, with mats placed beneath them. There are two benches placed at a distance either side of the ropes with two further benches angled at 60 degrees, hooked onto the wall bars on the facing wall. This apparatus is designed to encourage rope-climbing, swinging, pathways, and hanging, together with a sequence of each, involving shape and control. I stand hands on hips watching the gymnasts in action.

"Fish" is climbing up the wall bars. He sits himself astride the angled bench and slides down it with great glee.

"Yeeeeeee!"

He lands on his rump on the strategically placed mat, struggles to his feet and scrambles back up the wall bars to repeat the process and sound effect.

Ian and Shaun are both clinging to ropes while swinging backwards and forwards from one bench to another. As they traverse the gap between the two benches they both emit piercing screams.

"Ian! Shaun!... what is that meant to be and why are you making so much noise? It's totally unnecessary."

"Yeeeeeee!"

""Fish"... shut up too!"

I place my finger over my lips to reinforce this instruction, but he is already halfway back up the wall bars.

Ian points to the floor while keeping hold of his rope with the other hand.

"Sir, we're pretending that this is a river... and you have to swing across from one bank to another. If you put a foot down or fall in the water... the crocodiles get you."

(I may have missed it, but I noticed no mention of crocodile evasion in the Key Stage 3 Gymnastic syllabus).

I am completely stuck for any avenue of gymnastic advice.

"... Just don't make that noise."

The two other boys in the group, Muktar and Mustafa, are at least quietly absorbed on the equipment. They are sat at the top of the wall bars apparently deep in conversation.

"You two, how long are you going to sit up there doing nothing... it's not the social area, you know! Come on, do something... show me what you can do... you're supposed to be producing a sequence."

They reluctantly climb down the wall bars past Ian and Shaun who have now taken to sliding down the benches à la "Fish". They slide down in perfect synchronicity emitting stereo "Yeeeeees!"

"Don't make that noise!"

While my back was turned Muktar and Mustafa have joined "Fish" in the crocodile avoidance exercise, but to make their mission easier have tied knots in the bottom of the ropes. This is the equivalent of religious desecration; to knot a gymnastic rope. I try to restrain my apoplexy.

"Muktar, Mustafa... get off those now. I've told you, never tie knots in the ropes. Get them out now!"

They stand in the "river" and try to unravel the knots. Having stood on them, the knots are now too tight to undo. I have to do it myself with more blood vessel bursting efforts. I succeed eventually and wipe the perspiration from my forehead.

"Right, everyone... Stop what you're doing!"

Most of the groups begin to break off from their carefully rehearsed sequences and within a few seconds are sitting side by side on their respective benches. I quickly notice that Fabian is not: he is hanging by both arms from the basketball ring at the far end of the gym. This is not part of the apparatus layout and I am not impressed.

"Fabian, get down now – get off there!"

He hangs suspended; his legs are five feet from the floor. He lets go and I wince as he lands, but he is apparently unconcerned by the jolt and struts over to his group's bench.

"Fabian... I just don't believe you. How can you do that?" (It is done by running at and up the wall at great speed then springing up to grab the metal hoop ring holding the net). If you break one of those rings you'll be paying for it."

Everyone is sat down. I stand and wait for the mumbles and fidgeting to cease. Thirty seconds go by and they get the message.

Silence.

"Now I've watched every group and I have to admit there's some good original ideas. Some people are doing very well and are using their brains to think of a good sequence of movements. Others... well, you're just playing about."

I scan the room meaningfully, giving them chance to weigh up their own degree of guilt in the face of my accusation. They are all thinking about what I am saying except Damien. He is sat on his bench and has the end of a climbing rope protruding from between his legs. He nudges the boy next to him and pretends to masturbate this foot long, two-inch thick "penis".

"Damien! When you grow up you're going to be very disappointed... put that rope back and pay attention to what I'm saying."

He pushes the rope behind him, rests his chin on his hands and stares down at the floor.

"We're not here to play about – we're here to improve our gymnastics. All of you have the ability... now let's try to use it. We're going to change over now and move on to the next apparatus."

One or two boys immediately jump up and start to trot towards the next layout.

"Not yet... go back... sit down."

"When I say so, everyone will move round one place in an anti-clockwise direction... that way."

I motion with my arm slowly to indicate the direction of travel.

"Understand?... Wait for it... Go!"

Blue shirts hurtle in a blur of movement from their seated positions to their next destination. Fabian is immediately halfway up a rope, one or two start bouncing on the trampette and "Fish" is the first to dive in to a "crash" mat. I am not a happy gym teacher.

"Stop!... Sit down!... arms folded!"

I stand with my arms folded across my chest and let out an exaggerated sigh in the silence that follows. I feel like a lion-tamer with no whip and a chair too heavy to lift – the "lions" are definitely winning.

"That is just not good enough. If we are going to go on with this we have to do better than that. You are all to go back to where you just came from then sit down. Do not touch *any* apparatus."

The five groups return to their previous apparatus stations. We try again and this time... it's perfect.

"Now that's better – well done! Let's keep it like that. I'm going to watch you all; remember I'm looking for good examples of controlled sequences. Start!"

'Fish' immediately runs from his bench and belly-flops onto the "crash" mat again.

The lesson progresses. Each group experiences four or five minutes on each piece of apparatus and I look for good examples with which to demonstrate the standards we are trying to achieve. There are definite signs of gymnastic skills developing and with my continuous prompting one or two sequences are worth a viewing. In perhaps six or seven weeks time, we will have a class worth looking at, but the "pain barrier" of the early stages has to be gone through with all the irritating non-conformity purged, as far as possible.

There are ten minutes of the lesson left and after they have made their final change, they arrive back at the apparatus which they originally erected.

"Right, boys, well done. I'm pleased with what I've seen today. Let's keep improving on it. Now we have the real test of teamwork – putting the apparatus away. If it can be done properly we'll have a finishing game – if not then we'll do it again and you'll miss breaktime... it's your choice. Everyone is to do a job, everything is to be lifted in pairs... there is to be NO playing about. O.K? Once you've got your apparatus away, you sit on your team benches. Let's go!"

(At this point the whole group do a "runner" out of the gym door).

Well, actually they do not; they put the apparatus away with reasonable efficiency, alacrity and good sense except for Fabian, who manages a couple of reckless bounces on the trampette, and Damien who hangs on the ropes as they are being drawn in.

There was an occasion, however, when a group did run off. We had a young, inexperienced supply teacher in the department on a short-term contract for a couple of months. His name was Demetrios Propokopolous and understandably all the kids referred to him as Mr. P. He was a real character. He once phoned in "sick" only to be seen on that evening's national *News at Ten*, being interviewed for his opinion on England's performance in the European Football championships. He happened to be bedecked in England regalia and appeared a little worse for drink. He was also being interviewed in Holland!

He also distinguished himself by coming as near as anyone I have known to provoking Howard into physical assault. There had been a short period in a term when the Holte boys' kit appearance seemed as irreproachable as we could ever recall. There were very few kit defaulters and even the most regular of offenders seemed to be turning up in perfect blue chequerboard attire. It was discovered Demetrios, we called him Demi, had been so moved by the kit deprivation of the inner-city that he had seen fit to issue sets of neatly cellophaned, brand new kit to every deserving case he had come across. When Howard had noticed the serious kit deficit in the stores for which he was responsible, he had confronted Mr. Propokopolous. Demi had confessed. Howard was incandescent and I had to hold him back when he tried to pin Mr. P to the wall. I do not think I helped Howard's subsequent mood by referring to Demi as Robin Hood and singing the song:

"He robs from the rich
To give to the poor,
Robin Hood, Robin Hood, Robin Hood!"

Anyway, it was easy to get the picture when it came to Demi; he was an accident waiting to happen, even though his heart was, as they say, in the right place. When it came to teaching gymnastics, Demi admitted to having little confidence. Following a very uninspiring floorwork lesson, Mr. P had decided he would try out an apparatus layout for the class in question, and he hit upon the idea of assembling the apparatus himself in a preceding "free" lesson. He put together a wonderful layout that utilised every item of equipment. The pupils were able to use every kind of invention in exploiting the possibilities he had provided. Demi said afterwards that the class took to the apparatus immediately and that the whole lesson resembled "Pirates", the chasing game over gymnasium equipment, where no one is allowed to touch the floor. (The game had recently been banned owing to the growing number of casualties – a pity as children loved this game, and P.E. staff were also known to favour it as a good way of passing miserable winter afternoons with large numbers of pupils, when no other facility was available).

Mr. P's "piratical" gymnastics lesson went well, but alas, when it came to returning the equipment, from whence it came, the "pirates" fled. Howard and I had to help Demi round up the deserters in a breaktime playground "sweep". From that time onwards Mr. Propokopolous's gymnastic lessons were devoted to mats and floorwork only.

No one has run out on me and I am much relieved to be able to close the door of the apparatus store having squeezed every last item back into its designated place. The ropes are tied up, the climbing ladder is bolted back against the wall and there is no one left hanging from the ceiling. In fact, the whole class are sat in good order on their benches just as I had instructed them.

"Well done! Everyone – that was very pleasing indeed. When everyone does their job... it works. Damien and Fabian, you can both see me afterwards, alone – you know why!"

They both mouth mumbling protests of "innocence".

"Patrick, Boota, John, Kurt, Ali... I'm going to give you merits for good work... don't forget to get your card stamped at the end of the lesson."

There are a couple of minutes left, just enough time to finish with a game. It could be a "tag" game or some similar entertainment. It might have been "British Bulldog", a time-honoured favourite a few years before. This game consisted of two "tacklers" situated on mats arranged across the middle of the gym. On the teacher's instruction to "charge!" the rest of the class were required to run from one end of the gym to the other within a certain time limit, evading the tacklers who would try to restrain a "charger" for a few seconds. Anyone detained would join the tacklers for the next charge and so on until the last person surviving to charge was declared the winner. There were injuries; the authorities banned it.

"Right, lads, we're going to play 'Man the Lifeboats'."

(This involves no tackling and so far a limited number of non-life-threatening injuries so I am still waiting for the banning order).

"Remember, this is how we play it. If I say 'Man the Lifeboats!', you have to get to that end of the gym. If I say 'Back to the Ship!' this end. (I point). If I say 'Hit the Deck!' you have to be flat on the ground, and if I say 'Off the Deck!' you have to get up on a bench, wall bars or climbing ladder, your feet mustn't be touching the floor. The last person to do it goes down to the changing room. Last four left in get a little prize."

There is a hum of anticipation as they love this game.

"Man the Lifeboats!"

They all run towards one end of the gym.

"Back to the Ship!"

They make a quick about-turn before they reach the wall.

"Man the Lifeboats!"

They begin to hesitate and slow their running.

"Off the Deck!"

Ian, Muktar and Kurt all fall to the floor having made the wrong move. I open the gym door and they exit for the changing room.

"Man the Lifeboats!"

"Back to the Ship!"

They do not trust my instructions any more and jog slowly ready for the call to change direction.

"Hit the Deck!"

Another four stragglers are forced to drop out.

"Man the Lifeboats!"

"Hit the Deck!"

"Back to the Ship!"

"Off the Deck!"

I catch another three out and the numbers are dwindling fast. Most of them are gasping from their exertions to stay in the game. It is not the prize, it is the pride.

"Back to the Ship!"

"Hit the Deck!"

Shaun and Satpal are next to make an exit. We are now down to the last five survivors; "Fish", Fabian, Damien, Joseph and Dwayne, whose general gymnastic laziness has now disappeared. This is a test of fitness and the will to survive.

"Off the Deck!"

"Back to the Ship!"

"Hit the Deck!"

They refuse to buckle, no one wants to be last.

"Man the Lifeboats!"

"Back to the Ship!"

"Off the Deck!"

Damien slips and is clearly last. He collapses on his back, breathing heavily.

"That's enough lads, well done Damien. I'll count you as a winner too. You've done well, you're all very fit to keep going like that."

The other four boys lie along the benches with no breath left to talk. I reach into my bag by the gym door and pass to them each a Fun Size bag of Chocolate Buttons. I drop one on to Damien's stomach.

"Well done, boys... Damien, Fabian, next time don't play on the apparatus when it's time to put it away – do your job. Off you go!"

If only we could get "Man the Lifeboats" as a recognised gymnastics discipline, we could be going for gold.

Chapter Twelve

SEX, THIGHS AND VIDEOTAPE
(1973–2003)

INTRODUCTION

I am thinking of attempting a Master's Degree. I would like to submit as a topic for research, the hypothesis that Physical Education teachers of the male species are as a "profession" generally preoccupied with four predominant areas of thought:

- *Sex*
- *Sport*
- *Drink*
- *Gardening*

I feel I should leave it as a topic for others to attempt in defining the psychological bent of the female practitioners. I would strive to test my belief that the above four subjects tend to squeeze out most other foci of concentration in the average male P.E. teacher. I accept that cars, clothes, politics, wars, finances, holidays, family crises and other such trivia may often present a need for a passing pause for thought. In general company; social occasions, dinner parties and such like; the Physical Education teacher may rôle-play conversations and a semblance of coherent thought on the wide sphere of the world's affairs, but believe me when I suggest that his thoughts will never be far from "scores", "scoring" and % alcohol by volume. Should the conversation somehow turn, with his subtle prompting, to these avenues, he will become expert, philosophical and perspicacious.

His insightfulness in this respect is the result of an adolescent-into-adulthood practical preoccupation which has necessarily brought into play the need for a counterbalance; gardening. Having devoted so much time, thought and energy to the disciplines of *sex*, *sport* and *drink*, as the Physical Education teacher matures *gardening* becomes a fourth major source of thought and cause for constant regret.

Early in his career, the P.E. teacher's garden tends to be left as a neglected arena. He will think of it often, mainly with a sense of guilt, knowing he ought to attend to it more; that he should cut this, prune that, plant these and re-pot those. Often these thoughts will impinge upon his consciousness en route to a sporting engagement, upon return from a Bacchanalian encounter or in those moments of ennui, following a bout of energetic physical intimacy, when the mind begins to wander. Too frequently the P.E. teacher is too tired, too injured, too hung over or too "shagged out" to prune, clip, hoe or mow. However, it is my contention that they do think of these horticultural needs, especially when items begin to go missing (for example, their own small children) in the foot high grass and encroaching jungle that was once a neat back lawn and tidily beshrubbed garden.

There is nothing more heart-warming or gratifying to the P.E. teacher than to come across his loved one, be it wife or girlfriend, cutting the lawn or pulling up weeds, when he returns home on a late, balmy summer evening, having scored 50 and taken six wickets for 30 runs, then having stood several rounds at the cricket club bar. His feelings of appreciation and well-being may transform themselves into thoughts of a sexual nature. The returning "hero" may even forget his bruises sustained in the afternoon's combat and become a thoughtful and considerate lover should the amount of alcohol he has consumed not restrict his "longevity".

The Physical Education teacher, in his prime, always returns to his garden with regret, having thought of it often but being unable to escape the knowledge that he has been guilty of serial neglect. In my thesis I would also contend that the younger the teacher, the less he will think of gardening and the more he will ponder the possibilities of sex, sport and drink. Conversely, I would attempt to prove that as the watershed of the P.E. teacher's mid-thirties approaches, and wife, family, semi-detached house and medium-sized garden have somehow, remarkably, been acquired, he will, by necessity, think more of gardening. Having now to do more of it, however, he will tend to think of gardening less, for while engaged in the mundane menial tasks required of him he will instead be wistfully turning his thoughts successively to sex, sport and drink.

Should I decide to proceed with my research and test my hypothesis, I suppose I would be expected to produce verifiable statistics, attributable quotes and materials or whatever. I am already framing questions in my mind for a suitable questionnaire along the lines of the Catell 364 question, 16-personality factor trait interrogative that I sampled as a student at St. Paul's College in 1970. My questionnaire would be aimed at Physical Education teachers of varying ages and experience and would be geared to teasing out their thought processes, for example:

Which two of the following do you least choose to think about? *sex, sport, politics, drink, gardening, D.I.Y.*

Which four of the following activities are you at your happiest participating in? *shopping, sex, drinking, sport, gardening.*

If you had to give up two things for health reasons which two of the following would you choose? *sport, sex, visiting relatives, drink, D.I.Y.*

I believe that a couple of hundred questions along these lines would produce a psychological profile that would prove or disprove my hypothesis beyond any reasonable doubt.

My major worry in respect of the above interrogation would be that the subjects would not be entirely truthful in their answers and my psychological research would founder upon their mendacity. Good grounds for this anxiety are provided by the Physical Education teacher's job application form. Having completed all the relevant sections on the pro forma, with regard to Education, Qualifications, Experience and Courses Attended, there is always the problem presented by the Personal Interests section. In applying for a Physical Education post it is obvious that one should have a strong interest in sport. To declare at this Character Customs Checkpoint that one has a personal interest in:

Football	Basketball	Fitness
Cricket	Rugby League	Weight Training
Golf	Rugby Union	Beach Volleyball (on TV)
Tennis	Badminton	Scuba Diving (on Holiday)
Skiing	Table Tennis	Sky Sports TV

would tend to suggest the candidate is a little one-dimensional in their approach to life. In the cause of attempting to appear a more rounded character, on the path to educating young people, the P.E. specialist will succumb to the temptation to redraft and refocus these interests, presenting them in a more palatable form as well as embellishing some of his more peripheral hobbies and pursuits. Hence, a Personal Interest section listed below may well appear:

European Literature	Massage (Treatment of Injury)
Photography	Travel
Music	Sport of all kinds
Member of CAMRA	Film
The Theatre	Gardening

The above inventory could all be placed neatly under the subtitled headings of:

- *SEX*
- *SPORT*
- *DRINK*
- *GARDENING*

My credentials for producing an entirely subjective thesis are impeccable. I have worked with, trained with, attended courses with, exchanged personal and professional griefs and joys with, propped up the bar with and even shared communal showers and baths, naked, with Physical Education teachers of all ages and denominations for more than three decades.

"There are thee kinds of lies; lies, damned lies and statistics" (Disraeli).

I have decided I do not need statistical evidence – forget that questionnaire. Here is the "evidence".

SEX

I would like to start by examining the role of sex in the Physical Education teacher's life and career. However, true to form, I am going to start with...

SPORT

Anyone who has lived with, loved or made love with a Physical Educationist will testify, that generally, with specific unrepresentative isolated exceptions, Sport will usually take precedence over Sex. A sexual liaison is a tempting and often essential diversion for the testosterone fuelled "super-athlete". Physical Education teachers fall along the (very) outer fringes of this elite corps.

There has been regular debate as to the effect of participating in a sexual encounter prior to sporting activity at the highest level. One school of thought is of the opinion sexual abstinence is essential in creating the necessary competitive hunger for success. The opposite lobby would have one believe sexual release is a desirable relaxant prior to combat. Concentrated ongoing analysis of my professional associates had led me to conclude that P.E. teachers fall firmly into the celibacy camp. I would also draw attention to the rider that the risk of a groin strain, hamstring pull or dislocation would rank equally in terms of concern over loss of competitiveness through sexual "high jinks" on the eve of a crucial Division Five promotion clash, half-marathon or table tennis tournament. Friday evenings and Saturday mornings can prove to be a tense and often arid zone in a P.E. teacher's partner's erotic life.

Saturday nights on the other hand can prove to be just the opposite. Freed from the pressures to perform in the sporting cauldron of a Saturday afternoon with the local pub team or Veterans' Rugby XV, the P.E. teacher's readiness for intimacy may prove the sacrifice of the Friday evening to have been well worthwhile. His partner may see him return home the conquering hero or chastened culprit, bearing responsibility for a late reverse of fortune. It is likely he will be in the mood for reward or consolation according to preceding circumstances in the sporting arena. In either scenario sustained satisfaction is a likely outcome.

Physical Education teachers give a considerable amount of thought to Sex, but to fulfil their potential in the practical aspect, Sport has to be allowed to take its course.

They will have been raised on sport, having lived, consumed and breathed it in their formative years. Invariably, they will have been cruelly thwarted in their sporting ambitions somewhere between the ages of 14 and 18. They will believe they are still sportsmen, winning trophies to parochial acclaim with local clubs or teams; but they know in their souls they have flunked it. There will be no cup winning goal at Wembley for Aston Villa (or Huddersfield Town), no breaking of the 100 metres world record, no millionaire status of a Ryder Cup golfer and no possibility of an Olympic gold medal in the men's gymnastic floor work. Only wishful and wistful thinking of what might have been.

In seeing any youngster showing a glimpse of special talent, the P.E. teacher's spirits rise anew. In every gifted three-point shooting basketball guard, precocious tennis-playing youngster and impish, fearless teenage scrum half, the seed of the P.E. teacher's thwarted hopes is sown and given life again.

Surrounded by the constant green shoots of sporting promise, P.E. teachers always take sport seriously, living in self-deceit as to their own growing ineptitude, waistlines... and recourse to gardening.

SEX

Having established that there is no game to prepare for, selection meeting to attend, or training to undertake, the Physical Education teacher's mind will be able to fully focus on sex where previously it had been a passing provocation to distraction. This state of readiness is always helped if his mood has been mellowed by a suitable...

DRINK

"If music be the food of love

Play on. Give me excess of it..." *(Twelfth Night)*

The Art of Seduction often benefits from a little non-intrusive background music and the same might be said of ambient music as an aid in the clubhouse or public bar. Too loud and you cannot hear yourself speak. Just loud enough to seep into the hearing and the soul, and one drink may become several in the need to deconstruct thoroughly the ebb and flow of the afternoon's sporting encounter. The sense of camaraderie and "completion" in the hour or two spent at the bar is essential in separating the aggression of the sporting combat from the potential intimacy to come. It is highly possible that satisfactory lovemaking can be undertaken with not a single milligram of alcohol per litre of blood in the body. I believe that some Physical Education teachers may have achieved this state of purity under long-term medical supervision. In my not so limited experience I have yet to verify that phenomenon, as the Physical Educationists I have studied could always be judged to have some quotient of alcohol in their bloodstream. (This conclusion is based on the scientific fact that it would take several days of complete abstinence and flushing for the strains of alcohol and toxicity to disappear completely.)

Sport and drink appear to be inseparable even at the highest levels; football, rugby and cricket providing numerous examples. Even in an era of sports science, highly monitored diets and the all-seeing media, the need for a drink after sport is unlikely to be eradicated.

Ian Botham, George Best and every international Rugby Union pack have provided sufficient successful role models for the P.E. teacher, to justify the need for a relaxing drink as an essential aid to a sporting warm-down. In the same vein, where most P.E. teachers would doubt the desirability of expending sexual energies on a Friday evening, no such reservation would be expressed as to the efficacy of a couple of pints of "golden nectar" being consumed as an inhibitor of tension for the following day's important fixture. Whereas sex could clearly weaken the resolve, a carefully apportioned round of drinks or three will help with team bonding, and a diminution of stress and negative feelings that have arisen from the P.E. teacher's week gone by, (See previous chapters). A regulated amount of draught alcohol may quickly draw a veil over the previous week's trials and mishaps as well as giving the necessary injection of ego-boosting self-delusion; that he is worth a place in the Second XV at least, instead of the hapless Thirds.

If drink is an enabling lubricant in strengthening the psyche in readiness for the sporting battles ahead, it is an even more essential balm to aching limbs, wounded pride and contemplation of an unfavourable scoreline following that conflict. To have been dismissed for 32 all out having batted first and subsequently suffered the ignominy of taking tea only after the opposition have won the game in five overs without loss, one might see the retirement of many a P.E. teaching cricketer. The misery in the dressing rooms can only be alleviated by commiserations in the clubhouse bar. Several rounds of local brew later it will only then become apparent to the vanquished that it had been a crucially bad toss to lose, the South African professional playing for the opposition was definitely a chucker, the pitch had clearly been overwatered and a rumour had been heard that one of the umpires had needed to get away early for a wedding reception.

Drink and defeat are consolatory bedfellows. To have secured victory is to sup from the golden chalice, the promise of a hero's return and the prize of sensational...

SEX

Once victory has been thoroughly analysed and fairly attributed in the confines of the bar, only then may the sportsman's attention gradually begin to focus on intimacy. This may be inspired by a passing glimpse of a barmaid's shapely form as she retrieves a handful of bottles from the chilled cabinet, or possibly a diving glance into the inviting depths of the freckled cleavage of a W.I. lady passing round the sandwiches left over from her home-made cricketing teas.

These stimulating views may well provoke a stirring in the loins regardless of the tenderness felt in those nether regions; the result of a nasty inside edge on to the abdominal protector from the South African's second delivery.

P.E. teachers, defeated or victorious are attracted to the opposite sex. (It is highly likely they are also, in some cases, attracted to the same sex. However, in my essentially subjective hypothesis I would like to put this aside as an unnecessary complication.) Generally, P.E. teachers demonstrate a straightforward approach to life. They do not welcome complications in their lives nor much contemplation of them. When complications and potential adversity do arise, they will fall back on...

SPORT

Socrates, Nietzsche, Schopenhauer, Plato and Seneca made many profound philosophical contributions to the cause of coping with the ups and downs of life, yet none of them had the wit to discover the P.E. teacher's abiding philosophical credo:

"When all else fails, there's always sport."

Your wife might leave you, your children may not recognise you, your bank statement may be in a terminally deficient condition and your rust-raddled car may rest "deceased" on the hard-shoulder of the M42.

"Things won are done, joy's soul

Lies in the doing" (*Shakespeare*)

Win, lose or draw, there is always another fixture... or possibly another wife. P.E. teachers are not prone to suicide for, in the course of their careers, both in education and personal leisure, they have learned to treat those two impostors, success and failure, famously identified by Kipling, just the same. So your wife has left you, you are broke and your car is abandoned... but the Ryder Cup is on TV, the putt goes in and Europe win... life's so good. That calls for a celebratory...

DRINK

P.E. specialists tend to agree that champagne, as a celebratory drink, should be confined to weddings, or used as a water pistol by Ferrari drivers on the podium after leading the latest Grand Prix procession. Wine is not recommended as a suitable accompaniment to a victory celebration after a 56-0 win over the Old Shirtshiftians. "Six pints of Stinking Bishop and a glass of Chardonnay", shouted over an Old Boys' Club bar on a late Saturday afternoon, might bring an embarrassing silence to proceedings.

However, a bottle of Chardonnay, thoughtfully purchased, two hours later, from the off-licence on the journey home, is acknowledged by experienced P.E. specialists to be perfectly compatible with relaxed Saturday night...
SEX

The day's deeds are done. Victory or loss has been absorbed and dissected. The intimate dinner with the perfectly chilled Chardonnay has been consumed. The ambience of pleasant conversation with the loved one has created a frisson of expectation. When intimacy is at hand, it is at this crucial point that no viewing guide should be available for at this delicate point, if he is left unattended, the P.E. teacher may find after-dinner contentment, stretched on the sofa, highly stimulated by late-night...
SPORT

Where once the P.E. teacher's viewing of major sporting events and the television coverage of them was confined to Saturday afternoon *Grandstand*, an occasional evening treat of *Sportsnight with Coleman*, and that important part of English heritage, *Match of the Day* with Jimmy Hill, all brought into his home in sensible portions with no hint of excess or vulgarity, today's P.E. teacher is confronted with a whole host of televised sporting distractions. Dedicated channels provide wall-to-wall, hour-by-hour coverage to suit all his sporting tastes and predilections. Access to Test Match cricket, Rugby Union internationals, American professional golf, Grand Prix tennis, Premiership football highlights or even downhill skiing from Klosters can be available to him at any hour of the day or night.

To depart to kitchen or bathroom following that intimate dinner and to leave the TV remote control within easy reach of the encouragingly tumescent P.E. male should be regarded as irresponsible negligence on the part of his loved one. A press of the button and a sequence of Jonah Lomu crashing over the line for an unstoppable try is an invitation to an end to intimacy. Empathetic, considerate, mutual lovemaking demands the complete absence of any opportunity to view sport on a television screen. To be doubly sure it is advisable to hide all radios too. Many P.E. teachers' sexual partners may testify to an occasion of lengthy, considerate and intensely satisfying lovemaking brought to a sudden energetic conclusion which was followed by the casual depression of the 'ON' button raising the unmistakeable strains of the theme tune for *Match of the Day*. Loving afterglow completely shattered, it might be referred to as a specific Physical Education teacher syndrome: "Coitus Sportus Interruptus".

A professional footballer once admitted that the feeling of scoring a goal was better than sex. In his desire to watch goals being scored, often repeatedly, the Physical Education teacher is seen in his undeniably sad role as "voyeur". Sexual fulfilment and Sky Sport viewing schedules are not compatible and the P.E. teacher's partner would be well advised to disconnect the latter in the cause of achieving the former.

Despite this intrinsic flaw in their characters; one of constant sporting distraction, it needs to be stated that Physical Education teachers are often attractive, amiable and stimulating companions, hence their frequent magnetic appeal to the opposite...

SEX

The P.E. teacher's natural gregariousness, developed through a lifetime of belonging to groups, teams and clubs, transmits all the signals needed for attraction. They are outgoing, extrovert and confident socially. In being willing to take a chance and face rejection, they can be gauche, amusing, irritating and, at times, embarrassingly forthright. Any reticence they may have can quickly disappear if their hands hold a...

DRINK

However, in being attracted to the opposite sex and having had their limited inhibitions loosened by the above, the P.E. teacher has difficulty in the "art" of courtship. Too often he cannot separate this process from those which pervade his world of games or...

SPORT

The ever-present games playing traits in the P.E. teacher's psychological make-up can cause complete confusion in the mind of a potential partner when wooing is in evidence. When both male and female combatants in this process are Physical Education teachers the possibilities for perplexity are multiplied accordingly.

CASE STUDY

During my tenure at Holte I had the good fortune to guide, advise and mentor many personable and undeniably attractive young female P.E. students. There was one particularly talented 21-year-old who, I recall, was not only a formidable table tennis player and county standard at badminton but also a single handicap golfer. In addition, she had the positive personal qualities of being friendly and outgoing, blonde hair, striking blue eyes and a face with a model's bone structure that in ancient history might have launched a thousand ships. My professionalism does not allow me to make reference to her lithe, athletic and buxom stature. During her eight week teaching practice, as well as showing herself to be a talented teacher, she showed a welcome willingness to involve herself in staff after-school activities, particularly badminton and table tennis, along with the obligatory Friday evening get-together in the local public house. Let us refer to her as Y.

Among the many gentlemen who offered to partner her or oppose her in the above sporting activities, a certain gentleman we shall call X began to show more attention to her than most. He spent many hours attempting to better her in the badminton and table tennis disciplines and this friendly rivalry began to extend itself to occasional lunch hours and evenings when freedom from other P.E. commitments permitted it. This developing association became the source of some gentle ribbing and amusement in the P.E. department, although the innocent, competitive motivations of X and Y did not seem to be giving ground to any others of a carnal nature. Even in the bar, where X and Y would often be found in close proximity, the conversation would usually be mind-numbingly devoted to the finer points of the chopped backhand, the top-spin serve or the smash. It was apparent that their communion in sport was drawing them together, ever closer, and that X, who had never been counted as a womaniser or potential Casanova, was clearly smitten, if only by the voluptuous curves of her backhand slice.

Towards the end of Y's stay with us it was discovered that she had invited Howard (sorry X) to visit her parents' cottage in the Lake District over a half-term weekend. Although she would be travelling up with her parents earlier in the week, they had to return on the Saturday morning, thereby leaving Y and X, should he agree to accept the invitation, alone for the remainder of the weekend. In her subtle web of seduction Y also executed the effective "coup de grace" by adding the supplementary invitation to a game of golf on a local lakeside links. Any reluctance X may have had to travel the length of the M6 from Birmingham to the Lake District, and the necessity of making a start at an unearthly hour on a Saturday morning, was instantly overcome by this golfing sweetener.

X set out early in order to meet the tee-off time for the pre-arranged golf match. He arrived in the Lakes with perfect timing, sufficient to say a short and friendly hello and goodbye to Y's parents.

The game of golf went well (I believe X won 3 and 2). X and Y shared an intimate dinner together against the idyllic backdrop of a Lakeland setting. Y's soft, blue eyes deepened in the candlelight, her taut, firm breasts pressed languidly through her cashmere sweater as she leaned across the table to refill X's brandy glass, sparkling in the reflection of the flickering flame.

The inevitable denouement was at hand. It only remained for the pair to rise from the table and walk hand in hand out in the direction of X's car, where he bade her an affectionate farewell, thanking her for the game of golf and the dinner. Unfortunately X had to drive back to Birmingham as he had to get up early for his Sunday morning top-of-the-table clash for his other "love", Jumbo's XI.

This sad, salutary study is an example which may have been replicated in similar fashion many times by those who have experienced long-term or more probably very short-term relationships with Physical Education teachers.

The conclusion that might be drawn is that when Sport and Sex are in direct opposition in a P.E. teacher's motivations, the loser will invariably be...
SEX

In later life, when he begins to assume a slightly more mature, philosophical and balanced approach, the P.E. teacher will reflect on missed opportunities of this kind, all sacrificed in the cause of sport. These regrets and reproachful reminiscences may pass frequently through his mind when faced with unavoidable...
GARDENING

He will pause, then rest upon his spade.

His thoughts will turn to blondes:

And breasts betrayed.

When I was promoted in 1977, I joined the ranks of the Heads of Physical Education in Aston Schools. I look back on those 14 icons of sporting leadership and from my vantage point some 25 years on I count eight divorces, four deceased and one retired on a doctor's warning that it might become five.

I cannot help but wonder how their lives might have changed had they spent a little less time on sport, sex and drinking and given more attention to gardening.

Sex, Thighs And Videotape

Sex, Thighs and Videotape

Adventures with a Front Fastening Bra

A Sex Education

The Steel Band in the Showers

Dishevelled in the Darkroom

Cancelled... Surprise, Surprise, Home Early!

Leaving Party

Amsterdam

Save Water – Share a Shower

Tent

Tunnel of Love
Taking Stock in the Storeroom
Grounds for Divorce
Naughty Schoolgirls
Headmaster's Study – Meeting in Progress
Skylight: In Flagrante Delicto

1 *Sex, Thighs And Videotape*

In my early years as a Physical Education teacher in Aston I fell in with the wrong crowd. I was a small town innocent, uncorrupted by the ways and wonders of the Big City. I was peculiarly unversed in the leisure and lifestyle of an Aston P.E. teacher, though I was gradually making acquaintance with and beginning to recognise the other tracksuited exponents of the neighbouring Aston schools. In accepting an invitation to a fellow P.E. teacher's pre-wedding stag night, I had felt it presented the opportunity for a decent getting-to-know-you exercise.

I arrived at the door of the seedy, street corner, public house that early summer evening in the heart of Newtown. I loosened my tie, unbuttoned my tweed sports jacket, took a deep breath and entered the den that was thick with a smoky fug and bodies three deep shuffling to reach the bar. I soon had a pint of lager thrust into my hand by a six foot two P.E. teacher who had managed to get served and generously passed a series of full glasses over the heads of those behind to outstretched hands including mine. I was soon in the midst of the camaraderie of P.E. teachers and invited friends from the area. I recognised most of the faces and was pleased to be welcomed into their ranks so hospitably. I was introduced to the beneficiary of the evening who was to be married a few days later. He already seemed a little worse for wear from the drinks previously pressed upon him, as I shook his hand and wished him luck.

Our P.E. group took over residence of the whole of the small room adjacent to the bar. The conversation switched from football to basketball, cricket to cross-country and back to football again as I merged with the throng of new acquaintances and others I had met before through school fixtures.

I stood my expensive round of a dozen drinks which left me just about penniless with only my WMPTE bus pass to get me home to my bed-sitter in Moseley. I had never been to a stag night before and it seemed a very enjoyable male-bonding experience. The only women present consisted of a couple of local women customers in the opposite corner of the bar and the landlady herself, pulling a continual stream of pints.

Towards closing time, the atmosphere was suddenly changed by the appearance of two uniformed police officers; one a strapping 6 foot plus "bobby" sporting a neat moustache, the other a woman who I noticed was wearing rather heavy eye shadow and bright red lipstick. The former pushed his way through to the bar and loudly enquired of the whereabouts of the soon to be betrothed P.E. teacher. After several fingers had pointed him out, the policeman proceeded to arrest the protesting fiancé, seizing him by the arm and placing one wrist in a handcuff which he had drawn expertly from his belt. He then quickly attached the other bracelet to the brass bar rail.

The captive, in a drunken state, proceeded to struggle and shout to be released but none of his friends showed any sign of concern or intention of coming to his assistance. He was surrounded by heaving shoulders and the sound of laughter as derogatory comments were directed at him by his erstwhile friends. He struggled frantically to free himself from his manacled situation. The policewoman then came into the space cleared around the "prisoner" and, to cheers of encouragement and wholesale amusement, began to unfasten the captive's trousers. He continued to struggle but with much less conviction, particularly when two of his P.E. "friends" held his legs to allow the policewoman to unfasten his shoes and pull off his trousers. He seemed to accept his fate, as one item at a time, socks, shirt and vest were adroitly removed by the nail-varnished fingers of the policewoman.

I stood to one side at the bar and had a clear view as she stood up and confronted her captive, now attired in only handcuffs and red boxer shorts. He laughed nervously as the police officer threw off her flat hat with its chequered band and released a cascade of long auburn hair. To the encouraging claps of the surrounding drinkers, the policewoman, slowly and provocatively, began to divest herself of her blue tunic. In the suggestive and languorous manner of a striptease she removed her blouse and skirt, letting them drop to the floor from her extended arm. Observing her closely without these garments, I was able to judge that the underwear and teetering black stiletto heeled shoes that remained upon her person were not police regulation issue. The red brassiere, matching suspender belt and briefest of lace pants, atop sleek, black stockings was a combination that would forever prevent me from looking at a policewoman on high street patrol without some degree of wonder.

The policewoman, in this eye-catching attire, then edged forward and proceeded to wrap herself sensuously around the handcuffed prisoner who had by now completely accepted his part in this spectacle. A couple of flash cameras appeared and the policeman himself produced an impressive piece of photographic hardware. He proceeded to snap a series of daringly posed positions choreographed by the policewoman, involving herself and the by now almost passive fiancé. The final two poses involved captive minus boxer shorts while blindfolded with brassiere.

It was quite apparent that these were not bona fide police officers.

Once the "police" had departed, to much generous applause, the hubbub died down and the suspect was released from his bondage at the bar. He staggered to his feet and cursed his P.E. confederates, though he was soon placated by arms around his shoulders and a whisky placed into his hand. Though he referred to everyone as "bastards" he seemed to have accepted his humiliation in good humour through his alcoholic haze. Any real regrets with regard to his "arrest" would be delayed until a sober dawn and the incriminating photographic "evidence".

The evening appeared to be drawing to a close and I was fumbling to find my bus pass when someone announced a special viewing upstairs. In curiosity, I followed two or three others up the narrow stairs at the back of the bar. We stumbled into a small smoky room, noticeably cold after the heat generated in the bar below. A projector shot a grainy colour film onto a creamy end wall. There were only half-a-dozen chairs, all occupied, so I leaned against the nearest wall and tried to focus my eyes on the picture being projected on the "screen". My vision gradually adjusted to the images and I saw two young ladies, clearly not girls, dressed in what I recognised immediately as school uniforms.

They had appeared through two swing doors into an auditorium, tottering together on high heels. They wore very mini mini-skirts, white blouses with a school tie loosely askew. The cameraman zoomed in on ample breasts, their cleavages revealed by having several top buttons unfastened. Had they been in attendance at any school of my experience they would have been sent home immediately for improper dress.

The two long limbed women ("girls") lit cigarettes and sat side by side on a large blue mattress, sitting in a manner that revealed stockings, suspenders but a lack of underwear. (These two were definitely heading for long-term suspension). They lay back on the mattress, puffing and exchanging gossip. It was obvious this was a school gymnasium and they were sitting on a gymnastic "crash" mattress.

Seeing them lying there across the mat, pale thighs in view above sleek stocking tops I could not help a feeling of rising irritation at the thought of the damage those high heels could inflict upon the gymnasium floor. When one of the reclining pair casually flicked cigarette ash onto the mattress itself I felt I was witness to an act of desecration.

However, justice appeared to be at hand. The gymnasium door swung open to reveal a tracksuited figure. The P.E. teacher stood hands on hips, clearly outraged by the presence of the smokers on his hallowed "turf". He strode forward to confront the two miscreants.

The audience, probably all Physical Education teachers, including myself, held their breath. We leant forward as one in anticipation of the punishment that would be meted out for such blatant misuse of a gymnastic facility...

I will not bore you with the subsequent footage of the film. "Punishment" was inflicted upon the two "schoolgirls" by the "P.E. teacher". There was a "detention" insofar as they were both detained for the remaining ten minutes of the film. Several highly original and non BAGA gymnastics movements were executed. Some unusual balances involving all three participants were maintained, although there was a definite lack of poise and style accompanied by unnecessary moaning. In short it represented a totally reckless misuse of a gymnastic mattress. Needless to say, all of us present in that small upstairs room were appalled.

I can recall the film vaguely decades later. It was my first experience of a blue film. It was a far cry from the images presented by *Health and Efficiency* and *Parade*, the risqué magazines of our adolescent days, before Page 3 girls appeared with the breakfast cereal.

Two recollections of that film still shock me. One was the sight of that "P.E. teacher" baring his thighs and performing on camera, the other was a short and sudden glimpse of a blackboard on the gymnasium wall that briefly came into view above the undulating posterior of one of the "schoolgirls". The chalked marking on the blackboard had been rubbed out but a faint outline of hieroglyphics still remained. Just in shot I glimpsed the chalked remains of "23" under a heading of "AWAY TEAM – Holte". It was faint, but clear as day in that darkened P.E. teacher-filled room. I saw it for a second before bobbing buttocks obscured it and the camera's focus moved.

A few days later, as the sole basketball team coach at Holte School, I combed through the teams' previous season records and found what I was searching for; there it was: _____ 77 Holte School 23.

Several months later, the caretaker at a local school was taken into custody and charged with producing pornographic materials on school premises. He was found guilty. (*No* Physical Education teachers were involved).

To obtain the remaining chapters of *Sex, Thighs and Videotape*, please refer to *Are You a Proper Teacher, Sir – Volume 2*.

Chapter Thirteen

ANYONE FOR TENNIS?
(Summer, early 1980s)

JOHN McENROE is playing his fourth men's singles semi-final this afternoon. He is stepping out onto the Centre Court at Wimbledon trying to win his third championship in the last four years. At the same time it is an all Afro-Caribbean semi-final on Court One.

Yes, it is also Holte Tennis Fortnight, the 10th year of this traditional tournament having been held on the Holte tennis courts. Unlike Wimbledon, the school singles and doubles championships are played on a tarmac surface rather than grass. The courts are of the same dimensions but there end any similarities between the two venues.

There are nine courts on the Holte playgrounds and only Court One could be described as flat. The next five courts rise in a gentle slope up the playground to a grassy strip which separates these from courts seven, eight and nine which we regard as the "outside" courts in Wimbledon terms. These distant courts slope away in the opposite direction to the other six, in the direction of the inner city ring road.

They have the interesting playing feature of possessing a three feet difference in height above sea-level from the top of the court to the bottom. As a result players can experience the novelty of playing up or downhill. These three courts also have numerous gaps in their surrounding netting which would mean that ball boys, should there be any, would have to risk life and limb retrieving balls that have rolled across the busy road with its constant flow of traffic and Number 8 double-decker buses. We try to avoid using courts seven, eight and nine.

The netting around all the courts is generally in a very poor state of repair. This is not helped by the fact that these playground areas are used as a regular short-cut and thoroughfare by everyone in the neighbourhood. In the early days of the school, the perimeter fence was all-enclosing and secure. It did not stay that way for long.

Pedestrians came to resent having to take a half-mile detour around the new school's grounds to reach their shopping destinations of Newtown or the Lozells Road. Someone considerately, and perseveringly, spent an evening with wire cutters creating two or three passageways large enough for a reasonable sized adult to squeeze through.

Although subsequent repairs were effected, deterioration was inevitable and now there are more holes than intact sections. This wire mesh fence also curls up annoyingly at the bottom, allowing tennis balls to roll underneath and invariably just out of a player's reach. Of course, they can be easily retrieved by stepping through the human sized gaps in the fence.

At the lower end of the playground, near the sports hall, Court One is surrounded by this fencing on three sides. As well as being almost flat, it is the preferred court for important matches as ball-fetching is less frequent. The two Year 10 semi-finalists, Winston and Denzil, are warming up, knocking forehand drives backwards and forwards over the taut net. Errol, the specially appointed umpire, has been extracted from Maths and Music lessons this Friday afternoon.

He is needed to adjudicate on what is likely to be a heated and closely fought best of three sets contest. The players have even been handed two brand new Slazenger tennis balls for the occasion, although they have had to erect the posts and net themselves, just like my Year Eight group who are about to do the same for their afternoon's tennis lesson on the remaining courts.

"Come on, everybody... get a move on. Put your posts in the holes and get your nets fixed up. I'm giving you five minutes and then we'll have a warm up."

I lead the group of 24 boys past Court One as they stagger under the weight of the equipment. They are organised into groups of four and after six tennis lessons are now all familiar with their pre-playing rôles. "A" carries four racquets as handed out by me from the changing room store cupboard.

"No, you can't change that one... they're all the same. I know it's got a broken string but it won't make any difference... you're not Arthur Ashe, you know!"

"B" is responsible for carrying the neatly rolled up tennis net with its wire attachment cord protruding at each end, needed to hook onto the post's winding mechanism.

"I don't know who had this net last... it's in a right tangle. Don't try to straighten it out now... I'll help you once we get out on the courts."

"Cs" and "Ds" each carry one of the heavy green tennis posts. With the younger ones like these Year Eights, it requires the strength of both arms to lift them and the bearers need to set them down for an occasional rest in the process of transporting them the hundred yards or so from their store by the laundry room to the playground courts.

The group behind me resemble a Junior Corps of the Royal Engineers as they struggle across the scruffy litter-strewn grassy patch by the sports hall. I am carrying a wire basket of 30 yellow tennis balls (strictly seconds), one for each player plus a few spares. In my other hand I hold my finely-sprung Wilson racquet, ready to take on all-comers, should it be required. (No-one gets their hands on my racquet.)

I also carry the most important items in the Holte tennis inventory, which are worth more than gold. They are, in fact, gold in colour, being the six brass winding handles which I issue to each group of four players once their net begins to show some semblance of being attached to the uprights correctly.

The court surfaces do not look too bad today. The two caretakers have swept off all the broken glass and other detritus after I had recently put in my third written request. The nets and posts are being erected efficiently on each of the courts and I begin to hand over the precious "winders" to the 'Bs".

There seems to be a problem on Court Three where Hai, Phi, Kulvinder and Harinder are struggling to insert one of the metal upright posts. I trot over to find out what the problem is.

"What's up, fellas?"

"Post no go in... stuck hole."

Hai begins to poke the handle of his tennis racquet into the square hole which will not take the insertion of the upright. "Hai... don't do that! You'll damage the racquet... let's have a look."

Upon closer inspection I can see that a drink can has been neatly wedged into the footing and squashed perfectly to fill the cavity.

"Oh no... what idiot's done that... I don't believe it."

It will clearly require our gallant caretakers' time and specialist equipment to extract this obstruction. (Another written request form or two to be completed.)

"Look, lads... it's no good... take your posts and net up to the top courts, we can't put a net up on this one. Off you go... be quick."

The four of them mumble in disappointment as no-one wants to play on the "outside courts" with their "one-in-three" gradient and gaping fencing. Hai proceeds to roll up the net again while Harinder and Kulvinder in their matching navy blue patkas resume their post-carrying duties. Phi, carrying the four racquets, leads the way. I watch them stumble up the playground and disappear over the grass bank to the out of view hinterland of courts 7, 8 and 9.

I stand and lean on my racquet for a moment, observing the hard-working boys erecting their nets, one member of each group now winding vigorously on the brass handle. If John McEnroe, Björn Borg, Jimmy Connors or even our own Bobby Wilson or Roger Taylor had been required to carry out the posts and nets every time they played, perhaps they would have decided to turn to golf.

The simple reason we have to do this every day is that here at Holte we possess the only functioning tennis courts and equipment in the inner city. Should these precious posts and nets be left out overnight, it is a certainty that they would disappear forever.

We negligently left out a set of posts and a net on one occasion; one post was found hurled through the rear window of a parked vehicle in a nearby street, the other was discovered halfway up one of the few remaining trees in the neighbourhood – a feat of strength and perverse ingenuity. The net was never found, although fish stocks in Handsworth Park Lake have dropped alarmingly in recent years.

Holte tennis posts and nets have to be erected every day and taken in by lunchtime or evening. It is my group's misfortune that there were no tennis lessons this morning. Fortunately, Howard's group have tennis after mine so he can supervise the dismantling process.

"Right lads, well done!"

Kulvinder and company are apparently still erecting their posts and net, out of sight, over the crest of the hill so I decide to get the rest started.

"Right boys, everyone gather in... line up along this court."

The boys in their blue chequerboard kit jog over and begin to form up alongside Court Four, where I am standing. There are only two "lemons"; boys who have borrowed the spare canary-yellow ex-football team kit, having forgotten their own.

They provide a stark, though not unpleasant, contrast in the orderly line of royal blue, now facing me awaiting instructions and, impatiently, the chance to start playing.

"Now boys, before I give you a ball each let's remember... *Samson*!"

Everybody visibly jumps as I exclaim, having spotted Samson hitting a pebble with his racquet. "Samson... don't let me ever see you do that again. I've told you all, time and time again, do *not* hit stones with the racquets... you'll break the strings. You know how you all complain when you get a racquet with a broken string – well that's just how it happens."

Samson's parents knew what they were doing when they named him. He is a large, muscular, black boy from Tanzania. He has muscles on his muscles and I am sure there may have been a slight miscalculation in his date of birth, probably by three to five years. He can put the shot yards, threatening every school record; he hammers footballs, lashes badminton shuttlecocks, thrashes the water at swimming causing tidal waves, and hits the ball miles in tennis.

The latter capability is a major disadvantage in a sport requiring fine motor skills, even more so when you have to fetch the ball back yourself. In tennis, Samson spends a lot of time and covers long distances recovering tennis balls.

"Sorry, Sir."

Samson is also polite, gentle and always co-operative. "O.K. everyone, here's a ball each."

I reach into the basket and throw each boy in turn a bright yellow tennis ball. Being a good, skilful group they all catch them cleanly... except one. Christopher, a pale, mixed race boy, manages to miss the gently lobbed ball which rolls away, and under the curled-up wire fence.

"Can I have another?"

"No, Chris... get that one, you can reach it."

"It's too far... I won't be able to."

"Yes you can... use your racquet."

Christopher is a 'born again' sulker. There is no minor mishap in life that he believes cannot be resolved by sulking.

"Come on, Chris... go and get it."

He sticks out his bottom lip, turns and walks with a deliberate sulky sidle over to the fence, ten yards away.

"Right, boys... hold those balls still, listen. Ayoth, Suheel... hold your balls... keep those tennis balls in your hand."

I motion to Gareth, another mixed race boy, to join me on the court.

"Now remember how we warm up in twos. Start close to the baseline... go on, Gareth, you go over there."

Gareth jogs to the other side of the court and takes up a position of readiness on the back line.

"We play bounce-hit serving – no overhead serves to start with. Let's keep a rally going... remember racquet back... bounce... through the ball... follow through."

Gareth returns the ball well; he is a good player for demonstrations.

"Well done, Gareth! Remember, try to avoid coming in to the net... let's keep the ball going... forehand... backhand... bounce... hit... follow through... very good, Gareth."

We keep up a rally of ten to 15 strokes as I give an intermittent commentary after I strike the ball. Our demonstration ends when I mishit the ball into the net to ironic cheers from the boys at the side of the court.

"Right boys... got the idea... try to keep the rally going... no scoring!"

They all race off to their own courts, keen to finally get started. They love tennis.

Meanwhile Christopher has failed to retrieve his ball.

"Can I have another ball, Sir?"

"Are you telling me you haven't got it yet?"

"I can't reach it."

I turn on my heel and march over to the fence. In fairness, I find the ball is just beyond reach, even on hands and knees with racquet held with outstretched arm. However, there is a man-sized gap in the wire-netting fence for "right of way", only 10 yards further up the playground. I stride up to the gap, step through, pick up the ball, throw it underarm over the fence where Chris catches it without difficulty.

"You are such a lazy boy."

I step back through the hole and as I walk towards him he projects his bottom sulking lip another half an inch. He refuses to look me in the eye as he kneads the tennis ball in his hand.

"Just go and join your group, Chris... go on."

He drags his feet and sucks his teeth as he ambles over to Court Five where Leon, his patient partner, has been amusing himself by keeping the ball up, bouncing it at varying heights on his racquet. Leon is a lively, positive and cheerful soul. They make a highly contrasting pair as they begin to knock the ball backwards and forwards over the net. Leon is on his toes eager to play; on the other side Chris returns the ball with seething resentment. Somehow they sustain a rally.

The whole group seem to be practising as required. I suddenly remember that I have neglected proceedings on Court Seven. I jog up the sloping courts to the grassy bank where I immediately see Hai, Phi, Kulvinder and Harinder struggling to untangle the connecting wire from the net itself. I trot down the bank onto the court.

"What's up lads?... You're not having much luck today, are you?"

"Sir, the wires caught up in the net... we can't untangle it."

"Here, Harinder... you and Kulvinder pull that end tight and I'll try to free it."

By straightening out the whole net and its white top cord, I manage to extricate the coiled wire and inside two minutes we have the net attached. Hai winds it up vigorously using the brass handle.

I extract two tennis balls from my tracksuit pocket.

"Here, boys... have a couple of balls, you missed the get-together. Have a knock-up in pairs, half-court."

"Sir, can we have a doubles match... we know how to play by now."

I think of all the effort they have put in so far and the fact that we are nearly halfway through the lesson.

"O.K., Kulvinder, fair enough. Play one set, but let's have one serve from the baseline and if that's a fault, then your second serve must be from the line behind the serving box, bounce-hit, underarm. That will cut down on double-faults. Do you understand?"

The four of them nod in agreement as we have used this serving rule in most of our practices and half-court singles.

I leave them to it and walk back up the grassy bank above the court. I stand and watch as they have a brief knock-up. They pair off on opposite sides of the court, ready to start. It is clearly going to be an international Challenge match; India versus China. Harinder crouches, facing the net, as his partner Kulvinder serves from the back of the court, behind him.

The ball hits the net. He takes three strides forward and with the second ball hits a bounce-hit forehand serve which finds its target in Hai's half of the court. Hai returns it with a cross-court forehand to Kulvinder, who sends it back down the tramlines to Phi's backhand.

The ball just clears the net and Harinder has to sprint forward to dink it back into Phi's half of the court. Phi runs in and lobs the ball high over Harinder's head with its navy blue top-knot. Kulvinder runs in behind him and mishits a gentle return straight at Phi who manages a half-hit volley into the open space down the tramlines.

"Love – 15!" (I shout from the top of the bank). Not a bad rally for the first point.

They continue their game as I stand and gaze across the city landscape beyond Court Seven on this hot, late June, Friday afternoon. There is a jaundiced haze hanging over the skyline of Birmingham. Even though it is a cloudless afternoon, the sky cannot be described as clear or blue. The outlines of the distinctive buildings of the city centre are blurred by the heat haze and exhaust fumes which have congealed over the last few days. The whole landscape has a scorched and undefined appearance. On winter mornings with sub-zero temperatures, the silhouettes of the Post Office Tower, the Rotunda and similar Birmingham landmarks stand out clearly against the horizon. This oppressive afternoon, they can barely be identified under the warm smothering blanket that has enveloped the city.

I brush the perspiration from my forehead and return to Court Four where I call everyone in for further instructions. It takes a minute or two for them all to break off from their practices, retrieve balls and assemble again in front of me as I wait patiently.

"Right boys... well done. Everyone seems to be striking the ball well. Can anyone tell me the key points to remember when you're playing forehand and backhand drives?"

"Stay at the back of the court."

"Yes, well done, Suheel. Anyone else got an idea... put your hand up."

"Get your racquet back early."

"Good... yes, Amar."

"Step away from the ball to give yourself room and try to take the ball in front of you."

"Excellent, Amar... yes, Gareth?"

"Follow through after your stroke."

"Some great answers... well done! I'm watching you and you all seem to be hitting the ball well. Now what I want to do next is..."

The rest of my sentence is completely drowned by the sound of a police helicopter that hurtles low around the side of Clifford Tower, a 24-storey high block of flats which overlooks Courts Three, Four and Five. Hughie Quigley was once teaching tennis on this very spot when he was shot. Well, it was actually an airgun pellet. An ex-pupil, whom Hughie had apparently upset at some stage in his school career, had been living on the fourth floor of the tower block. Just happening to have an air rifle in his lap as he watched Hughie's tennis lesson from an executive box position, he succumbed, understandably, to the temptation to use Hughie for a spot of target practice. I believe three shots were fired, the last of which hit Hughie on the thigh. The pellet stung but, from that distance, Hughie came to no lasting harm. The sniper was tracked down and apprehended by the police.

Malcolm and I, once we had stopped laughing, were full of sympathy for Hughie and we raised the issue at the next Physical Education department meeting. It was agreed that in future all tennis lessons should be taught in bullet-proof vests. This was formally minuted. (We are still awaiting a management response or funding for this essential attire.)

The helicopter spins low over the rooftops of Lozells and I exaggeratedly put my hands over my ears as my tennis group follow its clattering progress, shielding their eyes from the dazzling sunlight. I am about to resume my tennis coaching monologue when there follows the distinctive wail of sirens. At least three police cars appear to be converging in the direction of the Lozells Road and again the din denies me the appropriate silence to continue any talking.

My heart has always sunk at the sound of police helicopter rotors or patrol car sirens. Riots, robberies, mayhem – Lozells has had its recent share and the ongoing threat seems forever on the doorstep.

"Anyone for tennis?"

The noise of police cars and helicopter subsides and I resume my instructions to the boys lined up alongside the court.

"Right boys... we're going to concentrate on singles today. To keep everyone interested we'll play 'King of the Court'."

This involves full singles rules but with the serving proviso of a second service delivered bounce-hit a few yards further forward from the baseline. A match consists of one game only, the winner staying on. A new challenger can have the option of taking the serves himself or allowing the "King" to serve. Anyone winning four consecutive games has to move to another court to issue another challenge, thereby giving others a chance on that particular court. Those players awaiting their turn to challenge knock up at the side of the court.

"Remember boys, winner stays on... come up for your second serve with a bounce-hit forehand. We've twenty minutes left, off you go."

They are quickly into the competition, though I can see Christopher deliberately hitting the net with his racquet on the court that Gareth and Leon are playing.

"Chris, stop that! Practise with Samson until it's your turn to challenge."

"I don't wanna practise... it's too hot."

"Come on, Chris, have a go... there's not long left, you can have a rest in Maths next lesson."

"It's not Maths next lesson."

"Whatever... come on, leave the net alone and have a knock-up with Samson."

Christopher turns and drags his feet to a position a few yards back as Samson bounces the ball repeatedly with his racquet. Christopher is far too close to receive the ball and start a rally.

"Go further back, Chris... you're too close."

"I aren't!"

He sighs and lifts his racquet half-heartedly as Samson throws up a ball. Samson's service is more of a smash than a serve and Chris fails to react in time as the tennis ball strikes him fairly and squarely in the groin. He flings down his racquet and doubles up in pain.

"Chris... you O.K? I told you not to stand so close."

"nnnnh... mmmh... fucking tennis... not fucking playing no more... nnnnh."

I lean over him, encouraging him to bend over from the waist, the time-honoured way of easing testicular pain. My sympathy is half-genuine, but

Samson seems completely oblivious to Chris's discomfort and he has resumed his "pat-a-cake" game with the tennis ball.

Christopher stumbles away from me, through the hole in the fence and flops down on the grass on the other side. I leave him to recover and decide to visit Court One to see how the singles semi-final is progressing.

"Game!"

Winston and Denzil change ends after Errol's announcement. Both of them take long gulps of water from the plastic bottles they have placed by Errol's chair.

Winston is sporting white towelling wrist bands, which contrast sharply against his shiny black forehead, glistening with perspiration which he brushes away with alternate sweeps of left and right wrists. Denzil, a tall, much paler Afro-Caribbean boy, is wearing a bright red headband which fits neatly round his head with its tightly curled mop of hair. It is the essential tennis fashion item of the day as promoted by Börg and McEnroe.

"What's the score, umpire?"

Errol, whose ancestors hail from Barbados, turns in his plastic chair and announces the score in a perfectly correct and officious manner.

"Winston leads 5-4 and is serving for the first set."

"Sounds like a good game... carry on."

Winston is stationed at the back of the court to my left. He clutches two tennis balls in his left hand. He throws one of the balls up above his head and hits a moderately powerful serve over the net and into Denzil's quarter of the court. The serve is in and Denzil hits it lazily into the net. He audibly curses himself as Errol formally announces, "15-love!"

Winston moves five yards to his left on the baseline. This time his first serve hits the net and drops to the ground. His second serve, a much gentler effort, finds its target and Denzil returns with a forehand drive to Winston's backhand. He lobs it high. Denzil allows it to bounce mid-court and then smashes the ball past Winston on his forehand side. From my position it would be difficult to decide whether the ball had stayed in or had gone into the doubles court sidelines.

"Out!"

Errol has no such doubts and he is the umpire.

"30-love!"

"That was in!"

"No... it was just out."

"How can you see sat there?... it was in!"

"I saw it... it was out, Denzil."

"The ball was in... easy."

Denzil tugs irritably at his headband and strides over to the exact place where, in his opinion, the ball had landed.

"It landed here."

He bangs his racquet head twice for emphasis on the "damned" spot.

"No it didn't, Denz... it just landed in the tramlines."

"The ball was in!"

"Denzil... it was out... 30-love."

"You cannot be serious!"

"Winston to serve... 30-love."

(Errol was not pulled out of maths and music for nothing.)

Denzil gasps in exasperation and trudges back malevolently to his position behind the baseline, all the while muttering obscenities to himself. He crouches down and gently taps his racquet on the line, shaking his head. He takes a few seconds to compose himself then focuses his attention on Winston, who throughout this whole episode has said nothing. Winston winds up to serve again. It is an ace, deep and straight, which Denzil fails to reach in his malaise.

"40-love... set point, Winston."

Winston delays his serve, bouncing the ball repeatedly on the baseline. He serves, it is in and Denzil returns the ball to Winston's forehand then rushes into the net. Winston's forehand passing attempt is met firmly by Denzil's stabbed volley straight into the net.

"Game. Winston wins the first set 6-4."

"... that ball was in!"

"Second set... Denzil to serve," Errol announces imperiously from his chair.

I leave them to the second set as I wander back up along the sides of Courts Two, Four, Five and Six. Everyone seems to be fully engaged in "King of the Court" as I had hoped. Only Christopher is not either playing or practising. He is lying on his back on the grass beyond the fence, surrounded by daisies and dandelions. He has one hand behind his head with his knees up, chewing a piece of long grass. It is a Friday afternoon, it is hot and it has been a long week. I decide to leave him to his meditation.

Then it starts. What little comparative peace we may enjoy on inner city tennis courts, surrounded by the continual subliminal traffic hum, is now shattered by the familiar "Boom, Boom, Karoomp... Boom, Boom, Karoomp".

It is the brain blasting bass of a big sound system. The thump and vibration always hits the senses first, almost like a depth charge on one's hearing. No tune can be discerned, just the heavy bass beats. The sound is coming from a wide open curtainless window on the sixth floor of the previously mentioned Clifford Tower.

Imposed upon the thumping beat are the instantly recognisable vocals of Bob Marley singing *Buffalo Soldier*...

Background musical accompaniment of this kind is a common phenomenon in outdoor P.E. lessons, particularly during the summer months. Music will either be provided from open windows, as in this case, or by some passing youth thoughtfully carrying a "ghetto-blaster" stereo system turned up to full volume as he makes his way through the "'hood". Non-ambient music of this kind does little to soothe the troubled brow on a hot, steamy summer afternoon. Bob's famous wailing continues.

Whoever the disc jockey is on the sixth floor, he now has, at least, one appreciative listener. Chris is sitting up and playing along on his tennis racquet, singing aloud with Bob and his Wailers.

The ongoing musical interlude has now reinforced my decision not to stop the group again for any further coaching feedback. I just let them get on with it. To stave off personal boredom I decide to intervene on Court Four where Gareth is clearly an undefeated "King", having just overcome Samson for a second time.

"How many games have you won, Gareth?"

"Four, Sir... nobody else wants to play me."

"Right, Gareth... then I'll give you a game. I'll serve, you give me a little knock-up first."

I hit a forehand over the net and Gareth returns it comfortably. We keep a rally going for a minute or so, using mainly forehands with the occasional backhand drive, until I hit the ball into the net.

"O.K... that'll do, Gareth. Here we go."

I serve accurately, without too much power, onto Gareth's forehand side. He takes the ball early and passes me comfortably.

"Good shot, Gareth... love-15."

I serve on the other side, this time to his backhand which he returns to mid-court. I have plenty of time to advance and place another deep drive to his backhand side. His return is weak and arrives invitingly as I wait at the net. I volley the ball into the open forehand court.

"15 all."

My next first serve hits the net but my second serve is comfortably in court and we share a 12 stroke rally which ends when Gareth hits a loose forehand into the "tramlines".

"30-15."

I double-fault on my next serve.

"That's what happens when I come in cold... 30 all."

I serve with more concentration and after Gareth returns well I hit a delicate drop shot just over the net. He scampers in and manages to scoop the ball back over. He's a foot from the net so I lob him with ease. The high ball bounces at the back of the court but Gareth chases back and succeeds in returning his own high lob which lands in the centre of my half of the court. By allowing it to bounce I have plenty of time to smash it past his backhand.

"Good rally, Gareth... well played... 40-30."

I serve to his backhand again. His return is weak and lands perfectly for my forehand which I hit smack into the net.

"Dammit... Deuce."

On the next point we have another back court rally of ground shots before I mishit one too long and leave Gareth at "advantage" and "King of the Court" point.

At this juncture I should remind you that Gareth is only 13 years old, and to beat me at "King of the Court" would be a source of much pride and joy to him and no real offence to me. He is a good player and I am his teacher, pleased that his skills are developing well, hopefully a part-result of my coaching expertise. However, I cannot allow myself to be beaten at "King of the Court". It is an unwritten part of my tennis lesson plans. I am not going to lose this next point – no way.

I take two, careful bounces of the ball and throw up the third with total focus. It is a good firm serve, it's in and Gareth does well to return it at full stretch. I chase across to play a backhand. I'm relieved to see the ball clear the net as Gareth strides in to send a deep drive to my forehand side. I have anticipated this and race across to hit a perfect 'pass' down the line leaving him stranded as he waits to volley at the net.

"Yessss!"

I punch the air in celebration.

"Deuce."

I have "King of the Court" point twice in succession but on each occasion Gareth somehow returns my forehand drives, which I am now hitting with maximum ferocity, to save the match. We arrive at our sixth deuce.

"Deuce... well played, Gareth!"

This is getting serious. I had not intended to play for ten minutes. Sweat is trickling down my forehead into my eyes, there are only five minutes of the lesson remaining and Bob is now belting out

"One love... one love...

Let's get together, it'll be all right..."

I face Gareth's forehand court again. There is no way that I am going to lose this. I bounce the ball on the floor twice, à la Jimmy Connors, and giving it my full power, leaping into the serve, I deliver a perfect ace that Gareth is unable to lay a racquet upon.

"Yes... come on. Match point."

I cross over to the backhand side and steady myself. With one finger I brush away the perspiration beading on my eyebrows. I look up at Gareth. He is swaying from side to side, totally concentrated on not conceding this crucial point. (This kid is a winner... but so am I.) Such is the "inner game" of tennis. The pressure is on him. I only have to get the serve in and make him play, force him into an error or wait for that vital opening, get into the net and make the killing volley.

I throw up the ball and as I swing my racquet in the serving arc I am totally distracted by movement in my peripheral vision. The tennis ball drops to the ground unhit as I turn to see two women pushing baby buggies, diagonally, across the middle of our court. The ball rolls away as I stand, hands on hips, in disbelief. Gareth and I watch and wait as the two young mums (I would guess them both to be no older than 17) push their toddlers across my half of the court. Their progress is slow, the buggies are laden with plastic bags filled with shopping and their pale, mini-skirted legs struggle to push the burden as they totter on precarious high stiletto heels.

There has been the isolated streaker at Wimbledon, halting play for a few minutes on occasions, but would Virginia Wade have won the 1977 women's singles had two women with pushchairs brought play to a standstill as she was about to serve for the match and a place in history? I think not.

I retrieve my ball and wait at the baseline, resisting all temptation to make any caustic comment as the two young mums make their way to the hole in the fence at the back of the court, behind Gareth. They have a knicker-exposing struggle to get their buggies, babies and baggage through the narrow gap in the netting. To his eternal credit, Christopher, witnessing their predicament, stops his "strumming" and hops up to give them a hand to lift the two buggies through. They readjust their shopping bags and mini-skirts then continue on their way in the direction of Newtown as I regather myself for the vital serve as Gareth crouches and sways in readiness.

"Right, Gareth... this is it... Match point."

My first serve smacks into the net. I put some slice onto a gentler second serve, making sure the serve is in. Gareth returns it to my backhand side. I hit it to his forehand. He returns a forehand cross-court drive. I place a forehand return down the line which he chases after and returns well. I drive another forehand across court which I follow in quickly to the net, going for broke. Gareth hits the ball directly at me and I somehow manage a stop volley in front of my chest. Gareth runs in and is able to scoop the ball up before it bounces twice. I put up a lob to the back of the court, but he refuses to give it up, chases back and with amazing agility returns the ball with his back to the net. The ball lands gently to my side, waiting to be dispatched and I do just that. I stroke a firm "put away" to the backhand side.

"Game!"

We are both gasping from our exertions. I wait at the net taking deep inhalations. We shake hands.

"Nearly had you there, Sir!"

"Well played, Gareth... a brilliant game. You really pushed me there – I'm knackered."

(I do *not* lose "King of the Court" – remember that).

"See me for a couple of merits afterwards."

Breathing heavily, my shirt wringing wet with perspiration, I have to shout above the "Boom, Kaboom, Kaboom" of the reggae backbeat as Bob and the Wailers move on to *Catch A Fire*.

"Right, boys... everyone stop playing now. It's time to pack up. Suheel, Shishu, don't start another game – there's only three minutes to the bell."

I am about to shout my instructions for them all to start dismantling the nets and posts when I thankfully remember that Howard has a tennis group for the last lesson of the week, so we are all spared further equipment hauling. I call them all down to the vacant Court Three.

"Well done, boys. I'm very pleased with the standard of your tennis to-day... how many people have been a 'King of the Court'?"

Six or seven raise their arms.

"Anyone win more than three times?"

Gareth, Ayoth and Kabir keep their hands held aloft.

"Very good, you three... see me afterwards for merits. You've all shown a good attitude and I'm pleased the way everyone's game is improving. Next week we'll pick up on doubles again."

One or two boys start to make off towards the changing rooms.

"Hold on, fellas... put your tennis balls back in the basket here. Everyone take your own racquets in and put them by the staff door."

Having spoken of doubles I suddenly recall that the "Davis Cup" tie between India and China is still in progress, out of view on Court Seven. I hand Ayoth the basket of balls as the group move off in the direction of the changing rooms.

"Here, Ayoth, take these will you... and can you stack up the racquets for me... I'll be back in a couple of minutes."

Ayoth takes the basket and I turn and jog up the playground to the top of the grass bank. The doubles match is still going on. However, it appears that

India have been eliminated as their representatives can be seen sitting side by side on the grass, minus their racquets, watching China now apparently locked in combat with Jamaica. The match now in front of me has Hai and Phi chasing about returning the ball over a sagging net, up the slope, to two Afro-Caribbean youths. The latter, playing side by side, have their backs to me and are wielding Harinder's and Kulvinder's racquets with some skill as a rally progresses.

One of the youths is wearing a large black woolly hat with the distinctive Rasta red, yellow and green coloured bands. His partner sports long matted dreadlocks which hang tied behind his head, a foot or more in length, below a bright yellow sun hat. The former is wearing a white string vest tucked into calf-length black shorts while the latter has stripped to the waist, having tied a T-shirt around the top of his faded denim jeans. Both of them wear ungainly, high-ankled basketball boots.

All four players are oblivious to my presence at the top of the bank as I stand and take in the proceedings. Phi serves to "dreadlocks" who returns the ball back diagonally across court. Phi plays a gentle high-arcing return to where "woolly hat" is waiting at the net. He executes a perfect forehand volley that bisects Phi and Hai's position mid-court.

"Game!"

The Jamaicans high-five each other, raising their left hands above their heads in mutual congratulation then make as if to change ends with the Chinese, who have now noticed me at the top of the bank.

"Sorry lads, it's time to pack in... the lesson's over... we have to go in."

"Hey, Mr. Boothroyd... how ya doin' there, man!"

It is woolly hat, who, having turned round, I now immediately recognise as Gaston, an ex-pupil who departed Holte a year previously. I do not recognise the youth with the yellow sun hat at all.

"I'm fine, Gaston... good to see you still enjoy your tennis... are you winning?"

"Yeah, Mr. B... we jus' passin' an see dese bwoys playin'. Jus' had to give dese Chinamen a whippin'. We winnin' easy eh, Lambo?"

Lambo just nods, not knowing what to make of me.

"Look fellas... I'm sorry to break up your game but these lads have to go in now... we're already late."

Gaston lights up his brightest smile, a memorable trademark of his years at Holte.

"Say, Mr. B... can we's borrow the bats for a while... we got nuttin' to do? Me and Lambo can have a game... we won't break 'em or nuttin'."

I am easily persuaded.

"O.K., lads... tell you what. You can keep the racquets 'til the end of next lesson. I'll tell Mr. Knight, who's got a class out here next. Make sure you give them back to him, O.K.? You can keep the two balls."

We leave them to it as I urge the four boys to run back to the changing room as we are already well into the next lesson, which for me is volleyball in the gym.

The two black youths take up their positions at either end of the sloping court.

"Raat Lambo... you son of a bitch... prepare for a rasclatin' whuppin'!"

The loose-limbed Lambo serves first and Gaston returns a pile-driving forehand down the server's backhand side. The ball just evades the gaping hole in the wire-netting at the back of the court, which separates it from the busy Inner-Circle road with its now nose-to-tail traffic on this hot, humid Friday afternoon.

"Yas... I'm da man... love-fifteen!"

I turn and begin to run back towards the school, leaving them to it.

So on Court Seven it is the Rastafarian Singles. On Court One Denzil and Winston are going into a third and decisive set for the honour of reaching the 10th Holte Singles Final. The umpire, Errol, is now standing on the plastic chair in order to obtain a better view of proceedings. He calls out the score in a professional monotone manner.

All this is playing out to the background, mesmerising beats of Bob's heavy reggae from the sixth floor window of the neighbouring tower block. By my reckoning, in the Year 2000, Britain's Davis Cup winning team will be all black and the days of middle-class nice and comfortable "losers" tennis will have disappeared into the archives.

Postscript

John McEnroe won his semi-final at Wimbledon and went on to achieve a hat-trick of singles championships. Winston became the 10th and last Holte Tennis Singles Champion. The school's tennis courts were soon to be condemned as unsafe. They were in need of resurfacing, renetting and required new post footings. None of these things was done.

Instead, the courts and playground area, without resurfacing work taking place, were marked out for a permanent 200 metre running track. Holte's six mile round trip to Holdford Drive Playing Fields, transporting pupils by double-decker bus, was no longer considered viable for financial reasons. Tennis ceased to be part of the Holte P.E. programme.

I believe that, as yet, no player of Afro-Caribbean descent has represented Britain at tennis.

Chapter Fourteen

FIRST AID
(Mid 1980s)

ANNIE LAY on her back as the headmaster leaned attentively over her. He gently pushed back the fringe of platinum blonde hair covering her forehead. Bob's lips firmly enclosed hers and contact lingered for two or three seconds until he broke free from this tender union.

"Bob's certainly not lost his touch with women," came the whispered aside from Simon, my fellow head of year, who was seated next to me on the bench, one of many set down along the walls of the Dance Studio, which the whole Holte staff now occupied.

Annie, whose pale lips received Bob's "kiss", was in fact "Resusci-Annie", one of two dummies which had been borrowed for the first aid course morning of a "Teacher Training Day", alternatively referred to by the whole profession as a "Baker Day".

"Resusci-Alf" was the male twin of the species on which we were being instructed in the vital exercise of mouth to mouth ventilation together with other essential first aid basics with which everyone, especially teachers, ought to be familiar. The earlier jocular and inevitable piss-taking comments:

"Andy, you should be excused this as you have enough practice every night on that inflatable doll."

and:

"I'm only doing that with Alf if he's a consenting adult!"

gave way to attentive silence as Bob Day, the headteacher, a qualified first aider, began to lead us through the resuscitation technique.

He had knelt over Annie and begun to go through the procedure to be followed in the event of a casualty being in need of this process.

"Check to determine if the casualty is breathing."

Bob had checked in an exaggerated manner, listening at her mouth and observing her chest failing to rise or fall. Annie had definitely looked distinctly unhealthy, particularly as she possessed no arms or legs.

"Having established that there's no breathing, check that the casualty's airway is clear of all obstructions."

Bob had then tilted Annie's head back by holding her chin and had then peered intently into her slightly open mouth.

"Airways clear. Now pinch the casualty's nose gently with thumb and forefinger."

I had leaned forward to observe Bob's next move.

"Now take a deep breath... place your lips firmly around the casualty's mouth and breathe smoothly and firmly until you can see the chest rise."

It was at this point, as Bob gave Annie a four or five second burst of exhaled air, that Simon had whispered his joke in my ear. I could see Annie's chest rise, then fall as Bob, kneeling on the square, blue gymnastic mat, withdrew his lips. He continued this routine for a minute or more to allow everyone the chance to absorb the exercise. Everyone appeared to be concentrating intently on Bob's words and movements for in a few moments we would all be required to practise our resuscitation techniques on Alf or Annie.

There were no jokes among the audience as we all contemplated the implications of having to administer this treatment in a real life situation in school.

Bob continued a procedure of ventilation and compressions for a further couple of minutes, talking through each stage to remind us of the "mantra" that should be repeating itself in our heads in any real crisis where this desperate process might be needed.

"If the casualty does recover and there is clear evidence of breathing and pulse, then place them in the Recovery Position."

Bob knelt upright from his crouched position over Annie and motioned in my direction.

"Gary... if you don't mind coming over here on the mat... I'll show you all the procedure for placing the casualty in the Recovery Position."

I lay flat on my back and Bob placed one of my arms across my chest. Placing the other vertically at my side, he gently tugged me over into a side-on position. Taking my body weight across his thighs he rolled me onto my front where he then pulled my right arm up to 90 degrees while resting my cheek on the back of my other hand. He completed the movements by tugging my right leg up to an angle of 45 degrees.

"This is the position to allow the unconscious person the freedom to breathe safely and prevent choking on vomit."

I remained prone with my face pressed cold against the surface of the mat until Bob tapped me on the shoulder.

"O.K., Gary... thanks for that."

I dusted myself off and returned to my position on the bench.

"Now everyone... as we have only two dummies, you're all going to have to team up in pairs to practise the ventilation-compression routines. Also, make sure you have a go on Annie or Alf. John and I will monitor your efforts on the dummies while the rest of you can practise in pairs on the other mats... O.K., thanks everyone."

There was much rapid pairing-off in same-sex combinations and although there were a few people left as wallflowers, thankfully I was not one of them as I had immediately turned to my right, and propositioned Shirley, one of the P.E. staff, to be my 'Annie.' Shirley had been in the P.E. department for a few years having completed a teaching practice at Holte from Anstey College, so we could consider ourselves to be on fairly intimate terms. I had kissed Shirley several times (at Christmas parties and on birthdays, I hasten to add) so we were on suitable lip to lip acquaintance for the task at hand. I took my turn on the mat first, lying limp for better effect.

"Shirl... I'm all yours... treat me gently."

"Oh my knee... I can't be doing with kneeling down. I got a real bang on the knee in hockey on Saturday."

"Shirley, you're just so romantic... whatever happened to foreplay?"

"Gary... shut up and let's get on with it. I'm just going to talk it through instead or I'll never be able to get back up on my feet. Right... now it's listen for breathing, tilt head back by holding chin..."

"Oh, come on Shirl... resuss me now. I can't wait any longer!"

"Shut up!..."

Shirley went through the routine verbally and as I lay there in a passive pose I glanced into the floor to ceiling mirrors that lined the far end wall of the dance studio and its dark brick walls, roof spotlights and half-drawn 20 foot curtains. I was able to see the reflection of the scene; 40 to 50 teachers in various positions of resuscitation, in casualty or recovery position with Bob striding from mat to mat, coaching technique, in his ever enthusiastic ebullient manner. Taken at a glance it appeared as a rather bizarre, unseemly tableau.

Mixed with the occasional bursts of self-conscious laughter inspired by the various manhandling and bodily proximity to each other, lay the ever-present reality that one day any one of us could be called upon to do this for real, not with Annie or Alf, but with a child's life resting upon it.

First aid is incumbent upon all teachers in an emergency, though there must be named, qualified first aiders available in every school. I have always felt that schools of reasonable size should have a full-time nurse and suitably equipped medical room where he or she should be in permanent residence. The number of casualties sustained in a normal school day, added to the frequent need for vaccinations and check ups at different points in the educational year would more than justify the validity of this appointment. A little expertise in stress counselling and anger management therapy would also prove to be a valuable additional asset. On reflection, however, the school nurse might have little time available to deal with pupil ailments owing to the ever-lengthening queue at the door formed by psychologically unstable members of staff.

The scope for accidents and injury in schools and Physical Education in particular more than supports my case for the above facility and personnel being readily available. I can honestly declare that I have never known a day when an injury, whether it be an abrasion, a tear, pull, bruise, gash, cut, fracture, concussion, headache, dislocation, earache, broken tooth, sprain, stomach upset or hangover has not been sustained at some point by a member of the P.E. staff. When adding to the equation all the degrees of pupil recklessness and potential for accident, risk is multiplied one thousand-fold when the playing field, gymnasium, swimming pool and showers are taken into account.

All P.E. lessons have to be considered generally higher risk zones of activity than academic classroom lessons, though I have to concede that I have walked into some of the above and borne witness to scenes resembling a battle in Beirut, only with the potential for higher numbers of casualties. I do accept the possibility of serious injury being an outcome of compass misuse in Maths, drill delinquency in Design Technology or cake conflagrations in Cookery. However, sporting activity does present more obvious and ongoing potential for mishaps.

Taking part in sport is risky – but only in the way participating in Life is risky. One must weigh up the probabilities, be aware of the dangers, stick to tried and tested rules and procedures, take care and avoid recklessness. Unfortunately, children, lacking experience, do not always fall into this cautious mode of thought. It is an essential role of the Physical Education teacher to be aware of the pitfalls and possible scenarios for injury or death and in so doing, remind, nag and, if necessary, terrify them into safe practice.

There was a time, perhaps in the early days of my teaching career, that the First Aid box was stuffed with all kinds of medical "goodies"; bandages, plasters of various shapes and sizes, eye patches, antiseptic cream, gauze, triangular bandages and even paracetamol or similar pain reducers. The modern Physical Education teacher can now resort to few of the above resources when presented with a minor casualty. It is highly probable that the pupil in question will have an allergic, religious or philosophical reaction to their application, with dire consequences for the P.E. teacher innocently administering them.

To offer a pupil an aspirin for a headache might be judged only slightly less worthy of condemnation than having tried to push heroin. In the event of having dabbed antiseptic onto a nasty looking grazed knee, the P.E. teacher responsible could face a hauling through the courts should the parents of the casualty be members of the "Anti-Antiseptic Association".

However, it has to be accepted that resuscitation techniques need to be an essential part of every P.E. teacher's first aid repertoire of expertise and be revised regularly in the sincere hope that he or she will never be called upon to demonstrate proficiency for real.

In most everyday, humdrum, sporting situations where minor "knocks" and "injuries" are sustained as a matter of routine, I have found that the best medical advice to give to the casualty is:

- Give it a rub
- Try to run it off
- Here is a note for the medical room.

Beyond these three tried and trusted remedies, a P.E. teacher is walking on very thin ice in attempting any treatment. (On no account should one attempt to give anything a rub oneself!) Speaking of ice, the administration of an ice pack to the bruised limb might be regarded as permissible if one is to hand in the P.E. department refrigerator among the cold beers. If this should not be available, the suggestion that the casualty places a packet of frozen peas upon the injured area once they get home could be regarded as a sensible piece of advice.

However, when considering injuries, prevention is to be entirely preferred to cure.

Physical Education teachers need to be well aware of every possible risk pertaining to each sporting activity. On sailing, canoeing, skiing, camping, diving and rock-climbing holidays or expeditions the risks are clearly considered and outlined with expert specialist instructors often accompanying the school party. In the daily commonplace routine of P.E. lessons, the risks may seem comparatively minor but potentially death-delivering, just the same.

For example:

"If the ball goes through the gaping hole in the perimeter fence – do not run across the busy inner city ring road to fetch it!" (Instructions to tennis group)

or:

225

"When at the top of the gym wall bars, do not believe you are Spiderman and attempt to jump across to a rope 10 feet away."

Similarly:

"When throwing the javelin; carry it point downwards at all times... only throw it in *that* direction *when I say*. Do *not* swing it round your head. Do *not* run to fetch it back... also *never* throw it back towards anyone after you've retrieved it."

(I always have recourse to Psalm 23 before javelin lessons – "The Lord is my shepherd; I shall not want...")

As for hockey:

"Keep your stick down below waist height and always have your hands well apart. Do not tackle from behind when someone's about to hit the ball..."

In basketball:

"Make sure you're not wearing rings or neck-chains or you're likely to have a dislocation or severed neck..."

In swimming:

"Never run on the bath side... remember *this* is the deep end!"

When it comes to weight training... I am beginning to think that video games are not so bad after all... well, apart from the possibility of eye strain.

Whatever the sport being taught, I have seen blood, bruising and tears, thankfully not many of the latter have been mine.

There is no field or facility that does not have the potential for injury; whether it be wet, icy, cracked, damaged, cold, hot or possessing perilous protrusions. In any event, I am always ready with that essential advice, not RICE (Rest – Ice – Compression – Elevation for the treatment of injuries) but the "3Rs".

- Rub it
- Run it off
- Retreat to medical room.

In the compensation culture of today it is also highly advisable that any Physical Education teacher should have a good lawyer at the ready. Invariably, the pupil who happens to have a minor finger injury while transporting gym equipment will several years after seek financial recompense at having a potential career as a concert pianist cruelly thwarted by the P.E. teacher's negligence in not providing industrial gloves.

No matter how many precautions the teacher may take and how much pedantic guidance is given to a class, a mishap is never far away. Staying calm while witnessing excruciating pain, uncontrollable crying and baleful moaning is a valuable asset.

Keeping one wary eye on the rest of the class while administering consolation, sympathy, as well as a quick diagnosis of the casualty's condition is a vital skill acquired only through experience:

"It's O.K. everybody, go back to what you're doing. He's all right... it's not serious. He's just shaken up, that's all. Don't crowd round him... that'll just make it worse. Let him breathe... go on back to your groups."

If the lesson is not to come to a complete standstill, the injured party has to be sidelined quickly until he or she has recovered sufficiently to resume.

This is not so easily achieved when blood enters into the equation.

I must admit to being good with blood, providing it is not my own. Cuts, gashes and abrasions from collisions or mis-controlled sticks or racquets can be staunched quickly with a handkerchief or spare team bib. I have not yet encountered a P.E. teacher who carries on his person the prescribed rubber gloves for blood injuries. (Spare goalkeeping gloves, in case he fancies a chance to exhibit his ability in goal... yes.) The subsequent cleaning with a "mediwipe" in the changing room and the chance to observe a wound needing several stitches requires a degree of 'sangfroid':

"It's only a nick, Ali... stop screaming. You're going to be O.K... we'll just get you down to the medical room. Hold this on the cut... come on, calm down... you're not going to die."

I recall this scene when Ali caught the full force of the backlift of a hockey stick across his forehead. I had run to attend to him as his piercing screams stopped a whole hockey group in their tracks. As he held his hand over his stricken eye, the blood poured profusely through his fingers, down his face and onto his chest. I had immediate visions of having to search for his eyeball on the Astroturf as he wailed,

"I'm going to die... I'm going to die!"

Arm around his shoulder, I led him away with the rest of the class gaping silent and open-mouthed in shared anguish. Having mopped his face with his team bib and somehow succeeding in prising his fingers from his forehead I was able to see a neat two inch gash along his eyebrow of the kind Henry Cooper sustained in nearly every fight. Five stitches put it right and Ali survived. However, he was scarred for life and I am still awaiting litigation, though I believe his battle scar gave him more street-cred.

Instant, calm action is vital in the first few seconds following a P.E. lesson mishap – unless the incident involves childbirth, which may take a little longer to resolve. I raise this possibility only insofar as a Holte 15-year-old sportswoman once gave birth to a healthy bouncing baby. The baby ought to have been in that condition as the girl had taken part in a netball lesson the previous day. The girl had claimed not to know of her condition and had not missed participating in many P.E. lessons in the weeks leading up to the joyous, though somewhat surprising, event. Needless to report, the women P.E. staff had a lot of heart searching to do when the announcement of the new arrival was made. Midwifery has yet to appear on Teacher Training Days for first aid.

In accepting the inevitability of casualties being sustained as part and parcel of school life generally, it should also be noted that the potential for serious injury is often at its greatest when a teacher least expects it.

For example; Howard once found himself registering his form group in the relative tranquillity of his top floor classroom one bright, sunny, summer afternoon. He was a little nonplussed a few seconds later to find two additional bodies in his classroom, particularly as one proceeded to pursue the other around the occupied desks, while wielding a machete. The pursued was a notorious Year 11 rogue, the pursuer a rather hot-tempered ex-pupil who obviously had a genuine grievance.

Fortunately, Howard knew them both well and somehow, in the company of his scattering, terrified class, managed to calm the situation, persuade the Mad Machete Maniac to leave while shielding the "prey" who had cowered behind a filing cabinet.

Howard's PSE skills were renowned but never were they put so effectively to the test as on that occasion. It makes one wonder what treatment is suggested in the first aid guide for multiple machete wounds. (Howard still awaits his George Cross or any mention in New Year's Honours Lists.)

Pupil altercations are also an inevitable fact of life in even the most well ordered schools. There will be School Rules, Codes of Conduct or various counselling systems put in place in an attempt to prohibit or reduce the severest forms of conflict. When tempers run high and emotions are unleashed the possibilities of injury through violence are greatly increased. Sport and conflict share a fine line in this respect. In a basketball key, the football six yard box, a rugby ruck or under a netball net, physicality may turn to fisticuffs. The P.E. teacher will step in, enforce the rules, dismiss the combatants and look upon the incident as part and parcel of the game's aggression, albeit unwanted and unacceptable. The offenders will be treated accordingly with warnings, suspensions or total bans being issued. Hopefully, injuries sustained will be minimal owing to the P.E. teacher's rapid intervention at the time.

In the other major arena of ritual conflict, the P.E. teacher as judge, umpire or referee is rendered virtually impotent. I am, of course, referring to the playground and its punch-ups.

In the playground, when conflict arises, normal codes of combat tend not to apply, nor does the Geneva Convention. Prisoners are not taken, particularly when adolescent girls are involved. There has been many a prop forward

P.E. teacher hospitalised after attempting to intervene in a playground fight between two welterweight girls. Elbows, fists, teeth and worst of all, nails, can inflict horrendous injuries on the gallant playground supervisor after he has laid down his coffee cup in the course of separating two female combatants.

This self-sacrifice may also result in him sustaining a few underhand blows from the surrounding crowd of eager onlookers who will be enjoying the whole gladiatorial spectacle while chanting:

"Fight! Fight! Fight!"

That was the sound that assaulted my ears as I walked along the pathway from the main building to the sports hall one Monday lunchtime. I was heading for an indoor cricket net practice with a group of boys awaiting my arrival by the door.

I could not ignore the shouts emanating from the back of the school kitchens so I told the cricketers to stay there while I went to investigate. I walked unhurriedly, though purposefully, in the direction of the din, hoping that by the time I reached the source of the disturbance my intervention would not be needed. I turned the corner by the large waste disposal bins and came upon a sight I would not choose to see again.

Two or three teachers were kneeling over a figure who lay on his back in the middle of the kitchen driveway. I ran forward to join them. It was a boy and he was lying in a pool of blood.

"What's happened?... what's happened?"

I stammered out as I crouched over the youth alongside Ruth, the Head of English, who was lifting his head gently and placing a rolled up jacket beneath it. I could see the boy's face – it was Sean, a Year 11 boy.

"He's been stabbed... I think... by one of those two."

I was aware of the blood soaking through the knees of my tracksuit trousers as I followed Ruth's finger pointing to the two figures standing at the school gates, 20 yards away. I recognised the two Asian boys immediately as they began to come forward hesitantly. They showed no aggression, only a clear look of concern at the growing realisation of the seriousness of what had happened. The crowd of pupils who had been drawn to the scene were now being coaxed and pushed back by other staff who had arrived in some numbers.

"Is he O.K.?" offered one of the youths.

"No... just go... just go!" was all I could begin to say. The two youths backed off and when they reached the gates strode off with anxious backward glances. No one pursued them.

It appeared surreally silent as the remaining staff and pockets of pupils who had not been shepherded into the building stood transfixed by the scene of carnage on the driveway.

"I think he's bleeding in two places... here in the neck and this side in the groin."

Ruth seemed calm and in control. My mind was reeling as I sought to regain composure.

"Sean... you're O.K. Can you hear me?... you're going to be O.K., son."

I tried to urge some comfort into his consciousness, for Sean lay still, his face ghostly pale. His usually freckled forehead was pallid beneath his curly sandy hair, now matted by sweat.

"Sean! Come on, son... answer me... look at me... come on."

His eyes flickered momentarily as if in recognition then closed again.

"He's in bad shock."

Someone crouching next to me voiced my own feelings. How to treat shock? Keep them warm, keep them conscious at all costs... what else?

Two coats were thrust at us and we placed them over him. Towels had been brought from the kitchens. Their new, soft white nap was soon soaked in blood as hands strove to staunch the pulse that was forming a crimson rivulet across the tarmac. I had a towel in my own hand and pressed it firmly to his thigh. I could not believe there could be so much blood.

"Sean, Sean... come on son, stay with it... the ambulance is coming."

That jolted me. Where was the ambulance? Someone said it had been called several minutes earlier, but still there was no sound of its reassuring siren.

Sean, myself and the three other teachers held still and silent as the seconds ticked by. I saw Sean's pale, drained face and felt his body shivering beneath its coverings. I witnessed the beleaguered looks on the faces of my colleagues, with Ruth, her hands and coat stained crimson. I glanced to see the trickling stream of blood disappearing down a drain a few feet away. I held a futile towel to Sean's blood-soaked trousers.

The sound of the two-tone horn could be heard at the front of the school. An eternity seemed to elapse before the ambulance turned in sharply through the open gates of the side entrance to the kitchens. Bob, the head, was there as Sean was lifted gently, the drip attached, on a wheeled stretcher into the haven of the ambulance.

Tracksuit changed, showered, but with the smell of blood still about me, I sat meekly silent in the back of the police car as it crawled slowly through city traffic. I tried to frame my thoughts as we approached the police station, making ready for the statement I would have to give.

I had been there. I was head of Sean's year group. I liked the lad.

I knew the other boy too, the one who had stabbed him to death.

They had both been members of the school football team.

Chapter Fifteen

ABSOLUTE BEGINNERS
(Autumn 1997)

THERE ARE many people in the teaching profession who have little time or patience to give to student teachers. They look upon them as troublesome, a risk to discipline, and a likely source of deterioration in standards. They see them as generally demanding of a considerable amount of work in guidance and advice to help them achieve a level of competency at which they may be unleashed without supervision upon someone's innocent, impressionable offspring.

Anyone who ever learned to drive will recall the early days of L -plates and the manoeuvring of a vehicle nervously and hesitatingly through busy traffic. How many of those drivers, now complacent with experience, show much patience when stuck behind a learner at a busy road junction as the car ahead is repeatedly stalled and numerous opportunities to pull out into the passing traffic stream are missed. Teachers who bemoan students remind me of those drivers who, in their impatience and irritability at the road junction, have forgotten that they too once sported L-plates. I do not count myself among their number.

I have to confess a complete empathy and undying admiration for the student teachers of any academic discipline. Of course, my greatest regard and affection is held for Physical Education trainees of either gender, for I know exactly where they are coming from. I recognise their outward air of irrepressible confidence and enthusiasm and their glowing appearance of health and fitness. I feel their desire to succeed and "make a difference", as the teacher recruitment advertisements exhort, but above all I realise that beneath this outer veneer there is an uncertainty, fear of mistakes and possible failure to match up to the requirements displayed by their role model; the

Physical Education teachers who inspired them, consciously or otherwise to pursue their chosen career.

Somewhere there must be an inner "desire" to emulate the character, lifestyle and general "je ne sais quoi" of their P.E. teaching idol, based upon total idealistic naivety. My sympathy and affinity for the student teachers' situation is understandable, for, of course, I wore those metaphorical L-plates myself.

The first occasion I ever stood alone in front of a class of children will remain in my memory as a salutary experience no matter how much, subsequently, I try to resurrect it favourably from the mausoleum of my teaching experience. It was a Workshop Teaching Practice in a small primary school in Cheltenham. The purpose of this exercise was to introduce gently the art of teaching to the recently inducted student. This involved six Physical Education students from St. Paul's College, accompanied by a P.E. lecturer, visiting local schools for practice. We were transported by minibus in our pristine, royal blue tracksuits with their striking, white zip fronts, immaculate white plimsolls and matching white Fred Perry tennis shirts with their minimalist blue laurel wreath on the left breast. "Sid", Mr. Elliot, introduced us to our prospective fresh-faced classes of nine-year-old boys and girls. We sat uncomfortably on hard-backed, low, wooden chairs at the side of the small assembly hall with its colourful papier mâché collages covering the high wooden-panelled walls. They, the children, sat cross-legged quietly, on the cold parquet wooden floors, a host of pigtails, short trousers, small chequered summer dresses and bare knees. Unlike theirs, mine were trembling.

Sid explained to them, with his incongruous Geordie staccato vowels, that they, the lucky (his words) boys and girls, would be taking part in extra P.E. lessons that term. He told them that they would be enjoying a chance to take part in football, gymnastics and country dancing and that "these enthusiastic young men here will be teaching you." The plump headmistress, stationed threateningly at Sid's shoulder, nodded her assent to this arrangement.

For the following week we were to plan and execute a follow-up lesson to that which we were to observe being taken by their regular class teacher. Our peers would observe this lesson and evaluate it with a critical eye. We were assigned in pairs to three groups participating in the above activities. Of course, I was allocated country dancing. Robbie, who had also been assigned to this activity with me, watched the chosen group go through their leaping and bounding paces in the hall while the rest filed out to football on the small, immaculate, school field with its newly painted picket fencing.

The dancers were a bright, lively and well behaved troupe coming neatly together and apart in well-drilled formation under the steely gaze of a strict-looking lady in her late forties who gave instructions in the way of one "who will be obeyed". On the surface, there did not seem much to it.

When Sid had pointed at me and uttered "country dancing", I might have thought, "fucking hell". However, at the time I was only 18, a fresh-faced teenager from the provinces who had never set foot in Birmingham and had yet to learn to swear. On returning to my solitary college room, country dancing had lost whatever slight appeal it may have had and I slumped on my unmade bed wishing Sid had pointed and muttered, "football". Thirty-five minutes of folk-dancing began to seem less enjoyable than the prospect of two hours in a dentist's chair, such was the degree of my escalating self-doubt.

However, there was no avoiding it. Desertion was not on the agenda and I steeled myself by considering that the SAS had to pass far more demanding psychological tests than having to teach country dancing to nine year olds. My student compatriots were equally nervous at the prospect of their first teaching appearances, though with the exception of Robbie, my similarly selected partner, were happy to remind me how glad they were not to have drawn the "dancing" short straw. The mickey-taking was unrelenting as I was asked if I would be getting measured up for lederhosen, or buying a nice check shirt and going to the Christian Union Folk Club on Sunday night to get a feel for it. There was one female CU student who I had often thought I wouldn't mind getting a feel of, but definitely not in the country dancing context. Robbie and I began to form a country dancing splinter group where we would furtively discuss our worries and discomfort at our approaching ordeal. We were in agreement that non-country dancing P.E. types were a piss-taking rabble.

We also confirmed to each other that we knew nothing of the finer points of this dubious discipline. My only previous experience of anything similar was back in 1959 at Junior School. One wet day, Miss Clarke, the mother of all battleaxes, decided our mixed rounders lesson in the school yard could not go on owing to poor surface conditions. We filed into the school assembly hall instead, to merge with class 1B for jigging about. I vaguely remember it not going well, in the folk dancing sense, as we boys hated girls and to come into physical proximity of one made us nauseous. The need to hold hands with a girl or swing one by the waist made this type of activity a psychological impossibility. Even Miss Clarke, with her malevolent glare, could not frighten us into co-operation and out of our self-consciousness. We moved about a bit but refused to enter into the spirit of the thing. It had not gone well and I remember two particularly silly boys being sent out into the corridor to face the wall outside the headteacher's office. The next time Miss Clarke was faced with inclement weather she decided upon a mass high jump. I remember this clearly as I won.

Country dancing had made its mark deep in my psyche and I had a few restless nights rehearsing my thought processes, key teaching points and "calling" routine. I played the dance tape selection for my lesson, repeatedly, in my college room. I am sure the sounds drew a few quizzical and sneering glances from my long haired, flower-powered neighbours whose selection of sleep-disturbing night-time beats ranged from Cream to Led Zeppelin to T Rex. I tried to keep the music as low as possible as I went through a few moves myself on the polished wooden floor alongside my narrow, single bed. I found moving to Otis Redding, The Temptations and Four Tops at several decibels higher a far more rewarding experience. My rehearsals were strictly in the line of duty to my future aspirations for a professional career.

I felt physically sick on the afternoon of the workshop as the minibus turned in through the school gates. I was second "on" and had difficulty focusing on the lively, enjoyable and well-organised football lesson taught by one of my pals. He was confident, knew his stuff and any criticisms would have been purely nit-picking (why could I have not had football?). We enjoyed a 15 minute interlude to analyse his lesson. The comments were all constructive and favourable. I did not participate. My mouth was completely devoid of saliva, my mind preoccupied with the ordeal to come.

We left the field where the football lesson had taken place and filed into the school hall. I felt like the condemned man being led to the scaffold. My companions, in their blue tracksuits, appeared to be licking their lips in anticipation as they made themselves comfortable on wooden chairs at the side of the arena.

My hands shook as I attempted, fumblingly, to place the tape in the large recorder with its single speaker which had been left on a table on a small stage at the front of the hall. Then they arrived; the 30 or so children.

I forgot to count them, something I do automatically with any group 30 years on (divide by four, divide by two, divide by three etc., when organising practices). They entered silently in their black shorts, white T-shirts and black elasticated pumps. I asked them all to sit cross-legged on the floor in front of the stage. This they did and no one spoke or giggled. Their bright, innocent Gloucestershire faces looked, as one, to me for guidance for I was to be their P.E. teacher for the next 30 minutes.

I put aside my nervousness by involving them in a few warm up movements to break the ice. They were all of a dancing nature; skipping, twisting, turning, hopping and leaping. I even managed a few myself without rupturing an Achilles tendon or casting a glance in the direction of my critical audience a few feet away.

Feeling much more at ease, and the sweat on my forehead more equally the result of my efforts rather than anxiety, I leapt in one bound onto the elevated stage. I motioned to the dancers to be seated on the floor and proceeded to give them a two or three minute motivational harangue concerning the qualities I wished to see in their country dancing style and movements. I gave them the psychological boost of telling them how impressed I had been with their performance of the previous week with their class teacher. Their little faces lit up with pride.

I announced that they should organise themselves into their groups or formations ready to do the Western Reel (or was it the Western Roll? – no, that's the obsolete form of high jump which I utilised to win Miss Clarke's competition). They moved quietly and with almost military precision into recognisable groups around the floor of the hall. My critics' eyebrows rose in impressed appreciation.

I depressed the 'play' button and the first few introductory accordion notes rang out on cue. The children, surely "wunderkinder", began to move in perfect order, style and formation. I helped them achieve a previously unattained height of performing excellence by calling out essential instructions in the way country dancing choreographers do.

"Turn to the left... link your arms, reel your partners to the right.

"Form an arch, go straight through... loop the loop...bow down low."
etc. etc. etc.

I threw in a few "dozy do's" as you do, or as I thought you did, and everything went remarkably, undeniably well. (I had what it took – I could do it. I could guide, teach, inspire and change for the better, the lives of impressionable young people, even in country dancing, an area in which I had no proficiency whatsoever. Just wait 'til I could expose them to football and cricket!)

The last chord of the Western Reel rang out. The children finished in perfect synchronised order.

"Well done, everyone... that was brilliant. Now on to our next one. Take up your positions for the Barn Dance."

Again, with minimum fuss or noise, the children moved into position in well drilled order. I pressed the play button again and after several silent seconds a loud dull click indicated the end of the tape.

Then it struck me. As the blood drained from my face I realised I had forgotten to rewind the tape from the previous evening's final rehearsal. The reel they had danced to was the last I had intended to play. I had called the moves to that dance while they, "superkids" that they were, had danced perfectly to the tune they recognised only too well. Those children had demonstrated skill, initiative, style and co-ordination in true country dancing traditions in spite of the distractions being presented to them by the imbecile on the stage in front.

I hastily rewound the tape to embarrassed silence from the children and bewildered looks from the tracksuited oafs to my left. There were two salutary lessons to be learned from this teaching experience which I have carried with me through the rest of my teaching life:

Always check beforehand that your resources are ready, working, and in the correct order,

and:

That it is always better to have good kids to teach – particularly if the teacher is hopeless.

It is through this kind of early experience that all teachers should feel able to temper their judgements of students with empathy and understanding, for surely no one is perfect and those who think that they are perfect are definitely not teachers. A lifetime of teaching mishaps has enabled me to temper all my judgements on student teachers. During my time at Holte School I mentored students on numerous teaching practices from St. Peter's College, Saltley, Birmingham University and several other teacher training institutions in the region. Mixed with undeniable skill, potential and motivation to become Physical Education teachers was the inevitable misplaced confidence, frequent disorganisation, total naivety and occasional downright cockiness. Of course, all these factors represent the ideal P.E. teacher in the making. It is for this reason I felt a great affinity for each and every one.

I have become particularly well-disposed towards them if they have been teaching my lesson in the graveyard slot; last period Year 10, on a Friday afternoon, which is a real character builder if there ever was one. This is the situation where rigour, teaching points and even lesson plans can dissolve during a tortuous hour. To observe a student's energetic, irrepressible efforts to maintain order and focus on learning with obstreperous youth whose attention is only on the potential recreation of the approaching weekend, is a joy to behold – particularly if it can be watched from a nearby bench with a cup of coffee and a chocolate biscuit in one's hand.

In recent years, the process of becoming a Physical Education teacher has altered drastically. The Postgraduate one year course has replaced the three-year teacher training programme of the Physical Education "Wing" colleges which were represented by institutions the like of St. John's York; Borough Road College, Isleworth; King Alfred's, Winchester; St. Peter's, Saltley; Loughborough; Carnegie and others of their kind. Physical Education teachers themselves are now more thoroughly and integratedly involved in "on-the-job" training and guidance.

Having gained a degree, trainee Physical Education teachers undergo a one year course that is intended to cover the theory, practice and experience of teaching, involving coursework, assignments and, most importantly, essential exposure to children. To achieve all this in one solitary year is a formidable task.

However, it is not an altogether unhealthy alliance that needs to be formed between the young enthusiastic student and the experienced career professional in this situation. There is nothing more energising than a youthful, spirited Physical Education student to act as a catalyst in keeping the old, arthritic, whingeing, cynical and elderly Physical Education teacher in a stimulated and analytical state of mind.

Every P.E. department should have a student for it helps to reaffirm what it really takes to be and remain a successful teacher. Often, in the day-to-day drudgery and routine of timetables, initiatives, paperwork and policies, that underlying philosophy and overview is lost. Anyone who has ever taught will know exactly what is required and how often and easily it is possible to fall short of the perfect practitioner we would all like to be. To have been good at sport and having subsequently gained a reasonable degree, becoming a P.E. teacher can appear to be a desirable career path for many young people. To progress from that vague notional foundation certain qualities have to be developed.

In teaching, National Curricula, government directives, guidelines, trends and tendencies will come and go and often if you stay in it long enough they will come around a second time. Having watched hundreds of lessons taught by trainee teachers and attempted to forget many of my own it has helped me become a little opinionated as to how easy it is to observe, criticise and inspect from the safe and comfortable position of a sideline observer. From that vantage point it is possible to be the unquestionable expert and theorist. In the thick of it oneself, surrounded by bats, balls and bolshiness it is not quite so easy.

What has become apparent to me through discussion with student teachers of the issues that have arisen through observation and analysis of lessons good, bad and indifferent, is that certain common key factors emerge in being successful as a P.E. teacher and in setting a standard. It is my opinion that they will be essential in becoming a successful practitioner regardless of any transient, political statutory conditions.

Please disagree with me, or better still add others, as I offer these qualities as essential in becoming a successful, professional Physical Education teacher.

Key Factors In Successful Physical Education Teaching

Look The Part. Dress appropriately for the activity, e.g. gym, football, cricket, basketball – be prepared to change when you have to, particularly footwear.

Be Organised. Be on time, have equipment ready, check out the facility, always be ahead of the game with pupils.

Record Keeping. Maintain up-to-date mark book, register, medical conditions, pupils' achievements, levels of performance, merits, etc.

Speak Clearly. Speak slowly, clearly and unhurriedly. Try to avoid shouting – give short, precise instruction, when everyone is listening.

Know What You Want. Standards of behaviour, dress, performance, listening, participation – keep to them. Know what your aims and objectives of the lesson and scheme of work are.

Rewards. Praise, encourage and reward success, no matter how small. Respect losing and make all participants feel valued.

Be Firm And Fair. Keep to your standards, be aware of unfairness, cheating, bullying, racism, etc. Pupils need to know you are impartial, even-handed, firm but fair to all.

Set A Good Example. In dress, attitude, enthusiasm, skill, knowledge, rules, standards, and again enthusiasm!

Authority. You are in charge, you set the agenda – keep your distance from pupils, beware of being too friendly or informal.

Planning. Plan lessons carefully and thoroughly, taking into account pupils' abilities and motivations. Always have contingencies and be prepared to be flexible if things do not go to plan.

Extra-curricular Activity. Be prepared to put in long extra hours on clubs, matches, camps, trips, performances, competitions, etc. *and* do not expect too much appreciation or thanks!

Chapter Sixteen

GOOD AT GAMES
(September 1961)

"Oh, dearest School
Beneath whose shade
Our childhood games
We oft have played
Whene'er our thoughts to thee are turned
We'll offer thanks for all we've learned.
Floreat schola,
Floreat schola,
Floreat schola, Almondburiensis."
Anthem – King James I Grammar School, Almondbury, Huddersfield.

THE INSPIRATIONAL strains of the school song, performed wholeheartedly by the boys' choir, provides the soundtrack as the picture frames the cricket ground. The camera pans slowly across the square with its paler strips and neat white batting creases.

Its gaze lingers on the newly painted cricket pavilion then slowly arcs away and drags its focus down through a leafy embankment to the three immaculate football pitches.

They are freshly marked, the stark, white lines and goalposts contrasting pleasingly with the texture of the swathes cut by the groundsman's mower. The picture on the screen is now one of the grass tennis courts on the lawn in front of the Jacobean period building which houses the headmaster's study.

The camera zooms in through an open stained-glass window of the adjacent high ceilinged library. It is unoccupied. The screen is filled with row upon row of books in old oak shelves above which are the honours boards dating back centuries.

"A charter granted by King James
Restored the School to loftier aims,
To him our gratitude is due, for him our praises we'll renew.
Floreat schola, Floreat schola,
Floreat schola, Almondburiensis."

The choir continues its anthemic strains as the camera focuses in close-up on the italic lettering on the boards. Slowly it draws its gaze downwards, taking in the inventory of headmasters from 1614 to the present day. Other boards that it briefly pans across reveal similar lists of champion houses, chairmen of the Jacobean debating society and Victor Ludorum. The board holding the names of ex-scholars who sacrificed their lives in the Great War is framed on the screen for a full ten seconds.

The camera now moves through the low library doorway and along the darkened wooden-floored corridors until it reaches a more modern 1950's style assembly hall. The doors are levered open to allow it access and the volume of the choir is increased.

"Beloved school to thee we raise
With voices loud our song of praise
Though from thy care we must depart
We yet will sing with joyful hearts.
Floreat schola, Floreat schola,
Floreat schola, Almondburiensis."

There I am. You would have got a three or four second glimpse of me as the camera's viewfinder rested upon the boy near the end of the front row, ten feet back from the stage.

The hand-held camera would have wavered slightly then remained steady as it picked me out for its singular attention. Had you been watching closely, slumped on your sofa for a Monday evening's viewing on your recently acquired black and white television set, you might have spotted me in this "fly-on-the-wall" documentary; "Grammar School" – had it ever been made, in September 1961.

Part One: First Day; the title would have been briefly superimposed on the centre of the screen. It would have used as its introduction the "welcome assembly", with the whole school in attendance. Mr. Taylor, "The Gaffer", would be seen leaning on his ancient lectern, centre stage, gazing with avuncular benignity upon the new intake of first years filling the front three rows of chairs.

In that four to five second shot, in which the camera held me in its view, you might have noticed my pale, white knees, held together on the monochrome footage. You would have smiled at the sight of my flat, brylcreemed hair, plastered to my head with a parting slightly to the left. My tie is slightly askew under the stiff collar of my grey shirt, not long unfolded from its cellophane packet by my irritatingly fawning mum. I am sporting a black blazer of good quality barathea with the school crest on the breast pocket, under which is a grey jumper with a black and amber V around its neck. This matches precisely the two bands that encircle the neatly folded-down tops of my long, grey school socks which end just below the aforementioned goose pimpled knees. Above these are the grey short trousers that complete the tell-tale uniform of the First Year, as seen upon the screen.

The only blemishes that betray my tailor's dummy look are the traces of mud and the scuffs on my black lace-up shoes, which are out of view. Similarly, the camera does not reveal my black school cap, with its King James's crest and green band along the back, signifying my membership of Siddon House. This hated cap, the butt of much baiting by older boys, is jammed firmly into my stiff, immaculate leather satchel which has been left under my form room desk with its lift-up lid, centuries of idle pupil compass carvings and half-full inkwell.

The camera now pans slowly along the serried ranks of identically attired, nervous eleven-year-olds. There are 60 of them, two new classes; "A" and "Alpha". Behind them can be seen, slightly out of focus, the older blazered boys, with the eldest sixth-formers to the rear of the hall.

The piano strikes a final, thunderous chord and the congregation, at some invisible sign, rise as one to face the choir of two dozen boys, of various ages, at the front corner of the stage. The choir lead the school in the rendition of the last verse of the school song. You would not have felt the tingle at the back of my neck as the whole male-voiced anthem engulfed the newcomers. Being unfamiliar with both tune and words, we first years could be seen to keep our heads down while fixing our eyes on our printed sheets, held tightly in our shaking hands.

"Oh dearest School,
Beneath whose shade
Our childhood games
We oft have played
Whene'er our thoughts to thee are turned
We'll offer thanks for all we've learned."

This last verse elicits some virtuoso frills from the music master at the piano, aimed at bringing the anthem to a climactic finale. The choirboys, heads held high, eyes clear, mouths wide from the unrestrained effort of giving force to their delivery of the emotional chorus, lead the assembled school in a final booming:

"Floreat schola...
Floreat schola...
Floreat schola...,
Almondburiensis."
Silence.

The picture on the screen now focuses upon the broad figure of the head-master, with his bulldog features and black gown trailing to the floor behind him. He motions to the choir to be seated. There is a scuffle of chairs and clearing of throats as the rest of the school take this cue and settle into their seats. The headmaster begins his oratory and the camera lowers its gaze slowly to pick out the prefects seated at intervals at the side of the hall. They sit bolt upright, hands on thighs, their status marked only by a small circular badge, fixed on their lapels, bearing the school crest. The head boy sits uncomfort-ably alone at the front of the hall, below the choir.

The camera spins back along the front row of silent, attentive boys, bring-ing me briefly back under its gaze. It slides past me to rest upon the figures seated at the other side of the hall; the masters. The camera fixes each one in turn for a few seconds' scrutiny. Each one would refer to the pale-kneed pu-pil on the front row, as Boothroyd. During his school career he would come to know each one intimately as "Sir". The masters, picked out singly by the camera, remain inscrutable as they give attention to the headmaster's words, which remain in the background of the soundtrack. The masters' look of aus-terity is reinforced by their black raven-like gowns which cloak their sombre suits beneath. The black and white picture continues to move from one to another towards the back of the hall until it finally comes to rest upon a con-trasting figure, seated alone against the rear wall.

This figure wears no gown, only a light, slightly crumpled, checked jacket, with leather elbow pads, a nondescript shirt with knitted tie, grey twill trou-sers and highly polished brown brogue shoes. Above his stocky frame, the well-fleshed face has a flush the black-gowned masters do not have. His fair, unruly, curly hair seems to bear witness to a relaxed, benign and outdoor life. Although well into his forties he still seems to have that unmistakeable bloom of youth.

The camera holds its focus firmly, fully on his friendly face... it is Mr. Ire-land, (Shamrock) "Sham", the P.E. teacher.

Of course, that one hour documentary special was never made. At that time, putting institutions under the TV microscope to observe human fallibility, discomfort and subsequent psychological dismemberment were not part of the popular viewing culture. Had the cameras been given the usual unlimited access and slanted provocative editing, who knows what educational horror story may have been revealed for the audience's delectation at King James's Grammar School? Which master's teaching style might have been the source of national merriment or derision? Who knows, "Sham" might have even become a C list celebrity and earned future fame on *I'm a Celebrity, Get Me Out of Here.* However, my feeling is that none of the masters would have made exciting, riveting viewing, least of all Mr. Ireland; fine body of men though they were.

There was Mr. Gill ("Fishy"), the physics master.

"Six point four. Six point four?

Six point four what, Boothroyd?

... yards of tripe?... buckets of steam?

Be specific, lad."

Or Mr. Waring, ("Eddie"), the art master.

"If that's a self-portrait, Boothroyd then there's something wrong with your bedroom mirror."

Then there was Mr. Addy ("Reg'"), the French master.

"Let your rrrrrrs rroll in derrière, Boothroyd".

They all had their nicknames which we used frequently and mostly affectionately, though never within their hearing. Each master also had his foibles and eccentricities, honed and perfected through years of teaching in the cloistered, traditional confines of a provincial grammar school.

Each morning at assembly they would be seated at the side of the hall, glowering at our multitude as we clutched our hymn books to give our rendition of "Holy, Holy, Holy" or "For those in Peril on the Sea". They would watch for inattention, missing or worse still deliberate corruption of verses:

"While shepherds washed their socks by night..."

Amongst those long-serving pedants could be seen:

"Tex" Mr. Western, the chemistry master;

"Beaky" Mr. Heywood, the french master with his prominent Roman nose;

"Soapy" Mr. Hudson, the geography master and deputy headteacher, who wrote the definitive text book on North American geography (I should know, as he made us copy it out);

"Twig" Mr. Bush, the young Latin master (my favourite subject until I achieved 86% in an end of year test, yet came last, which resulted in my losing interest);

"Happy Harry" Mr. Gledhill, the music master. He was the assembly piano player and also the accredited composer of the school song.

He earned his label because every line in his near-retirement face reflected the effort and heartaches he had suffered, cajoling adolescent boys to sing – even the "grunters", of which I was one. He would insist everyone sang one verse solo in music lessons, in an attempt to discover talent for the choir. After one line in my case.

"No... you're a 'grunter', lad."

(Forty years on, this instant diagnosis has restricted my singing to solitary moments in the bath.)

"Isaiah" Mr. Bareham, the history master, known as such owing to his lopsided face (one eye was higher than the other... Isaiah... geddit?)

I could go through the whole staff list: "Jack" (Mr. J Taylor, not the "Gaffer"), the biology master.

"Caecum, it's pronounced 'secombe', laddy, not caycom... as in Harry Secombe. You wouldn't say Harry Caecum, would you?"

"Dimwiddy", Mr. Mallinson the chemistry master, a lookalike for Jimmy Edwards's sidekick in the much loved TV comedy *Whacko!*; "Jim", Mr. Toomey the Catholic scout master with seven children (we had heard); and "Wally", Mr. Haigh the maths master, who chain-smoked through all our lessons under the pretext of arranging stock in the store cupboard as we deciphered algebra from the rows of hieroglyphics he'd left us on the blackboard. Everyone was a character but I will stop here at the risk of inducing boredom. They all taught and educated us in their own peculiar styles. They all made us suffer. There was not a woman among them... until Mrs. Hebblethwaite arrived, and what a woman she was!

Mrs. Hebblethwaite (she had no nickname, we held her in too much awe). She taught French and had a passing resemblance to Grace Kelly. She was beautiful and, what is more, she had breasts, which became the focus of every libidinous schoolboy who ever conjugated French verbs in those deadly dull language rooms. I was never happy with French and eventually failed miserably but looked forward as a spotty 14-year-old to lessons with Mrs. Hebblethwaite with lick-lipping anticipation. She had a classical bone structure, warm hazel eyes beneath a carefully groomed cumulus of blonde hair. She wore a hint of lightly applied pale pink lipstick and her smooth, elegant neck led one's surreptitious gaze to those two ample mounds pressing firmly and, occasionally, sullenly, against a well-fitting jumper or, better still, loosely hanging sheer summer blouse. Her hips would be sublimely encased in a tweed or plain pleated skirt, below which her perfectly proportioned calves could be observed as she turned to scrawl "Je t'aime" across the board. Those legs, with the stocking seam plunging vertically to elegant ankles, "Madame Hebblethwaite, je t'aimai en 1964!" (*sigh*).

My memories of "Sham" are just as vivid though far less erotic. He was an enigma in my formative, sport-obsessed years. A stocky five feet nine(ish) in height, with a soft, west-country accent, Sham was neither a "character" nor disciplinarian. He never presented himself as a sporting role-model, or demonstrated to us performing excellence in any activity. In his baggy, faded tracksuit with its zip fastening at the neck and elasticated bottoms, he was as far from the motif-laden, logo-sporting P.E. practitioners of the 21st century as it is possible to be. Nike, Reebok, Puma, Ellesse, Diadora and other globalised brand names as worn by every high street layabout and sport-phobic had yet to make their mark upon everyday culture. (I believe Mitre, a respectable and irreproachable *Huddersfield* sports equipment company, may have been the trailblazer in the growth industry of branding.)

No, Sham did not wear labels. He was very difficult to place in any category at all.

In his quiet, efficient, unobtrusive manner he would inflate the footballs, allow us to select our teams, send us out to play, stroll out to ascertain the score and switch on the showers for our return. At other times he would point us in the direction of the cross-country course, blow the whistle for the "off" and 25 minutes later hand out the finishing tickets by the changing rooms. He would pin up the team sheets for the Saturday morning football fixtures against similar schools at exotic venues such as Heckmondwike, Sowerby Bridge, Cleckheaton, Mirfield, Penistone and Batley, also making sure that the pick up time by the Hanson's coach that he had pre-booked was clearly underlined.

In summer, Mr. Ireland would oil the cricket bats, whiten the pads and make sure all the necessary equipment in the school 1st XI bag was packed. He would umpire serenely in his white coat and supervise the interval teas. He would walk around the tables full of youthful cricketers in their whites, pouring tea into cups from a heavy aluminium pot.

Sham was not in the business of team talks or motivational oratories before the contest or at half-term. He rarely criticised and left us to our own thoughts in defeat. His acclaim at victory was restricted to a begrudging "well done". He was no "kingmaker".

Sham kept the sporting house competitions on track, which were contested in football, cricket, tennis, athletics, swimming and cross-country. He totalled up the points and kept the house scores meticulously on the P.E. noticeboards, much to everyone's ongoing interest. In his way he kept sporting rivalry going, but in a modest, unspectacular, non-aggressive manner. I cannot recall him shouting at us for any reason other than to urge us to throw ourselves recklessly over some piece of gymnastic equipment as he stood waiting to give physical support by its leather-topped surface.

Mr. Ireland was the perfect role-model in as much as he was even-tempered, amiable, well-organised, favoured no one and was always there.

P.E. seemed a bit like sex at that time – you just had to pick it up as you went along. One talked about it, thought about it, tried it out, liked or disliked it and went on from there. You just had to get stuck in, do your best and if you had it, make the most of it. Sports science was in its early stages.

Sham never made up the numbers if we were one short in any football lesson. He certainly never hit any young fast bowler for six in the Staff and Old Boys v School 1st XI annual cricket match. (As ever, he umpired and made the teas.) He never challenged anyone to a race over 200 metres and under no circumstances would he have risked splitting his crotch to show us how to execute a flik-flak in gymnastics. Sham saw his task as one of making sure we ran, swam, kicked, hit, served and generally played the game. Above all, that we played and did all those things in the "right spirit". In modern terminology he might now be referred to as a "facilitator". Sham facilitated a school life that was brimful of sporting opportunities. In a school founded to develop academic standards and traditions and that still existed with that ethos, Sham provided the perfect counterbalance, the facilitation of a love of sport.

My first interim school report at the completion of the Autumn term of 1961 makes riveting reading, if you can spare the 15 seconds required. My performance in the various subjects is reported as follows:

Religious Education	*Satisfactory*
Physics	*Satisfactory*
History	*Fair*
Geography	*Steady*
Chemistry	*Poor*
Biology	*Fair*
Latin	*Very Satisfactory (very?)*
French	*Disappointing*
English Language	*Sound*
English Literature	*Satisfactory*
Art	*Weak*
Physical Education	*Good at Games*

Perhaps it was Mr. Ireland's expansive reporting style, in using three words where one might suffice, that gave me the first essential impetus that was necessary for a future glittering career in sport. However, at games, was I that good?

When it came to the subject of sport, I guess that I could have been a contender. At the age of nine I was an above average swimmer and surprisingly discovered myself the Huddersfield Primary Schools champion at backstroke. Any possibility of my development into a child swimming prodigy was reduced by the anxiety I felt waiting for my races to be called. I felt physically sick in the cold, cavernous changing rooms, sitting there shivering on the wooden benches with a towel around my shoulders. This aversion to the possibility of fame in competitive swimming was compounded by the routine necessity of having to attend squad training sessions at 7.00am at a distant pool with an ambient water temperature just above arctic conditions. Although I continued to be a big fish in the small pool of house swimming competitions at King James's, I determinedly shied away from representative swimming and possible honours, knowing only too well the commitment and cold-tolerances required.

When it came to cricket, my dad had been taking me to his local club, Bradley Mills, from the age that I had been first able to walk. As my mum made the teas and dad stayed out on the field as long as possible to keep away from us, I showed myself capable of scoring hundreds – on the spare ground alongside the pitch, against other "orphans". We played for hours into the dusk, on the outfield, as the adults repaired to the bar. I developed an interest in girls for the first time; they proved to be very useful extra fielders. I played for the youth team as I got older and even made appearances for the adult teams when they were short-handed, during holiday fortnight. At school I was a regular in all the teams, finishing my sixth form career as an average opening batsman and lively wicketkeeper, just like my dad. Just like him too, when it really mattered, I nicked one for a duck and missed a crucial stumping. I was good, but not that good.

At cross-country I was able to grind it out with a reasonable degree of stamina, usually scraping into the first 20 runners home. At sprinting I was pedestrianly fast and usually made it as last pick for the relay team. In the discipline of running I never found a distance suited to my ability. The 800 metres was the nearest I came to being a record breaker. Pressed reluctantly into running this distance in the inter-house sports day, I felt I had no chance at all. Purely as a joke, I ran the first lap almost at a sprint to reach the finish of the first lap, pretending I had won, which I had by nearly half a lap. I proceeded to jog on rubbery legs the remaining lap looking over my shoulder and waiting for every other runner to pass me. On the final straight I still found myself in front of a tiring pack and somehow found sufficient wind to run the last few yards to stay ahead and take the gold. Having won, I was selected for the District Athletics championships. I tried this tactic again and, of course, came last. I gave up my ambitions in middle distance running and will never know just how close I might have pushed Coe and Ovett.

Badminton, basketball and tennis were looked upon as minority recreational activities in the 1960s and although I was quick to master the basics, opportunities to play and develop potential in these areas were very limited, so I did not.

Then of course there was football. (Rugby did not exist – we were a footballing grammar school.) I was always the captain which meant I had a prominent place on the front row of all team photographs. You will always find that, in all the archives, I am the one holding the ball (we did not win trophies) next to Sham on the front row. I was a quick (over 10 yards), skilful player with a push and run style reminiscent of my boyhood hero, Kevin McHale (Huddersfield Town's legendary right winger 1955–1968). Heading the ball was never a problem to me, I avoided it at all costs, though I did score one headed goal in my glorious career. I was acting as a decoy runner to the near post on an inswinging corner, ducked too late and saw the ball glance off my forehead and unerringly into the far corner (A brain scan showed no lasting damage – those leather footballs were hard!).

I admit to half believing I could make it as a professional footballer and play for Town. One night after Latin homework I wrote a letter asking for a trial. I was 15. Remarkably, Huddersfield replied and on one evening on the car park at Leeds Road, where Town held their training sessions, I impressed them sufficiently to be invited to regular youth team training at Beck Lane in Heckmondwike.

Cloyingly muddy pitches on freezing February evenings under dim floodlights at Beck Lane are not among my fondest footballing memories. I stuck it out for a month and held my own in terms of fitness, athleticism and skill with the ball at my feet. It was in other aspects of the game I was found wanting. Those crucial aspects were desire, determination and the total self-belief needed to become a professional. Playing alongside and against future Town icons; Trevor Cherry, Frank Worthington and Geoff Hutt ("brick outhouse" would have been more appropriate, he was *that* hard); I found I lacked the motivation and psychological make-up required, and I knew it. They and most of the footballing apprentices of my age were made of the "right stuff", the essential qualities needed to succeed in a hard, unforgiving game. They displayed skill, courage and no little vision of themselves as players of the future as well as a high threshold for enduring pain. I witnessed it at close quarters; they had it and I did not. It was back to biology and art homework on Wednesday nights.

Yes, it was true, I was good at games, but I was never going to be good enough, strong enough, fast enough, or mentally tough or motivated enough to be a star or make a living from any of them. I would never live in a mock-Elizabethan style manor house behind high security gates in a leafy suburb of

Cheshire, and be rewarded handsomely for photo-shoots for *Hello!* magazine. However, thanks to "Sham" I was to have a career in sport and have the enviable opportunity to wear a tracksuit for the best part of my waking life.

Having staggered into the King James's Sixth Form on the back of (very) moderate O-Levels and to great surprise, not least my own, having gained three (very) decent A-Levels, Sham came into play in his other role as part-time careers master. He suggested I considered a future career in Physical Education teaching. Where my sixth form friends were considering offers from Manchester, Liverpool, Bristol, Leeds, Oxford or Cambridge (the universities, not the football teams), my destination in waiting was St. Paul's College, Cheltenham. This attractive venue with its traditions, leafy boulevards, spa town location and seductive sister college was described to me in wistful terms by Sham himself, for, of course, he had been a graduate there years previously.

I was to follow in his footsteps both physically and metaphorically.

The camera sways and returns in a slow arc to focus back on the first years on the front row. They all stand as the choir strike up a familiar refrain:

"And did those feet in ancient times

Walk upon England's mountains green..."

My pale, innocent face lifts from the hymn book and I begin to mouth Blake's emotive words. To my right, a little taller than I am, is Cunningham (now a top banking executive in Surrey). Next to him is Bradley (something in futures in the far east). To my left is Barton (a BBC producer for *Newsnight*), next to him Wood (a lawyer). At the end of the row is Orme (a local GP) and behind him is Walsh (a bit of a rogue, not singing, did not bother with the sixth form after disappointing O-Levels. He is a multi-millionaire now, he made it in mountain bikes).

The picture on the screen slowly slides across the eleven-year-old faces of the "Class of '61", in the front three rows. The closing titles begin to scroll upwards.

"... Nor shall my sword sleep in my hand

'Til we have built Jerusalem

In England's green and pleasant land."

I recall them all now; bank managers, executives, doctors, lawyers, judges, media men and even millionaires and then there's me, the P.E. teacher. I think of them and I cannot help wondering... just where did they all go wrong?

Chapter Seventeen

THE ONLY PRIZE
(July 2000)

"Things won are done, joy's soul
Lies in the doing"
Troilus and Cressida

THE CAMERA clicks into action again, only this time it is for real. Brian, the assigned amateur photographer for the annual Holte Prize Presentation, snaps away at the front of the hall, his Nikon capturing each young prizewinner as he or she steps onto the raised stage to receive a trophy and accompanying book award from the special Guest of Honour. This year a "star" has been secured; Judy Simpson, the well-known British international heptathlete.

The assembly hall is bursting to the brim with pupils, governors, guests and a few proud parents. The fire doors have been left wide open to allow a gentle breeze to circulate on this hottest of midsummer days. Three wide beams of sunlight fall across the tightly packed ranks of pupils sitting sweltering on the rows of brown plastic moulded chairs. They present a pleasing scene of community and conformity in their immaculate white shirts and blouses. The latter are all open at the neck, the former contrasted by loosely fastened black ties with amber and blue diagonal stripes. The faces focused on the stage are predominantly brown and of Asian origin with an occasional Afro-Caribbean countenance and more contrasting isolated white face. The perfect sheen of the Asian girls' sleek, shoulder length hair is highlighted by the sun's rays invading from the playground beyond the open doors. The solitary royal blue of a Sikh turban provides the greatest contrast in the row upon row of heads.

Several of the staff members seated at the side of the hall are also of multi-ethnic origins. Asian, Afro-Caribbean and far-eastern, alongside their Caucasian colleagues of both sexes. Most of the women teachers are wearing bright, colourful dresses and blouses in keeping with the summer, while the male staff sport a variety of light cotton shirts with ties unfastened in the manner of the pupils. There's a general air of informality in the stifling heat of the assembly hall as the prize-giving routine proceeds, each recipient being applauded and photographed in a pre-rehearsed routine.

The staff on either side of the hall sit beneath large, daubed, colourful paintings which are positioned at intervals on the dark brown brick walls. They have been painted by past pupils. One depicts a racing motorcyclist taking a hairpin bend, the next a modern pop singer gyrating with a microphone held tightly in his hand, a striking pose on the six foot by four foot canvas. The one nearest the stage shows an image of a footballer in Aston Villa colours volleying for goal and yet another on the opposite wall portrays a black woman athlete sprinting to break the finishing tape.

Beneath each painting the members of staff continue to applaud as the line of prizewinners, in carefully pre-arranged order, stride confidently to the front of the hall. Each one is announced by Eric, the master of ceremonies, and then upon reaching the stage accepts their prize from Sue, the organiser, with a handshake from the international athlete as a posed photograph is taken by Brian, who perches on the edge of his chair, pointing his camera. Bob, the headteacher, just to his left, next to the chair of governors, Councillor Bert, beams and applauds as each prizewinner poses with Judy.

The majority of the applauding staff are young, with four of their number, Alan, Powelly, Andy and Suzy having just completed their first year as newly qualified teachers. The older staff, though frayed around the edges, still have a look of vigour and enthusiasm about them. Howard (forever youthful) claps loudly when one of his own particular form receives an award.

The certificates, trophies and book awards begin to dwindle on the white linen that covers the trestle tables. The ceremony is drawing to its close. The steel band in traditional Jamaican dress, who earlier played "Soul Limbo" as the guests took their seats, now sit restlessly fiddling with their drumsticks. The woman music teacher seated by the piano gesticulates in irritation for them to keep still. They wait impatiently to play their grand finale.

An array of awards has been made for every school subject; maths, English, science, art, drama, history and the rest, each area nominating its candidate for achievement. However, it is the sporting awards that appear to have gone on for the most interminable period of time. Six cricket championship trophies, two football league trophies, four Birmingham badminton championship shields, netball, cross-country, athletics and table tennis cups and each sporting discipline from swimming to dance, basketball to trampoline having its award winner or "Player of the Year".

The remaining three trophies sit in isolated splendour on the table at the centre of the stage. Two young people, the Sportsman and Sportswoman of the Year, stride up together to receive their cups and encyclopaedias of sport. A stocky, bright-eyed Asian boy and a slim and sinewy Afro-Caribbean girl stand proud and beaming as they have their photograph taken either side of Ms. Simpson.

She towers above them in her wonderfully striking vivid salmon pink two-piece suit. She has the legs of a supermodel perched on her matching pink stiletto heeled shoes. Her long muscle-toned legs shine in the sunlight's reflection, as does her face, with its attractively proportioned high cheek-bones. She has clear, confident eyes, a smile that wins by miles and all set to perfection beneath a startling arrangement of braided hair. From each lock is suspended a scarlet bead, which falling together forms a tapering curtain to either side of her magical face.

She is the essence of health, athleticism, beauty and charisma. Her smile lights up for Brian's camera without the merest hint of pose or fabrication. She is an Amazon upon whom everyone's gaze has become transfixed.

The moment passes, the prizewinners leave the stage clutching their silverware and the applause subsides. The headteacher rises from his seat and turns to face the audience of pupils and guests. He thanks everyone for their enthusiasm and patience on such an oppressively hot morning.

"... but there is still one final award to be made."

Bob points to a cricket bat on a supporting stand, now alone on the table. The bat bears a silver plate on its face, below the handle. It has been engraved.

"As most of you here will know, today is a bit of a landmark in the history of Holte School. We are losing someone who has been a part of this place for 27 years. I think we should acknowledge his contribution in making sporting achievement such a major factor in our school's life. The number of successes seen in these awards today bear ample testimony to that."

Numerous heads begin to turn to try to identify the subject of this eulogy.

"He would like to make a special presentation today... to commemorate his leaving Holte School... Mr. Boothroyd!"

The P.E. teacher rises from his chair at the rear of the hall near the dining area serving hatches. His tie is still tidily fastened beneath his cream linen jacket. His back feels stiff, his palms are moist as he makes the short journey along the side of the hall past the row upon row of eyes that follow his progress. He wipes his hands surreptitiously on his navy blue trousers as he climbs the steps up to the stage. He shakes the international athlete's outstretched hand.

Her grasp is firm and warm as she meets him eye to eye. She looks and feels young, fit, supple and alive. She releases his hand with a whispered "well done", then backs away diplomatically to one side of the platform, leaving him alone to face the silent audience. He clears his throat.

"Thank you, Mr. Day... for those very kind words. This is certainly a memorable and yet extremely strange day for me... to be leaving somewhere that has been so much a part of my life."

He pauses and looks around the assembly hall, absorbing the upraised faces giving him their full attention.

"However, I feel I must correct him. I've actually been here 27 years and 204 days exactly. In terms of teaching that means I've probably taught... let's see... at 20 lessons per week... subtracting holidays and weekends..."

He pretends to count on his fingers.

"... yes... that comes to 17,005 lessons, mmm... so with an average class size of... let's say 25 to make it easy, as my maths isn't too hot... now I make that about 425,125 kids that I've taught.

"I suppose if I add on clubs, teams and trips I could claim half a million!"

There is plenty of laughter from the body of the hall, the loudest from the staff, Bob in particular, with his irrepressible good humour on "state occasions".

"Well believe me... I'm not really counting... but I hope it will help you to understand why I'm looking so tired. Just standing here next to Judy... one of Britain's super-athletes, makes me feel weary... I mean just look at her... she's fantastic... look at me – see what I mean?"

The kids in the audience laugh loudly at that. Judy shakes her head deprecatingly.

"Anyway, here I am... and it's the last time you'll ever have to listen to me giving you an ear-bashing from this stage. So I'll make the most of it by saying a few more things."

The P.E. teacher steps to the very edge of the stage.

"I want to confide in you all that there are many reasons for wanting to become a teacher... in case any of you are thinking about it down there."

There are one or two "mock" groans among the seated guests.

"Of course, there are the long holidays... then there's the fantastic pay..."

This is interrupted by several ironic cheers from the younger members of staff.

"Well... there's also the continual praise and appreciation teachers get for the brilliant job we do, especially from politicians... yes, all these things make a difference... but what I really want you to understand, is what's at the heart of it... the only real prize for being a teacher. That's seeing young people like you succeed and having been a small part of that process."

He turns and picks up the cricket bat which stands behind him on the table.

"I would like to leave this as an annual award to the boy or girl who best represents success in the true sporting ethos and tradition of Holte School. In selecting Nasair Iqbal as the first winner of this I hope you will begin to understand what I mean about teaching."

A small boy sits alone, self-consciously, on a chair near the door at the front of the hall. The P.E. teacher indicates in his direction.

"Before I ask Nas to come up I must tell you a little bit about him to illustrate my point. When he first came to Holte, he was only a little "dot"... about 4 feet and 4 stone in weight... he's not much bigger now... only joking Nas!"

(Nasair was also quiet, stammered, was physically frail and without confidence in academic areas, but the P.E. teacher did not recount that.)

"I saw him running in the cross-country teams where he would keep chugging along in all conditions. He would battle away in the school football team, tackling tenaciously boys as big as grown men. Sometimes he'd get hurt... but he'd never give up.

"I remember him swimming in the gala. His class were one short in the relay team... he nearly needed rescuing from the deep end but he finished the length for his team. When it came to sport, Nasair always had a go and never complained."

The boy's face began to redden as he sat there looking at his knees, his fingers rolling up his presentation programme.

"However... it was at cricket that I saw the genius in him. His first ever match for the school team was against King Edward VI, Aston. I stood as umpire as he came out to open the batting with his cousin, Yasser. Nas was wearing pads that came so high up his legs that he could barely walk... let alone run. He wore a batting helmet that I'd virtually tied on to his head to stop it falling over his eyes... even though it was the smallest we could find. Even his bat looked too heavy for him."

The P.E. teacher raised the engraved bat to emphasise the point.

"Well... I remember feeling fearful for him as a fast bowler as big as Darren Gough pounded in and sent a bouncer past his head first ball. Nasair fell over trying to avoid it. Anyway... we had to dust him off and while this was happening, the King Edward's captain called in the fielders to surround this little chap. I remember one rather 'cocky' lad coming in very close on the leg side at square leg... (I'm sorry to blind you with cricketing science but it was like this you see)."

The orator stepped away from the edge of the stage and using the trophy cricket bat indicated where the fielder was in relation to the batsman.

"Anyway... you get the picture... O.K? The big brutish fast bowler comes pounding in again towards this little kid encased in pads and helmet, barely able to lift his bat... only this time he pitches the ball right up on Nas's leg stump... about here... see?"

He indicates with the bat, a point just in front of his left foot, and then proceeds to swing the bat with a smooth vertical arc in emphatic demonstration.

"Well... Nasair middled it with the timing and perfection of Gavaskar, Boycott, Lara and Hussein all rolled into one. He cracked the ball like a rifle shot... straight onto the shin bone of the fielder who had come in cockily close.

"He went down shrieking in agony... we had to stop the game while he was carried off to the pavilion."

The hall was filled with laughter, as the audience pictured the described scene. Nasair's head began to drop even lower in embarrassment.

"Of course, Nas went on to make one of his many fifties and start a cricketing career that's given me much joy to watch; just as many more of you have in all our sporting activities."

The P.E. teacher could have told several other cricketing tales involving Nasair, all of which would have demonstrated this little lad's guile, skill, intelligence, resilience, courage and love for the essence of the game... but he didn't.

"In short, Nasair, to me... perfectly represents what sport should be about. It is about excellence... but it's more about playing any game with pride, good sportsmanship, persevering under pressure, accepting defeat with good grace and winning, which everyone want to do, with honour. It's about giving your best... especially in adversity... it's about sport and it's about life...

"I'm presenting this trophy to Nasair Iqbal because he represents to me what is the best thing about being a P.E. teacher... he represents all of you who've come up here for awards today... and all those who are just as important... who didn't make it because they didn't win."

He beckons Nasair up onto the stage.

The young lad, with a shuffling gait, smart in his school uniform, hair neatly combed and gelled, climbs the five steps up to the stage. The P.E. teacher hands him the new Slazenger cricket bat with its shiny, engraved silver plate, fixed firmly to the blade.

It reads:

THE TYKE TROPHY
Presented by G. D. Boothroyd
Head of Physical Education 1972–2000
To the pupil who best represents
the ethos and spirit of sport
2000 Nasair Iqbal

Judy Simpson shakes the young man's hand and the three figures on the stage present a smiling tableau for the camera. The shutter clicks and captures:

The youngster, his sporting future ahead of him;

The international athlete, the image of present excellence;

The ageing P.E. teacher.

The applause resounds around the hall. The headteacher rises from his chair. The P.E. teacher makes his exit from the stage, his vision blurred.